Tacitus' History of Politically Effective Speech

Also available from Bloomsbury

Tacitus, Rhiannon Ash
The Roman Empire, Peter Garnsey and Richard Saller
The Historians of Greece and Rome, Stephen Usher

Tacitus' History of Politically Effective Speech

Truth to Power

Ellen O'Gorman

BLOOMSBURY ACADEMIC
LONDON • NEW YORK • OXFORD • NEW DELHI • SYDNEY

BLOOMSBURY ACADEMIC
Bloomsbury Publishing Plc
50 Bedford Square, London, WC1B 3DP, UK
1385 Broadway, New York, NY 10018, USA
29 Earlsfort Terrace, Dublin 2, Ireland

BLOOMSBURY, BLOOMSBURY ACADEMIC and the Diana logo are trademarks of
Bloomsbury Publishing Plc

First published in Great Britain 2020
This paperback edition published in 2022

Copyright © Ellen O'Gorman, 2020

Ellen O'Gorman has asserted her right under the Copyright, Designs and Patents Act, 1988,
to be identified as Author of this work.

Cover image: *The Orator*, c.1920, Magnus Zeller (1888–1972).
Digital Image Museum Associates/LACMA/Art Resource NY/Scala, Florence.

All rights reserved. No part of this publication may be reproduced or transmitted
in any form or by any means, electronic or mechanical, including photocopying,
recording, or any information storage or retrieval system, without prior
permission in writing from the publishers.

Bloomsbury Publishing Plc does not have any control over, or responsibility for, any
third-party websites referred to or in this book. All internet addresses given in this
book were correct at the time of going to press. The author and publisher regret
any inconvenience caused if addresses have changed or sites have ceased to
exist, but can accept no responsibility for any such changes.

A catalogue record for this book is available from the British Library.

Library of Congress Cataloging-in-Publication Data
Names: O'Gorman, Ellen, author.
Title: Tacitus' history of politically effective speech : truth to power / Ellen O'Gorman.
Description: London ; New York, NY : Bloomsbury Academic, 2020. | Includes bibliographical
references and index. | Summary: "This study examines how Tacitus' representation of speech
determines the roles of speakers within the political sphere, and explores the possibility of
politicallyeffective speech in the principate. It argues against the traditional scholarly view
that Tacitus refuses to offer a positive view ofsenatorial power in the principate: while senators
did experience limitations and changes to what they could achieve in public life, they could
aim to create a dimension of political power and efficacy through speeches intended to
create and sustain relations which would in turn determine the roles played by both
senators or an emperor. Ellen O'Gorman traces Tacitus' own charting of these modes
of speech, from flattery and aggression to advice, praise, and censure, and explores how
different modes of speech in his histories should be evaluated: not according to how they
conform to pre-existing political stances, but as they engender different political worlds in the
present and future. The volume goes beyond literary analysis of the texts to create a new
framework for studying this essential period in ancient Roman history, much in the
same way that Tacitus himself recasts the political authority and presence of senatorial
speakers as narrative and historical analysis"– Provided by publisher.
Identifiers: LCCN 2020019022 (print) | LCCN 2020019023 (ebook) |
ISBN 9781350095496 (hardback) | ISBN 9781350095502 (ebook) |
ISBN 9781350095519 (epub)
Subjects: LCSH: Speeches, addresses, etc., Latin–History and criticism. | Oratory, Ancient. |
Rhetoric, Ancient. | Communication in politics–Rome–History. | Communication–Political
aspects–Rome–History. | Political culture–Rome–History. | Tacitus, Cornelius.
Classification: LCC PA6083 .O36 2020 (print) | LCC PA6083 (ebook) | DDC 875/.01–dc23
LC record available at https://lccn.loc.gov/2020019022
LC ebook record available at https://lccn.loc.gov/2020019023

ISBN: HB: 978-1-3500-9549-6
PB: 978-1-3501-9501-1
ePDF: 978-1-3500-9550-2
eBook: 978-1-3500-9551-9

Typeset by RefineCatch Limited, Bungay, Suffolk

To find out more about our authors and books visit www.bloomsbury.com
and sign up for our newsletters.

For Synnøva

Contents

Preface ix

Introduction 1
  1 Imperial regimes of truth 1
  2 Senatorial business 15
  3 Entering the archive 24

Part One Modes of Speech

1 *Turpe servitium*: The Political World of Flattery 31
  1.1 The agency of *adulatio* 34
  1.2 The art of *adulatio* 43
  1.3 *Adulatio* and *honor* 47

2 *Pro incolumitate principis / ex calamitate civium*: The Political World of Predatory Accusation 53
  2.1 *Delatio, maiestas*, and distributed agency 57
  2.2 Majesty and harm: the world of *maiestas* 66
  2.3 The speech of *delatio* 73

3 *Servitium rupit*: Counter-speech 81
  3.1 *in adulationem lapsos cohibebat* 82
  3.2 *de praemiis accusatorum abolendis* 92

Part Two The Critical Archive

4 *Existimatio vitae*: The Judgement of Character 109
  4.1 Emotion, speech, and moral principle 112
  4.2 The critical archive of character 123

5 *Narratus et traditus*: The Transmission of *mores* 139
  5.1 The social network 140

5.2 Genealogies of practice 148
 5.3 Future communities 156

Conclusion: *sententia* 167

Notes 169
Bibliography 197
Index 211

Preface

The research for this book was supported by a University Research Fellowship from the Institute of Advanced Studies at the University of Bristol, and by a Margo Tytus Fellowship from the Faculty of Classics at the University of Cincinnati. I am immensely grateful to both funding bodies for this support, without which I would not have completed the book, and also to the Faculty of Arts Research Fund at Bristol, for covering the costs of the book cover. My heartfelt thanks also to our indispensable subject librarians, Damien McManus and Tim Riley, for all their help over the years. My colleagues in the Department of Classics and Ancient History have offered intellectual challenges and collegiality for longer than I care to admit: Emma Cole, Lyndsay Coo, Will Guast, Kurt Lampe, Bella Sandwell, and Edwin Shaw. In particular, the friendship of Bob Fowler, Pantelis Michelakis, and Vanda Zajko have kept me going in darkest times. The last stage of writing was enhanced immeasurably by the presence of Aske Damtoft Poulsen, who shared with me many discussions of Tacitus and generously read several draft chapters: his insights have sharpened many of my thoughts in this book. My graduate students have taught me more about writing than anyone, and I am lucky to have supervised them: Hannah-Marie Chidwick, Richard Cole, Corbin Golding, and Dana Lungu. Four generations of undergraduates studying 'Roman Emperors: A Survival Guide' have helped me to clarify my thoughts about the experience of imperial subjects: I thank them for their energy and engagement.

Papers related to this research have been delivered over the years at Bordeaux, Bristol, Exeter, Jerusalem, Liverpool, Lund, Rome, and St Andrews, where I have been fortunate to discuss and refine my ideas with various audiences whose responses have helped me greatly. Four months spent at the Faculty of Classics in the University of Cincinnati was transformative in all the best senses, and I am profoundly grateful to Steven Ellis for managing my visit, Emilia Barbieri, Marion Kruse, Daniel Markovich, Carina Moss and Susan Prince for much hospitality, and my fellow Tytans, Peter Day and Lisa Mignone, together with Lindsay Taylor and John Wallrodt, for community feeling and much laughter. Conversations with Lauren Donovan Ginsberg about Tacitus were immeasurably helpful and delightful. Over at Xavier University, Tom Strunk contributed further stimulating exchanges on Tacitus and politics, and provided helpful comments on the whole draft in its near-to-final form.

Fellow Taciteans and para-Taciteans over the years have made me think and rethink Tacitus' politics and the meanings of his texts: Rhiannon Ash, Shreyaa Bhatt, Olivier Devillers, Tom Geue, Elena Giusti, Elizabeth Keitel, Simon Malloch, Victoria Emma Pagán, Amy Russell, Lydia Spielberg, Henriette van der Blom, and Chris Whitton. Elizabeth Keitel and Andrew Feldherr generously read and commented on an early book draft, and Christopher Pelling and Andrew Feldherr (again) very kindly wrote in support of my grant applications. None of the aforementioned is responsible for the errors or infelicities of what follows.

The editors at Bloomsbury have been models of professionalism and friendly encouragement at every stage of the project. Alice Wright prompted me at just the right moment to get on with saying what I've been thinking for a long time. Lily Mac Mahon has provided invaluable advice for every issue, large or small, that came my way. Goretti Cowley has been a patient and precise copy editor. The referees for the manuscript administered a salutary dose of well-founded scepticism and made me think again and argue more carefully.

Outside of academia, my friends and family were (mostly) understanding when I couldn't come out to play. My thanks (and apologies) to the Bristowe consort, Collingwood viols, Crumscrum, Mosaik, Pink Noise, RRV, SkWirrals, and Stanton Prior voices and viols. The O'Gorman-Harings, Sillen-O'Gormans, O'Gorman-Kellys, and Bannons have all been wonderful, and they can stop reading now. My husband, Duncan Kennedy, has been a tower of strength, silliness, and incisive comment, and I expect him to read to the end.

Introduction

1 Imperial regimes of truth

In the tenth year of Tiberius' reign (AD 24), the eminent consular Marcus Lepidus successfully argued to reduce the severity of a sentence upon Sosia Galla, charged along with her husband with treason. The episode prompts Tacitus to reflect on the principles underlying a successful senatorial career under an emperor.

> *unde dubitare cogor, fato et sorte nascendi, ut cetera, ita principum inclinatio in hos, offensio in illos, an sit aliquid in nostris consiliis liceatque inter abruptam contumaciam et deforme obsequium pergere iter ambitione ac periculis vacuum.*
>
> Ann. 4.20.3

> Hence I am compelled to wonder whether it is through fate or the chance of birth (as other things are) that the favour of rulers is bestowed on some men and their dislike upon others, or whether there is something in our conscious behaviour which enables us to steer ourselves between brusque defiance and shameful compliance and to pursue a path clear of ambition and dangers.[1]

Tacitus has not arrived at this question unexpectedly, for it shapes his thinking from *Agricola* to *Annals*: what is the relationship between what senators can control (their avoidance of ambition) and what they cannot or can only partially control (the dangers of a ruler's disfavour)? Does control over their own behaviour as senators enable them to avoid or limit the dangers of imperial disfavour and its potential to destroy their careers and the future of their families? Can senators consciously adopt a mode of behaviour through which their political career can flourish, without damage to their honour and integrity? Tacitus and his readers devote much energy to identifying what mode of behaviour might achieve this. In this book I want to address the question from a slightly different angle, which

I will articulate by looking more closely at the passage just quoted. For the desired career (*iter*) of the successful senator here is described as an absence of negative qualities – *iter ambitione ac periculis vacuum* – and characterizes senatorial activity in terms of reaction and avoidance. Yet if we look at Tacitus' narrative, we see senators busily engaged in activity, often taking initiatives, making proposals and counter-proposals. Throughout their activities, to be sure, imperial senators are keeping in balance their desired outcomes and the possibility of serving or crossing more powerful political actors (just as their Republican predecessors kept such factors in mind). In this episode, for instance, Lepidus reviews, along with other senators, a *maiestas* charge where the offence felt by the emperor is made very clear (*Ann.* 4.19.3). Lepidus steers his path away from pointless opposition by upholding the condemnation and the sentence of exile. But he also avoids shameful capitulation by using legal precedent to secure Sosia Galla's property for her heirs.[2] Thus his actions conform to Tacitus' description of the senator's ideal career, to steer a middle way between defiance and complicity. But they also highlight how limited that description is, for it says nothing about the concrete achievements of Lepidus, or what those achievements might mean for Sosia and her descendants. The empty path of success, clear of ambitions and dangers, is actually filled with smaller, incremental gains for the social and political culture of the imperial senators.

My central argument in this book is that, by looking at senatorial activity as it is narrated in Tacitus' works, we can recover a representation of what was politically effective in the imperial senate and can explore its productivity for good or ill. My contention is that Tacitus saw and presented in his works the possibility for a senator to engage in effective political action, and that such a possibility becomes visible to us when we consider a senator's action as having multiple aims and outcomes. Again, while Tacitus' reflection on the principles of senatorial success in *Ann.* 4.20 are oriented entirely around a subject's relationship with the ruler, the narratives of senators' actions show that effective political action is not always along that single axis. Lepidus' proposal may be prompted by commitment to the law, rivalry (or even alliance) with the proposer of the original sentence, or by friendship with the condemned, as much as by his relationship with Tiberius.

Hence the title of my work – *Truth to Power* – might seem initially misleading. The phrase 'Speaking Truth to Power' usually conjures up a scene of exchange between a dissident speaker and a powerful addressee, and demonstrates both the danger and necessity of maintaining integrity in the face of coercion.[3] The 'truth' in this formulation is imagined initially as external to power relations between speaker and ruler: it is the truth that the ruler does not want to acknowledge. The dissident speaker shows her commitment to that truth and by maintaining truth she transforms the power relation. In my analysis, many speakers are far from dissident, and their scenes of speaking involve multiple addressees. 'Truth' is the product of their speech, and the 'truth' that they produce is a political vision in which the conceptual positions of ruler and subject, as well as their ideal relations, emerge as by-products of the speeches' ostensible aims. Lepidus, for instance, speaks in order to preserve the status of a fellow senator's children and in the process expresses a sense of how senators should engage with each other and with the ruler. Political visions of this sort draw on established networks of associations which concretize citizenship, senatorial status, and authority through metaphors of physical protection or abuse, fertility or sterility, propriety or transgression. Crucially, these networks provide avenues for senatorial activity – or close them off. For instance, the speech of flatterers, which we will examine in chapter one, makes it nearly impossible for the senator to act as an impartial advisor to the princeps and thereby forecloses on ruler–subject relationships of this kind. The political vision projected by flattery generates a new kind of truth-regime within which certain modes of speech, such as deliberation or advice, lose their validity.

In using the phrase 'truth-regime', I draw on the insights of Michel Foucault, who outlined ways in which systems of knowledge were profoundly implicated in the power-systems of any particular era. Focussing on knowledge systems often considered 'non-political', such as science or medicine, Foucault investigated what effects of power emerged from their 'disciplinary constraints' – the specific procedures which ensured verifiability within these systems. He thus showed how empirical knowledge determined the limits of the sayable and thinkable, effectively structuring human experience, and how the development of such disciplines both drew from and contributed to the ordering of human subjects within the state. Following Foucault, Andrew Wallace-Hadrill has examined how knowledge systems of religious tradition, calendars, civic space, and ancestry were transformed in the Augustan cultural revolution so as to shift social control away from the senatorial and into the imperial domain.[4] In section 1 of this introduction I will show how Foucault's understanding of 'non-political' knowledge systems can be extended also to explicitly and traditionally political knowledge systems such as rhetoric and historiography. Tacitus' recording of senatorial speech in his historiography thus participates in the creation of the Principate's truth regimes, as we will see in a moment. The second part of my argument is that Tacitus' historical narratives perform the double task of participating in and simultaneously critiquing truth regimes. Foucault encourages readers to uncover a society's regime of truth by paying attention to 'the types of discourse which it accepts and makes function as true; the mechanisms and instances which enable one to distinguish true and false statements, the means by which each is sanctioned; the techniques and procedures accorded value in the acquisition of truth; the status of those who are charged with saying what counts as true'.[5] Tacitus produces a discourse which can be analysed in this way, but his writing also produces its own analysis along Foucauldian lines. He achieves this most often by his notorious ambiguity or irony, which denies objective authority to the 'sanctioning' of truth in his account of imperial politics.[6]

We can observe how this works by examining a 'truth universally acknowledged' in the Roman Principate: that autocratic rule was necessary to ensure peace in the state. Tacitus expresses this truth at the start of *Histories*:

> *postquam bellatum apud Actium atque omnem potentiam ad unum conferri pacis interfuit.*
>
> Hist. 1.1.1

After fighting concluded at Actium and it was in the interest of peace that all power be conferred on one man.

Tacitus combines two statements at the same level of objectivity: the Battle of Actium and the expediency of the Principate. The latter is clearly a truth which structures relations between ruler and subjects, not least by setting up the emperor as the protector of citizens. But this is a truth which is not self-evident so much as *produced* by various discourses which concretize peace as security, prosperity, and victory,[7] and thereby organize the experiences of Roman subjects so as to attest to the truth. The production of this truth becomes more visible when we consider how it universalizes particular concepts of security, prosperity, and victory, which are necessarily only experienced by some subjects. The overall effect of this statement is one of constraint: truth and power just *happen*, and all subjects can do is recognize them as the conditions of their existence. This illustrates how Tacitus' narrative participates in the Augustan truth-regime, but as his preface unfolds, we see him explicitly considering the consequences of this new truth for traditional knowledge systems. The change wrought in the state after Actium is associated with the loss of great historical writing which exemplified both skill and commitment to its own criteria of truth.

> *multi auctores ... res populi Romani memorabantur, pari eloquentia ac libertate: post bellatum apud Actium atque omnem potentiam ad unum conferri pacis interfuit, magna illa ingenia cessere.*
>
> Hist. 1.1.1

> Many writers ... recorded the activities of the Roman people, with eloquence matching their independence: after fighting concluded at Actium and it was in the interest of peace that all power be conferred on one man, those great historical talents dwindled out.

Tacitus thus implicates changes in power with a transformation in discourses of knowledge, so that a new truth-regime is produced. Initially he seems to represent this as a one-way process, with imperial power acting upon knowledge. But as the preface unfolds, we see Tacitus using historical distance to represent the imperial truth-regime as relative rather than absolute. As part of this relativizing, he reserves the word 'truth' for the practice of history before it degenerated in the Principate. He thereby implies confidence in historical perspective and its potential to uncover – or even dismantle – regimes of truth. We will follow the implications of this below. But Tacitus also resists a top-down model of regime change when he recounts how the transformation of historical discourse affects the imperial truth-regime itself. He thus not only shows knowledge acting upon power, but also observes how this knowledge is supported by senatorial agency: in Tacitus' account, the senators' understanding of the Principate affects historical writing, which propagates the truth of power. We see this in Tacitus' elaboration of his claim that history has degenerated, in the same passage.

> *magna illa ingenia cessere; simul veritas pluribus modis infracta, primum inscitia rei publicae ut alienae, mox libidine adsentandi aut rursus odio adversus dominantes.*
>
> Hist. 1.1.1

those great historical talents dwindled out; at the same time truth was fractured in various ways, first because of ignorance of the commonwealth, as (if it were) the property of another, then because of passion for compliance or alternatively because of hatred against those holding supremacy.

The discourses of the Principate 'fracture' the truth-criteria of Republican historiography, but the reinvented discourses of flattery and invective will produce their own political truths, as we will see in subsequent chapters.[8] The important phrase here is *veritas . . . infracta . . . inscitia rei publicae ut alienae*, which shows knowledge, discourse, and power acting upon each other in multiple ways. The truth of historical discourse is broken, Tacitus says, because of ignorance about the workings of the state. This ignorance is in turn explained by the phrase *ut alienae*: because the state was in the possession of another. This is usually taken to be the extra-senatorial princeps, but the lack of specificity emphasizes the dispossession and alienation of the senate.[9] It is possible to take this as an objective condition, which is developed through Tacitus' coinage of the term *arcana imperii*, 'Secrets of State', and the idea that it is in the interest of the state to bar its citizens from full knowledge of state workings.[10] Dio's more extensive explanation of how the Augustan regime inaugurates this bar of knowledge implicitly takes such an objective stance.[11] But the interdependence of *inscitia* and *ut alienae* also betrays the lack of external support for this truth. That is, the 'recognition' that the state is the property of another comes from those existing in a state of ignorance: it may be a *misrecognition* which exemplifies that ignorance, reversing the tenor of cause and effect. The ambiguity of *ut*, which I've rendered 'as (if it were)' points to how this truth about power is never accorded absolute objective status.[12]

What difference does this make? My point here is that the discourses which produce truth under the Principate (in Tacitus and other authors) are not simply responding to changes in power; they are generating those changes through their own discursive transformations which determine what can be perceived and spoken as the truth. Tacitus does not present a simple picture of a power grid descending upon and constraining the speech of senators and historians. He shows us their speech marked by passionate engagement with different modes of addressing imperial power – 'passion for compliance or hatred of those holding supremacy' – which radically determine how that power is perceived and experienced. The Principate becomes a co-production in the dialogues between subjects and ruler.[13]

Thinking about the Principate as a regime of truth which is produced by discourses opens the way for considering how, and by whom, different political truths can be propagated. This provides a space for considering the agency of imperial subjects. The choice between compliance and resistance, for a senatorial speaker like Lepidus or a historian like Tacitus, ceases to be an ethical struggle within an unyielding system and becomes an ethical-political act of engagement with a continually evolving and partially responsive domain. This is not to overstate the agency of senators and historians in the Principate. In this, Lepidus' participation in a treason trial serves as a salutary reminder of the limits to what a senator can achieve. Nor are these limits all exclusively the effect of the imperial regime;[14] the boundaries of what can be thought and known by the Roman senatorial class also impose restrictions on what new political truths can be propagated. But neither, I suggest, should our awareness of those limits lead us to discount the effects of senatorial actions and the use senators can make of what agency they claim.

Throughout this reading of the preface to *Histories*, I have increasingly interpreted what Tacitus says about historical writing as applicable also to the practice of senatorial speech. I do so because there are clear parallels between the two discourses as vehicles of political knowledge, where the pressures of imperial life are manifested and negotiated. This is evident from the similarity between the extremes of resistance (*contumacia*) and complaisance (*obsequium*) in Tacitus' discussion of the Lepidus episode, and those of hostility (*odium*) and desire to flatter (*libido adsentandi*) in his presentation of imperial historiography. But the conflation of history and speech may obscure a significant difference: that the historian, speaking about regimes of the past, has a greater degree of freedom than does the orator, addressing the present ruler. Historical distance, in this view, enables Tacitus to uncover the workings of earlier imperial truth regimes which could not be accessed by the senators of the time. This is an important difference between history and political speech, but it has too often been overstated in such a way as to deny any potential effectiveness in either discourse. For example, Tacitus' careful analysis of truth and power in the preface to *Histories* has often been seen as fatally vitiated by his concluding praise of the emperors under whose rule he writes.

quod si vita suppeditet, principatum divi Nervae et imperium Traiani ... senectuti seposui, rara temporum felicitate, ubi sentire quae velis et quae sentias dicere licet.

Hist. 1.1.4

But if enough life remains for me, I have set aside for my old age the subject of the divine Nerva's principate and the reign of Trajan, in that rare happiness of times when it is permitted to think what you want and say what you think.

It is difficult for contemporary readers to read this as anything other than the sort of flattery that Tacitus has just condemned as corrosive to imperial politics. The solution is to assume that Tacitus here does not mean what he says.[15] When he refers to the new regime as a time when he *can* mean what he says, Tacitus implies a self-consciousness which further destabilizes the truth-claim and suggests that the reader needs to take up the task of critique which the historian lays down. Certainly, recent scholarship has been sceptical of 'taking Tacitus at his word' here, a position which has also been adopted in relation to the speech of imperial subjects more generally.[16] It is important to explore this more fully in order to recover a position where we can take Tacitus at his word when he declares a belief in the efficacy of speech in an imperial regime. For the rest of this section I will examine the theory of figured speech, which has become the default interpretative position for scholars of Roman imperial texts, and will outline its limitations for understanding senatorial speech in Tacitus. I will then return to Tacitus' praise of Nerva and Trajan to propose an alternative interpretation of it as a declaration of truth guaranteed by the authority of the historian.

Terms such as 'figured speech'[17] and 'doublespeak',[18] as well as 'irony'[19] and 'poetics of conspiracy',[20] have been used to map out how the discourses of imperial subjects accommodate a suspension of meaning. Carefully calibrated statements require the audience to complete their meaning, but are fashioned in such a way that an alternative meaning always remains available. This enables the speaker or writer to steer their way between dangerous criticism and ignominious flattery, by maintaining 'plausible deniability' about the final meaning of their discourse. Readers who take this approach to Tacitus' praise of Nerva and Trajan, for example, see it as deliberately ironized by its context: uttering this praise demonstrates its necessity at the same time as its terms have already been emptied of significance.[21] Tacitus 'saves face' with rulers and fellow subjects alike, while conveying an important truth about the Principate.

A neat episode from *Annals* illustrates how figured speech of this kind might work in a senatorial context. Thanks to the machinations of Claudius' wife Messalina, Poppaea Sabina has been accused of adultery and driven to commit suicide before trial. The senate proposes various condemnations after the fact, which compels Poppaea's widower, Cornelius Scipio, to contribute to the debate.

> *rogatus sententiam et Scipio, 'cum idem' inquit 'de admissis Poppaeae sentiam quod omnes, putate me idem dicere quod omnes', eleganti temperamento inter coniugalem amorem et senatoriam necessitatem.*
>
> *Ann.* 11.4.3

> Scipio, also required to give his opinion, said 'since I feel the same way about Poppaea's crimes as everyone, take it as read that I say the same things as everyone', a measured statement, judiciously balancing a husband's love and a senator's duty.

Scipio explicitly calls on the principle of the audience completing the meaning of his words, while also implicitly commenting on the possibility that the rest of the senate does not say what they feel.[22] His statement is even taken by some scholars to be an ironic reference to Claudius' strictures on senatorial participation in debate.[23] It thus encapsulates what readers of figured speech find compelling: a statement that leaves open the possibility of diverse readings, while also constituting a reflection on the difficulties of speech in relation to power. It is a posture which, in modern eyes, redeems many imperial subjects from an attitude to the ruler which we find impossible to respect; the idea of figured speech is therefore often invoked when we encounter material (such as praise) which challenges our sense of a subject's integrity.[24] But figured speech does not exemplify most senatorial speech acts in Tacitus' narratives.[25] Here I will point out some of the limitations of focussing exclusively on figured speech, before delineating another way of approaching Tacitus' praise of emperors, as well as the discourse of praise more generally. This will provide the groundwork for considering the productive potential of senatorial speech acts in section 2.

We may start by observing the referent of figured speech, what transforms it from suspended meaning (or meaninglessness) to pointed meaning: it is taken to refer to the conditions which produce the speech itself. The terms in which Tacitus speaks of Nerva and Trajan's regime 'conveys something about the Principate, where it is so difficult to be sure that anything said ... can be taken straight'.[26] Figured speech, in short, talks (obliquely) about its own production – if it has anything to say, that is, beyond the exigencies of the immediate situation. A less salutary example than that of Scipio shows another Claudian senator using ambiguous language simply to avoid committing himself, without commenting further on the power struggle which he aims to survive.

> *inter diversas principis voces, cum modo incusaret flagitia uxoris, aliquando ad memoriam coniugii et infantiam liberorum revolveretur, non aliud prolocutum Vitellium quam 'o facinus! o scelus!' instabat quidem Narcissus aperire ambages et veri copiam facere; sed non ideo pervicit, quin suspensa et quo ducerentur inclinatura responderet.*
>
> Ann. 11.34.1

> While the emperor's self-contradictory remarks wavered between accusations of his wife's crimes and recollections of their marriage and their little children, Vitellius made no declaration beyond 'oh, the crime! the wickedness!' Narcissus, to be sure, put him under pressure to clarify his ambiguous words and elaborate the truth of his thoughts; but he did not prevail, in that Vitellius replied with words where the meaning was not completed, and which could be interpreted whichever way the emperor led.

Vitellius' speech suspends meaning to the point of non-intervention, while that of Scipio provides a wry commentary: both are inherently reactive, and the primary aim is avoidance, another instance of the 'path clear of ambition and dangers'. Many other instances of speech, however, show us different and more active modes: prosecutions and defence pleas; proposals and counter-proposals in senate; justifications and altercations. Senators are, for the most part, trying to do things with words, so their speech needs to be more proactive and for the most part more concrete than the suspensions of figured speech would allow. The references of their speech become a world they want to act upon, whether (for instance) by acquitting or condemning another citizen, instituting or annulling honours for rulers, limiting the payment of advocates, or establishing the sanctuary status of provincial temples.[27] Some of the aims and achievements of speech may be trivial or degrading (issues I will address again in later chapters), but in seeking to act upon the world, such speeches exceed the descriptive and analytical capacity of figured speech.[28]

The open possibility for interpretation presented by figured speech draws readers into a world characterized by what Shadi Bartsch has called 'linguistic bankruptcy'.[29] As she puts it in relation to Tacitus, 'terms like *freedom*, *happiness*, and *safety* are always already undermined by their unveiling as hollow in the very works in which they appear'.[30] The suspension of meaning, as well as the thorough excavation of ideology by Tacitus, continually brings us to this point of bankruptcy, and its effects are not to be underestimated. But senators and historians also continue to deal in the currency of speech, even ambiguous speech, as (if) it held purchase on the world. Is this, as Bartsch suggests of Pliny's *Panegyric*, a failed attempt to restore meaning? Let us return to Tacitus' declaration about the present regime, and ask the question, 'In what way does it act upon the world?'

First, we should be clear that this is not an attempt to dispel ambiguity from Tacitus' text, but rather to explore the potential effects of his statements in order to conjecture what they might do for the historian. As I've already suggested, earlier in the preface, Tacitus has distinguished between imperial historiography's transmission of the regime of truth and a more rigorous historiography's critique of that regime, such as he already begins to offer with this account. The next stage of critique, if it is to move beyond reactive commentary or critique, is to propose an alternative, a modification, or even a reaffirmation of the existing regime. What happens if we take Tacitus' declaration seriously as just such a proposal?

Foucault provides a way of thinking towards such a reading when he discusses how any truth – no matter how 'self-evident' – depends upon a non-logical element. It is significant that he conceives of this element as a speech act: an assertion. He calls it 'an assertion that does not belong exactly to the realm of the true or false, that is rather a sort of commitment, a sort of profession ... that consists in saying ... it is true, *therefore* I submit'.[31] The non-logical 'therefore', he maintains, constitutes a 'profession' because it is in this assertion that the speaker comes into being as a subject (that is, a subject who can declare 'I' and who is subjected to the truth). Importantly, the assertion grounds the subject as a practitioner within the discourse that produces this acknowledged truth. Hence, 'profession' is both disciplinary (the profession of the historian) and non-logical (the profession of faith). Let us consider this again in relation to Tacitus as a practitioner of history.

As soon as Tacitus declares 'I', he grounds himself in both politics and history by orienting his attitude to previous emperors around his political career and his commitment to the truth procedures of historiography.

> *dignitatem nostram a Vespasiano inchoatam, a Tito auctam, a Domitiano longius provectam non abnuerim: sed incorruptam fidem professis neque amore quisquam et sine odio dicendus est.*
>
> Hist. 1.1.3

> I would not deny that my senatorial status was begun by Vespasian, it was considerably advanced by Titus, and promoted much further by Domitian: but no emperor should be spoken of with excessive affection or hatred by those who profess incorruptible truth.

The impersonality of the final phrase signals the separation between Tacitus' experience and the discourse to which he will now submit. But his promise, immediately following, to speak of Nerva and Trajan in the future, 'internalizes' historical discourse, which now becomes the truth not imposed from without but emerging from within: to feel what you like and say what you feel. Tacitus thus declares not just his willing subjection to the disciplinary regime of history, but his emergence as a senatorial historian through that subjection. It is only through Tacitus' willing subjection that the happiness of the present regime can be constituted as truth, for it cannot be self-evident.

Now, it could reasonably be objected that this, first, is only one way of reading these notoriously elusive sentences, and, second, presents an overly optimistic view of a speaker's agency in the Principate. These are valid points, and I will take a moment to address them together. I have assumed a progression here between Tacitus' two statements about speaking: no one should be spoken of (by historians) with excessive love or hatred; (I will write a history of) the rare happiness of times when you can feel what you like and say what you feel. This progression could, however, be a disjunction, especially if we emphasize Tacitus' introduction of *quod* – 'but' – and the ambiguity over whether the rare happiness of times is the present regime, or Tacitus' anticipated old age.[32] One possible alternative reading could be: no one should be spoken of with excessive love or hatred, *but* if I live, I will make a history of the present age, when I am old enough to say what I really feel. A reading like this produces a statement of future dissent and coheres with the image of Tacitus as the exposer of ideological facades.

My first point about such a reading is that it does not substantially alter the way Tacitus makes (his) history the discourse which guarantees the truth. Whether we characterize Tacitus' discourse as a commitment to a new regime or an ongoing destabilizing of regimes, we still have to proceed by way of this discourse. Where there is substantial difference between these two readings is in the degree of optimism – or I would prefer to say faith – with regard to what this discourse produces. Does Tacitus look forward to stripping bare the falsehoods of Trajan's principate, once it is safe to do so? Or does he choose to believe in a new regime of speech and, by choosing, take one step towards making it true?[33] The non-logical element in Tacitus' commitment to truth would then be his commitment to the truth of the present as a time of true speech.

Tacitus' declaration of truth then becomes a profession of faith which produces and sustains truth. It can also exemplify the effects of speech I want to pursue in this book; for Tacitus' formulation concretizes the regime he professes in strongly experiential terms. We have already seen how Tacitus identifies affective orientations towards power – 'hatred and excessive affection' – as detrimental to independent historical discourse. But he positions himself in the present regime (or in a future old age) which is defined affectively as 'happiness' (*felicitas*). This constitutes an intervention in what Carlos Noreña has called a 'politics of emotion', where discussing the nature of happiness – the activities and experiences through which it is felt and expressed – entailed a debate about the role and place of a citizen in the imperial state. As Noreña observes, a difference emerges between expressions like Tacitus', which link *felicitas* to senatorial autonomy and agency, and other perspectives where *felicitas* is associated with abundance of material benefits, positioning the citizen not as an agent but as a consumer.[34] Noreña, following Seneca, associates this latter experience of happiness with the depoliticizing of the imperial subject, encouraged to concentrate on leisure and material comfort. Against this, we might evoke Vivasvan Soni's vision of a lost politics of happiness which reconnects speech, thought, and action on the one hand, and physical well-being on the other, thereby 'encompassing all concerns germane to a life's narrative'.[35] In this light, Tacitus' concretizing of senatorial autonomy and agency as 'when you can think what you want and say what you think' – *ubi sentire quae velis et quae sentias dicere licet* – encompasses the experiential modes of feeling and thinking (both senses of *sentire*), wishing and desiring (*velle*), potential and capacity (*licet*), and the vocal and bodily expression of these modes (*dicere*).[36] Because all of these verbs are used quite commonly, it takes conscious effort for us to revive the connotations of mind, body, and affect in which these actions are embedded, but it is important for understanding how Tacitus' concept of political *felicitas* is that of a senatorial body working in perfect harmony across its intellectual, physical, and emotional operations. Tacitus makes this more explicit in his preface to *Agricola*, where he talks about the absence of such *felicitas* in Domitian's reign by using the metaphor of bodily health (*Agr.* 2.3–3.1). But his metaphor is not purely metaphorical; in both prefaces he expresses modes of being under different emperors as the experience, or lack, of mental and physical well-being.[37]

When Tacitus associates well-being with the capacity to speak, he situates himself as both historian and political agent. As Christopher Whitton has observed, 'the final words of *Hist.* 1.1.4 … evoke the last three words of the traditional formula with which the presiding consul summoned the Senate: "*senatores quibusque in senatu sententiam dicere licet*".[38] The phrase thus also communicates a recognizable sense of authority and socio-political status, of being summoned to a space of deliberation. The *felicitas* of the historian, then, is rendered concrete as the embodied experience of the senator, and this signals, I think, the way Tacitus' narratives will concentrate on senatorial speech as one of the primary modes of political efficacy (a point to which I return in section 2).[39]

Tacitus' choice of *felicitas* to describe the productive potential of the era for senatorial historiography is provocative, since *felicitas* has a long history as a term for the emperor's beneficence and seems to have been pointedly revived for Nerva's reign. *Felicitas temporum* is used not only at the two points where Tacitus refers to the new regime (here and *Agr.* 3.1), but in an edict of Nerva's preserved by Pliny (Plin., *Ep.* 10.53.7).[40] Since *felicitas* is recognized as an imperially sanctioned and disseminated phrase, it is often assumed that Tacitus is doing no more than following an official line, responding to an established ideology.[41] Such assumptions overlook the way the terms of imperial ideology originate from different sources of representation;[42] the choice and particular attributions of Nervan/Trajanic *felicitas* likely emerged from dialogue between senatorial and imperial circles.[43] Pliny and Tacitus, belonging to both circles, can be seen as initiating contributions to such dialogue and helping to form, rather than passively echoing, imperial value-terms. This gives added force to the way we read their association of *felicitas* with senatorial agency, as inflecting but not rejecting the association of *felicitas* with imperial beneficence. Instead of a model which emphasizes the emperor's bestowal of a happiness which subjects can only passively enjoy, Tacitus lays claim to happiness as a gift from the emperor which is only ratified in its active enjoyment by subjects. He declares that it is *only* when subjects say what they feel that the truth of the regime, the happiness of present times, is guaranteed.

In this section, we have looked at how the constraints and possibilities of speech are imagined in Tacitus' works, and the theoretical underpinnings of how we might interpret them. I have argued for an understanding of speech in Tacitus which gives more account of the speaker's agency in maintaining or modifying the truth regimes of his political world. In section 2, we turn to the imperial senate and the representation of its activities in Tacitus.

2 Senatorial business

'Does the imperial senate deserve the prominence that Tacitus gives to it?'[44] Discussing Tacitus' portrayal of senatorial behaviour, Stephen Oakley suggests that the historian's focus on the senate was prompted by the traditions of historical writing, against his 'realist' understanding that senators 'no longer wielded real power'.[45] In this section I will argue that, on the contrary, Tacitus' attention to senatorial business derives from his understanding of political agency as rooted in speech. For him the ultimate loss of agency is to lose the capacity to speak and listen, and he equates this with the condition of slaves (*Agr.* 2.3).[46] I will start with a brief overview of the imperial senate's functions and how these enhance the senate's collective prestige; active participation in these functions therefore provides significant opportunities for individual senators.[47] Then I will turn to how this understanding of the senate reflects on Tacitus' portrayal, which is generally more negative. Here I will focus on the honorific activities of the senate and associated speeches of praise since, as we have already discussed in section 1 of this introduction, these are the elements of the Roman imperial world which modern readers find most repellent. While Tacitus seems to share our distaste for the most part, this is because he concentrates primarily on moments where honorific speech tips over into dishonourable flattery. Finally, I will present the criteria by which Tacitus evaluates speech not in terms of 'Republicanism' but rather in terms of productivity and integrity.

The traditional narrative about imperial Roman rhetoric emphasizes declamation as the predominant rhetorical activity of senatorial and non-senatorial speakers.[48] In this narrative, senators find an alternative outlet for their energies in the declamation hall as exchanges in the senate become ever more ritualized and politically meaningless. Declamation therefore becomes an activity associated with political alienation – though recent scholarship has reclaimed this mode of speech as a dynamic site for the formation of the elite male subject[49] – and with the exercise of political agency in a differently regulated sphere.[50] It is striking that Tacitus pointedly ignores declamation, with all its cultural and political implications: with the exception of a few comments in *Dialogus*, he effectively proceeds as if this site of speech did not exist.[51] This omission is worth noting because it points to how Tacitus recentres the senate as the site of his investigation into effective speech.

The main kinds of activity Tacitus' senators engage in are reflective of what we know from other sources about the imperial senate: they ratify the authority of emperors, receive delegations from provinces, legislate, and review the state's finances. Predominantly, in *Annals* especially, the senate sits as a judicial body on trials concerning the public interest and determines honours for the ruler in response to particular achievements. These functions dominate Tacitus' narrative because they elicit the modes of speech he considers to be most damaging to the state – predatory accusation and flattery. They are also the activities which support a view of the imperial senate as a sterile site, where speech does no more than retrace situations it has no capacity to alter. Against this, recent historians of the early Principate have drawn attention to the way in which the additional formal powers of the imperial senate not only increased its prestige, but extended the creative potential for senatorial speech in this sphere.

First, the diversification of what constituted political speech in the senate demanded new deployments of technique and knowledge. Matthew Roller, in a detailed reading of the senatorial business narrated in some of Pliny's letters, observes that 'the Imperial senate's *interconnected* legislative, judicial, and deliberative functions generate some highly non-Republican political dynamics … Cicero could not comprehend the parliamentary *virtuosity* Pliny claims to have displayed.'[52] The consequences for the senate is to configure it as a new kind of political space, with greater capacity for more diverse modes. Beyond the curia, the heightened prestige of the senate consolidates its identity as a collective,[53] while in the conduct of meetings there is still space for the individual to achieve prominence. Roller's image of the senator skilfully mediating his different roles as prosecutor, legislator, and advisor shows the opportunities available for a speaker to exercise – and display – his mastery of these various modes of political speech, and thereby to shape his authority. What these modes also offered was a broader conceptual vocabulary with which a speaker could engage, and they promoted different political worlds and ruler–subject relations. The language of law and justice, in particular, provided ways for speakers to project citizenship as a commitment to deploy laws, whether in defence of the ruler (an implicit claim of those bringing trials for *maiestas*) or to protect fellow citizens (a claim made on all sides, but with particular charge by speakers opposing the practice of *delatio*).[54] The interconnection of the different functions of the senate, in short, enabled political discourse to be versatile in moving across different modes of senatorial activity. This perspective will inform many of my analyses of how Tacitus presents senatorial tactics in the following chapters.

The language of praise and honour can also be re-evaluated in this light. Two problems face ancient and modern critics when dealing with a subject's praise of the ruler: the pressure on truth brought to bear by the unequal power relation and the apparent unproductivity or limited productivity of praising and honouring a ruler.[55] More simply: we cannot believe that the senator who praises a ruler 'means what he says' (a problem already observed with reading Tacitus' praise of Nerva and Trajan), and we cannot see what is achieved by such speech beyond pleasing, mollifying, or even irritating the ruler (and fellow subjects). This becomes a stumbling-block for understanding why the senate spends so much time proposing and voting on honours for the princeps, an activity seen as 'getting in the way of real politics'. Pliny, speaking of Domitian's reign, lends weight to such views when he presents the necessity to praise the ruler on every occasion as an obstruction to the business of senate.

> *Nihil ante tam vulgare tam parvum in senatu agebatur, ut non laudibus principum immorarentur, quibuscumque censendi necessitas accidisset ... quasi prolatis imperii finibus nunc ingentes arcus excessurosque templorum fastigium titulos, nunc menses etiam nec hos singulos nomini Caesarum dicabamus ... At nunc quis nostrum tamquam oblitus eius de quo refertur censendi officium principis honore consumit? ... in curiam non ad certamen adulationum sed ad usum munusque iustitiae convenimus.*
>
> <div align="right">Plin., <i>Pan.</i> 54.3–5</div>

Previously, there was no matter brought before the senate so commonplace, so minor, which was not held up by encomia of the rulers from whichever senator whose duty it was to speak ... as if speaking on the extension of the empire's borders, we discoursed on mighty arches, and inscriptions which would not fit on the tops of temples, and even the months, renamed wholesale after the Caesars ... But now who among us, forgetting the subject before the house, uses up his whole allotment of speech in honouring the ruler? ... we gather in the senate now not to compete in flattery but to exercise and deliver justice.

The language of delay, of time being eaten up, and of issues being forgotten, strongly polarizes praise and politics in Pliny's view (this is, of course, a speech in which he inaugurates a new mode of true praise for Trajan, a profession of faith analogous to that of his colleague Tacitus).[56] Interestingly, the productive alternative to useless praise is described as the exercise and delivery of justice, illustrating how that (imperial) senatorial function becomes the mode of expressing political action at this point in Pliny's discourse. This statement supports the view that praise (of Domitian) is a synonym for flattery; it is not a vehicle but an obstructor of productive political action. In the same way, the proposal of honours is represented in terms of expansion and constriction: the senators could be discussing the extension of the Roman Empire in space; instead they propose honours which extend beyond the architectural and temporal spaces on which they are imposed.[57] The result is not amplitude but depletion: honours and praise crowd out and exhaust the spaces of empire and the span of senatorial political attention. A similar point is made in Tacitus' narrative by the Neronian senator C. Cassius, who remarks that 'the whole year will not be enough for the proposed supplications in honour of Nero' (*Ann.* 13.41.4).

Recent scholarship on both honours and praise has provided persuasive alternative views of the political work these might perform. Egon Flaig's influential studies of 'consensus rituals', deriving as much from Republican as imperial practices, invite readers to re-examine the political significance of all forms of communication between the ruler and different subject groups.[58] As he repeatedly observes, 'a great part of the political process in the Roman empire consisted in mutual expressions of consent'.[59] Flaig is not the only scholar to examine imperial interactions in terms of consensus,[60] but his particular focus on ritualized actions is valuable for de-investing honorific proposals and decrees of their association with political irrelevance.[61] As Andrew Wallace-Hadrill had already observed, the language of such decrees 'was vital for the construction of imperial power, and ... represented a transformation of the language of public life'.[62] Not only did the Principate as an accepted system depend on repeated consensus rituals of this nature; the senate gained authority and prestige because it was the prime (if not the only) site for honorific proposals. Amy Russell points out that the importance of such decrees is evident in the fact that they were recorded even when the ruler refused the honours: in other words, the pronouncement by the senate had significance beyond the execution of the honour itself.[63] Under such circumstances, the degree of attention that senators collectively and individually devoted to honorific proposals seems more understandable: they were dynamically engaging with a process which held considerable stakes for their capacity to intervene in the life of the city and the empire.[64]

This is our modern understanding of why the senate would devote so much energy to devising honours for the ruler, but it is not clear that Tacitus sees this activity in the same light. Rather, his representation of the honorific process concentrates more on instances where the senate as a whole, or individual senators, degrade themselves with excessive and inappropriate proposals. When honours seem appropriate, on the other hand, Tacitus usually passes over them with extreme brevity, but if they are read more carefully, we can see that there is an underlying sense of propriety which often guides Tacitus' evaluation. Adulatory honours are improper because they over-represent and therefore do not successfully represent what has been achieved. Early in Nero's reign, for example, a military campaign against Parthia's involvement in Armenia is celebrated with triumphal honours in the first stage of action (*Ann.* 13.8.1). Because these honours would be more appropriate at the end of a campaign, they lose the capacity to symbolize effectively the events they mark.[65] Tacitus refers to the proposals for these honours as exaggeration – *in maius celebrata* – and as *adulatio*, setting them off against the senators' real joy in the qualities of Domitius Corbulo, the commander of the campaign. Critical accounts of this nature implicitly rely, however, on a sense that some honours *are* appropriate and that good judgement is required to arrive at a suitable speech, object, or ceremony to symbolize the ruler's achievement.

The performance of suitable honours remains for the most part as 'background noise' in Tacitus' narrative: comments such as 'the usual honours were voted' could be taken in this way rather than being seen as scornful.[66] One notable exception is early in Vespasian's reign, when Tacitus presents Helvidius Priscus' successful delivery of honorific speech from which 'false things were absent' (*Hist.* 4.4.3), an achievement which we will examine in more detail in chapter three. There are also moments where we can discern Tacitus' acknowledgement of the work involved in devising appropriate honours. On the death of Tiberius' adopted son Germanicus, for instance, the way in which Tacitus introduces the senate's proposals is revealing.[67]

> *Honores, ut quis amore in Germanicum aut ingenio validus, reperti decretique.*
>
>   *Ann.* 2.83.1
>
> Honours were sought out and decreed, as each proposer was authorized by his love for Germanicus or by his ability.

Tacitus here highlights not the collective decision of the senate but the activity of each proposer, reflecting his awareness that individual senators would be remembered for their contribution to this debate.[68] Tacitus' reference to each speaker as *validus* could refer to his motivation for speaking – he is 'energized' by affection – or to his effect on the audience, being 'authorized' by his ability. In a more incidental episode near the end of Tiberius' reign, the senate decrees honours for the emperor to mark his support of those dispossessed by fire. These honours are implicitly appropriate representations not only because of the genuine good Tiberius brings to the community, but also because he refuses to glorify his own acts (*Ann.* 6.45.1). The senate's importance in symbolizing these acts is therefore reinforced and perhaps accounts for the care that senators put into their suggestions: *et pro ingenio cuiusque quaesiti decreti in principem honores* (*Ann.* 6.45.2). 'Honours were devised and proposed for the princeps according to the talent of each proposer.' The reference to researching or devising honours in both episodes (*reperti, quaesiti*) suggests the critical judgement involved in adapting suitable precedents as well as in justifying these proposals.[69] Tacitus maintains his jaundiced view of honours, but in both these instances the worst he can conclude is that the honours do not stand the test of time. Given his capacity to undermine the actions of senate and ruler in other episodes, we should take his forbearance in these episodes seriously.

What these readings suggest is that it is worth our while to consider more carefully whether every instance of bestowing honours is dismissed by Tacitus as flattery. Instead, I would argue, there are signs that the historian discriminates between different kinds of honorific proposal. Policing the boundaries between honour and flattery in this way indicates acceptance of the new role of imperial senators but emphasizes the importance of conserving their dignity and integrity. When Tacitus renders judgement on a speaker who has transgressed these boundaries, he touches once more on issues to do with the truth produced by speech.

In the first chapter we will look at the truth produced by flattery, but here I will turn briefly to Pliny to illustrate how a productive discourse of honour can be sustained. Honour and praise work as a discourse of commonly held values, whether sanctioned by the gods, philosophical canons of virtue, or the consensus of the speaker's community.[70] Evoking this discourse in a speech of praise, or as an element of deliberative or forensic speech, is often seen as persuasive or didactic, pointing out to the audience and/or addressee a desired path of behaviour. Pliny's formulation on his own *Panegyricus* is very influential:

> *Sed parendum est senatus consulto quod ex utilitate publica placuit, ut consulis voce sub titulo gratiarum agendarum boni principes quae facerent recognoscerent, mali quae facere deberent.*
>
> Plin., *Pan.* 4.1

> But now I must obey the decree of the senate, which it is pleased to make in the public interest, that through the voice of the consul delivering a speech of thanks, good rulers should recognize what they have already achieved, and bad ones realize what they are required to achieve.

What good rulers have already achieved is to be good rulers: panegyric will be descriptive for them as it is prescriptive for bad rulers. It is usual to excerpt the concluding phrase of this passage,[71] but I have retained the context, which has important consequences for the discourse of virtue here presented. Pliny presents this discourse of virtue as filtered through to the ruler by way of a senatorial process – a decree commanding the consul, with reference to the interest of the Roman people as a whole – and by way of a consular voice which articulates the will of the senate. He thereby presents proper political process as an inversion of imperial hierarchies, with *utilitas publica* as the primary concern of the senate, with the consul obedient to the senate's will, and, finally, with the ruler shaping himself, at the consul's word and the senate's will, to the interests of all.[72] The discourse of imperial virtue is authorized by the political structure of the state. Although Pliny's reference to himself as 'the voice of the consul' seems to deprive him of agency, it also augments his authority: the speaker of praise is the mouthpiece of the community, articulating its values.

Pliny's practice illustrates the political work done by honorific speech. Nevertheless, the extent to which such speech can enhance a speaker's authority remains partially dependent on the nature and actions of the ruler as beyond the speaker's agency. In that respect speakers of praise, like all orators, are poised between responding to external conditions, and shaping those conditions through their speech,[73] a point made explicitly by Pliny in the passage quoted above. But it is important not to focus on the representation of the ruler as the singular effect of speech. Insofar as praise is a performance of evaluation and an affirmation of communal values, it projects an image of the senate as a site of judgement, which holds considerable political potential.

The discourses of praise and advice are not limited to the senate; both formal and informal councils convened around the ruler also provide opportunities for senators (and non-senators) to act directly upon the world of the Principate. A few illuminating instances will show up in this book: the military council of Otho before the first Battle of Bedriacum in AD 69 (*Hist.*

2.32–33); various scenes of accusation and defence in the emperor's 'private' quarters (*Ann.* 11.1–2; 14.52). But for the most part I focus on the senate, because this was the primary site where speech could be directed towards multiple audiences, and particularly towards the senators as a political collective. It was also a site where the formal requirement to speak and the order of speaking could be deployed creatively, not only to press a course of action but to develop and sustain a sense of what a senator should be.[74] Finally, senatorial business and decisions were in different ways recorded, which – to a degree – gave a certain self-consciously public direction to the speech acts of senators.[75] Tacitus exploits these procedural and archival elements in his narratives of senatorial sessions,[76] showing how senators take up opportunities in debate to promote their own status and enhance their own fame as well as to project their understanding of ruler–subject relations and of citizenship.

It will be noticed that I have not so far referred to any senatorial action, or to Tacitus' perspective, as 'Republican'. Approaches of this nature do not seem to have yielded much detailed insight into specific episodes in the narrative, perhaps because 'Republic' is a term capacious of many different positions and behaviours. It seems to me that most attempts to classify every political intervention as an appeal to 'Principate' or 'Republic' are too abstract and therefore too sweeping in their claims.[77] The Neronian senator Thrasea Paetus, for instance, is often regarded as a 'Republican' and his interventions in the senate are interpreted (and disparaged) accordingly as unrealistic attempts to restore a political constitution long obsolete. But many features of his interventions, such as participation in a treason trial, praise of the emperor, and reinforcement of the senate's prestige in the provinces, show how he fully inhabits the thought-world of an imperial senator.[78] To investigate senatorial politics in the Tacitean narratives more extensively, I consider how it operates at an experiential level: how citizenship and relations with a ruler are conceptualized through existing, recognizable social roles and hierarchies. In this, I draw on the influence of Matthew Roller, who showed the importance of modelling imperial authority and power on convivial and paternal ideas.[79] Following Roller, I am interested in how such ideas and concepts can be both conservative and transformational: they can maintain the status quo, or enable change or restoration. Hence my focus is on how these ideas are deployed politically both as vehicles for specific arguments in a given situation and as the broader, longer-term effects of speech beyond its immediate, local aim. In my conviction that imperial senators did find some limited space of efficacy in their political sphere and that Tacitus records political action to identify and preserve modes of efficacy, I share some approaches with Thomas Strunk. He boldly conceives of Republicanism as 'the choice made for the common good over that of personal advantage', a sense of 'Republic' based in pragmatism and capacious of different points of view.[80] This enables an analysis of Tacitean narrative which is ideologically informed and engages with the concrete detail of senatorial action in the city and on military service. My analysis will differ from Strunk's in moving away altogether from the polarity Republic–Principate and in exploring the broader conceptual worlds engendered by senators, whether their concern is for personal advantage or for the common good.

In this section we have examined the role of the imperial senate from the perspectives of both modern scholarship and Tacitus' own writings. I have sought to move past the idea that Tacitus' representation of the imperial senate is relentlessly negative. Instead, by focussing on what we can see of senators strategically deploying their deliberative practices, I have tried to uncover a sense of what senatorial speech might produce in the world of imperial Rome. This presents a paradigm for the sort of reading I will pursue throughout this book.

3 Entering the archive

In his famous digression on historical writing, Tacitus outlines what he considers to be the use of history in the Principate.[81] The framework for his claim is definitively political: he begins by expressing the uses of history in democracy and oligarchy, where he says it is important to understand fully the nature of the powerful group (*populus* or senators) so that the reader of history can successfully negotiate with them. When he turns to the Principate, however, Tacitus does not advise the reader to understand the nature of the princeps.[82]

> *sic converso statu neque alia rerum <salute> quam si unus imperitet, haec conquiri tradique in rem fuerit, quia pauci prudentia honesta ab deterioribus, utilia ab noxiis discernunt.*
>
> Ann. 4.33.2

similarly, when the whole status quo has been overturned, and there is no safety for the Roman commonwealth unless it is under the command of one man, it would be relevant to inquire into and transmit these events, since few people can through their own wisdom distinguish honourable acts from worse, or expedient from harmful.[83]

The actions of historical research and writing – *conquiri tradique* – encapsulate what I have termed the 'critical archive' that Tacitus produces: researching, commenting on, and passing down practices from which future readers can learn. It is significant also that, instead of knowledge about the ruler, Tacitus offers the fundamental skill of deliberative rhetoric: the capacity to perceive and articulate a situation in terms of what is honourable – *honesta* – and what is expedient – *utilia*.[84] Thus Tacitus grounds senatorial political knowledge in the traditional craft of oratory, but posits history as the archive in which this knowledge can be preserved and transmitted.[85] In the following chapters, I will explore how Tacitus represents effective speech, the political worlds it creates, and the transmission of effective practice across and in his narratives.

The following three chapters examine in more detail the ideas rehearsed in section 2 of this introduction. I investigate how Tacitus represents the political effect of speech acts by reviewing how different modes of speech draw on certain social and political relationships. Tacitus views deleterious modes of speech as damaging in their effects because they project ruler–subject relations in sterile or hostile terms and because they pervert and hollow out the socio-political relationships on which they draw. Attempts to counter these damaging modes of speech, therefore, face the challenge of revitalizing existing relationships, but also continually risk being assimilated into the speech that they oppose.

Chapter one examines the problem of *adulatio* or flattery as a mode which draws on both the discourses of praise and advice and the social structure of friendship. Reviewing Tacitus' representation of flatterers through the lens of ethical philosophy shows how acts of flattery are fundamentally anti-social, in that they involve the willing abandonment of independence on the part of the speaker and aim to decouple the addressee from his social network. In senatorial contexts, flattery is exposed as inimical to the practice of deliberation. At the same time, competitive displays of flattery, and the pressure to continually innovate, call upon precisely the rhetorical skills that the senatorial class has carefully cultivated. The aesthetic dimension of flattery, therefore, engages the energies of orators even as it depletes their political independence.

Chapter two turns to the second deleterious mode of speech, the practice of *delatio* or predatory prosecution. This practice draws on the civic requirement to uphold the law and evokes a relationship with the ruler centred on the idea of security. Just as the ruler's existence ensures the safety and flourishing of the state, so subjects' main concern is to safeguard the personal safety of the ruler. I examine how this concept is elaborated from Cicero's *Pro Marcello* to Tiberius' Praetorian Prefect Aelius Sejanus to project the ruler as continually under threat and requiring vigilant protection from citizens. This nexus of ideas enables lawful acts of violence against fellow citizens; the tradition of conducting prosecutions with more than one prosecutor, I argue, alleviates the anxiety of this civic violence by distributing the agency of prosecution and depersonalizing the process. Tacitus exploits this distributed agency in his narrative of the Tiberian regime in order to create uncertainty about whether the *delator* is an independent agent or a pawn of the ruler. Around this uncertainty is built one of the most important debates about the imperial subject: the extent of his responsibility for his actions. Attacks upon former *delatores* and their speeches of self-defence become the site for discussing senatorial agency in imperial politics.

Chapter three reviews the strategies available for countering these modes of speech. Because they are seen to be parasitic upon social and political institutions such as friendship, the *consilium*, deliberation, the exercise of justice, and the lawcourt, those who speak up against *adulatio* or *delatio* have to work from within these same institutions to effect change. The strongest opponent of *adulatio* is the Emperor Tiberius himself, who (not entirely consistently) emphasizes his concrete achievements and relationships with the senate as a collective. Meanwhile, the senator Helvidius Priscus, early in Vespasian's reign, seems to inaugurate a new way of addressing the ruler which combines truth-telling and honorific speech. Opposition to *delatio* implicates speakers in the most difficulties, because this mode of speech is inherently agonistic and because the commonest approaches to countering *delatio* are through the law. Consequently, attacks on this practice risk becoming assimilated to the aggression of the *delatores* themselves. A significant factor that speakers focus on is the reward of money or status which *delatores* gain from prosecution; this enables them to project *delatio* as a form of predation rather than civic duty. Finally, as we have already noted at the start of this chapter, speakers who intervene in and mitigate the sentencing of trials engage indirectly with the *delatores* and thereby promote the idea of senatorial participation and the exercise of judgement in the service of preserving fellow citizens.

The final two chapters of the book examine ethical and pragmatic aspects of the presentation of speech in Tacitus' work. Here I am concerned with how Tacitus makes his historiography a critical archive of effective speech by both representing and commenting on speakers. Chapter four identifies ethos, the performed self of the speaker, as an important way of distinguishing between productive and deleterious modes of speech. Ethos works by engaging the audience's evaluative and emotive responses, and a successful performance of the speaker's self affirms or redirects community values. This provides a solution to the problem identified in chapter three, where the actions of the *delator* are disturbingly similar to other forms of judicial and legal speech. Tacitus isolates the *delator* from engagement with shared emotions, which become the site for resisting his persuasive recalibration of community values: I pursue this through an examination of Eprius Marcellus in both *Dialogus* and *Annals*. Ethos as it is performed and received in speech mutates into character-representation in narrative, enabling the narrator and his readers to join in the evaluative engagement with speakers. Tacitus pointedly intervenes as a narrator, to 'correct' the contemporary audience's estimation of Helvidius Priscus in *Histories* and Marcus Lepidus in *Annals*. He thereby demonstrates his anxiety to transmit the appropriate judgement of these individuals to the future.

Chapter five moves from ethos to *mores*, conceived not just as character but as modes of behaviour, skills, and strategic actions. Tacitus' narrative shows us certain patterns of senatorial intervention, repeated across years or even generations, which propagate a sense not just of traditional values but of specific tactics for effective action. This tradition reaches beyond the limits of the narrative to encompass the narrator and potentially the reader. Here I focus on Thrasea Paetus as the central figure in a 'genealogy of virtue' reaching back to Marcus Lepidus and forward to Tacitus himself. While this genealogy has often been structured around the ideas of a 'Stoic opposition', I argue that the strength of Thrasea as an exemplary figure rests on the diverse modes through which he forms connections with his contemporaries and with the future. In particular, the pointed parallels between Lepidus and Thrasea suggest a transmission of political tactics and senatorial principles which can then be traced between other senators of different generations. The work of Pliny the Younger, and its intersections with Tacitus' narratives, illustrates how these tactics and principles are extended into the Trajanic era.

We have already seen how Tacitus characterizes that era as a time when inner thought and feeling (encompassed by the verb *sentire*) can be expressed. The concluding section of this book briefly reflects on how the expression of thought – the *sententia* – in Tacitus' works denotes both the formal speech act of the senator and the distinctive epigrammatic style of the historian. Tacitean style becomes the vehicle through which the ideals and techniques of efficacious speech are transmitted to the future.

Part One

Modes of Speech

1

Turpe servitium: The Political World of Flattery

In AD 35, the Emperor Tiberius appointed Lucius Vitellius, consul of AD 34 (and father of the future Emperor Aulus Vitellius), to the important position of governor of Syria with the mission of supporting changes of rule in Armenia and Parthia. Vitellius' exemplary success is presented in an account which combines two years' campaigning: Tacitus explicitly draws the reader's attention to this as an episode designed to relieve the mind after contemplating the deterioration of the Tiberian regime (*Ann.* 6.38.1). But even as Tacitus introduces the new governor whose actions are worthy of his heroic narrative,[1] he looks ahead to Vitellius' inglorious career under later emperors and reintegrates his character into the sordid world of Roman politics.

> eo de homine haud sum ignarus sinistram in urbe famam, pleraque foeda memorari; ceterum regendis provinciis prisca virtute egit: unde regressus et formidine C. Caesaris, familiaritate Claudii turpe in servitium mutatus exemplar apud posteros adulatorii dedecoris habetur, cesseruntque prima postremis, et bona iuventae senectus flagitiosa obliteravit.
>
> *Ann.* 6.32.4

As regards this man, I am not unaware that he has an unfortunate reputation in Rome and that many disgraceful acts of his are recorded; but in ruling provinces he acted with old-fashioned virtue: returning from there and switching to disgraceful servility from fear of Gaius and intimacy with Claudius, he became the prime example for posterity of the dishonourable flatterer. So his first deeds gave way to his later acts, and the good of his youth was eclipsed by the reproach of his old age.

L. Vitellius is explicitly introduced as *exemplar adultorii*, evoking the sort of 'sententious character type' analysed by Patrick Sinclair,[2] which encapsulates a mode of being in the world of imperial politics. Sinclair concentrates on character sketches which perform the move from the individual to the general type by concluding with a universalizing *sententia*. Here, Tacitus gestures towards the general with the noun-heavy term *exemplar adulatorii dedecoris*, where both *exemplar* and *adulator* suggest that Vitellius stands for a practice more widely adopted by Roman imperial subjects.[3] Around his character sketch congregates much of the evaluative language associated with flattery throughout Tacitus' work: predominant is the language of dishonour – *foedus, turpis, dedecor, flagitiosus*. At the centre of the sketch, the returning governor's new mode of behaviour is called *servitium*, and the concluding 'premature epitaph' picks up on the opening comments about memory and reputation, warning readers that the cost of *adulatio* is eternal infamy.[4]

What makes a talented and successful senator court such infamy? Tacitus presents two motivators for Vitellius in his relations with two rulers, and these too are exemplary of the wider problem of flattery in the Principate. The more understandable is Vitellius' fear of violence from the uncontrollable Emperor Gaius; as Daniel Kapust has observed, flattery often emerges as a form of coerced speech in situations where inequality of power is reinforced by the ruler's capacity to inflict pain and death.[5] Kapust rightly observes that this is a less morally reprehensible form of flattery. Indeed, if we read Dio's account of what occasioned Vitellius' fear and flattery, as he is dragged before the emperor to be put to death and seeks salvation by prostrating himself before his ruler (examined further in section 1.1), we might find it difficult to see any dishonour or degeneracy in such desperate measures. (Dio 59.27.5–6) The second cause requires a closer look: Vitellius' intimacy with Claudius should, ideally, release him from the constraints of speech under Gaius and enable him to speak openly to the emperor. Instead, Vitellius' continued exercise of *adulatio* illustrates a near-universal tendency for this mode of speech to undermine the social interchange of friendship and with it the practice of friends giving advice.[6] In a world where decision-making is carried out in private council as much as in public senate meetings, *adulatio* has an immediate and disastrous political impact.

Flattery, then, emerges out of and is a mark of the damage that is done by unequal power relations such as subsist between the emperor and his subjects. At the same time, however, the practice of flattery does its own damage, corrupting and degenerating modes of speech which underpin social and political interaction. It thus illustrates the 'co-production' of the imperial regime which I outlined in the introduction: the imperial subject may turn to flattery in conditions of violence and coercion imposed by the ruler; the subject may also initiate a discourse of flattery without prompting – or with only the barest of prompts – from the ruler. It may be objected that, even in this latter situation, the subject is still under the coercion of a latent threat from the ruler, that Vitellius, for example, is prompted by fear of Claudius as much as by familiarity. But it is important to keep a space open for the agency and responsibility of the imperial subject, as Tacitus does: however common it becomes to speak of senatorial experience under the emperors using the metaphor of slavery, there is still a range of options and opportunities available to senators, unrealizable in slave experience.

The association of flattery with slavery, nevertheless, is crucial, because it evokes a model of speech which is the antithesis of senatorial speech – non-advisory, lacking independence, following the contours of the master's will and desire. In this last aspect, therefore, *adulatio* is fundamentally false, either externally or internally and sometimes both at once: it does not provide a faithful representation of the world and/or it does not express the true opinions or feelings of the speaker.[7] Because it lacks these fundamental ties to a speaker's mind or to the world, it is empty speech, sometimes described as inert or absurd. In that it is entirely dependent upon the will and desire of the master or ruler, it is degrading for the speaker: hence, as we've seen in the case of Vitellius, it is associated with corruption, foulness, dirt, and dishonour. What will also emerge as we look further into flattery is its (initially paradoxical) association with innovative forms of speech. We see how the dynamic of flattery leads to competition with and eventually aggression towards peers. These aspects of flattery mimic the behaviour not so much of slaves as of orators: part of the damage done by flattery is in the way it 'shadows' elite practices of formal speech and social exchange, emptying them of significance.[8]

Before we turn to Tacitus' exploration of *adulatio* and the world it creates, it is worth noting how this mode of speaking crosses different modes of existence and creates a new political commonality of imperial 'parasites'. In place of agonistic debate, *adulatio* substitutes a false speech associated with slavery and the household, with the threat of violence and (as we shall see) the 'reward' of life. When it is deployed in the senate or the *consilium*, the dissonance between servility and senatorial status is felt. In the political domain, moreover, the standard by which flattery falls short is constructed on the ethical model of friendship, but the extent of distance between the friend and the senator as advisor remains unstable. Finally, Tacitus' sharpest reproofs of *adulatio* are directed at neither slaves nor senators, but the people, whose political disenfranchisement he does not acknowledge. In holding the people accountable for their meaningless flattery despite the absence of any more meaningful communication environment within which they could operate, Tacitus makes a rigorous point about responsibility which, I argue, should be held as applicable to the senatorial class as well.

In section 1.1, I will situate Tacitus' treatment of *adulatio* in the context of ethical philosophy in order to explore these issues of agency and responsibility. Here the social and cultural expectations of friendship in conditions of inequality are sketched out, as is the damage done to social relations by the practice of *adulatio*. This is vividly illustrated by Tacitus' accounts of emperors whose access to the truth or to any meaningful interaction with their subjects is foreclosed.

1.1 The agency of *adulatio*

When Lucius Vitellius turns to the discourse of flattery, as we have seen, he does so in extreme conditions which are imposed by a violent emperor. Gaius, we are told, feels hatred and suspicion for successful men of ability like Vitellius: such feelings are characteristic of the tyrannical ruler.[9] In response, Vitellius puts on a very careful performance of humility and adulation:

> Adopting a demeanour much more humble than his status would suggest, Vitellius fell down at the emperor's feet with tears and lamentations, prostrating himself before Gaius and worshipping him as a god; finally he vowed that if he lived he would offer sacrifice to him.
>
> Dio 59.27.5

Vitellius' deliberate self-abasement draws the scorn of Tacitus (and of posterity), but Dio's account of his interactions with Gaius makes it clear that Vitellius' agency is severely limited. Many scenes of flattery draw attention to the way in which the *adulator*'s words take their direction from the will and desire of the addressee, to which they must conform. This is caricatured in the line of Terence which Cicero quotes, where the flatterer's habit of speech is reduced to pure repetition: *negat quis, nego; ait, aio; postremo imperavi egomet mihi omnia assentari* (Cic., *Amic.* 25.93, quoting Ter., *Eun.* 250): 'A man says "no", I say "no": he says "yes", I say "yes"; in short, I have made it my rule to agree with him on all matters.' Plutarch, in *How to Tell a Flatterer from a Friend*, uses the analogy of mathematical geometry to liken the flatterer to an imaginary line without substance or independent existence (Plut., Mor. 63c). More commonly, the *adulator* or *kolax* is likened to an animal who produces sounds without *logos*. The verb *adulari* is first attested in a context which presents human voice as an extension of the different sounds made by animals, and particularly by dogs.[10] Cicero picks this up in his invective of Piso, when he concludes that his opponent has been reduced to a creature 'without voice, without independence, without authority, without any appearance of consular status, shivering, trembling, fawning on (*adulantem*) all men' (Cic., *Pis.* 99). Philodemus and Plutarch in their treatises on flattery liken the flatterer to a dog or a monkey,[11] and Philodemus makes it explicit that the notion of being a *tame* animal or a pet is as important as the debasement of voice.[12] The role of the animal lies in its responsiveness to a situation initiated by its master, whether that situation is the animal's original domestication or any subsequent interaction between master and pet.[13] We can already see that the example of Vitellius involves a much higher degree of creativity, but the caricatures of flatterers in ethical writings point to an important question of agency: to what degree can we hold these speakers responsible for the way they address a person, when that person so evidently holds mastery over them?

The question becomes ever more pressing when we turn to the last figuration of the creature without *logos* whose default speech mode is flattery: the slave. We already saw Tacitus speaking of Vitellius' return to Rome as a transformation *turpe in servitium*, 'into disgraceful servility', performed in Dio's text as prostration at the emperor's feet. In the preface to *Histories* Tacitus identifies the *adulatio* of historians as *foedum crimen servitutis* (*Hist.* 1.1.2), the 'foul dishonour of servitude'. And when in *Annals* he records Tiberius' reign as *tempora . . . adulatione sordida* (*Ann.* 3.65.2), 'times disfigured by flattery', his judgement is once more validated by the emperor: *memoriae proditur Tiberium, quotiens curia egrederetur, Graecis verbis in hunc modum eloqui solitum 'o homines ad servitutem paratos!'* (*Ann.* 3.65.3) 'It is recorded that Tiberius, whenever he departed from the senate house, would exclaim in Greek: "O men, self-prepared for slavery!"[14] The evaluative language of disgust – *turpe, foedum, sordida* – is directed specifically at those of high political and cultural status, senators and historians, descending to such levels of dependent speech. In *Dialogus* Tacitus brings out the internal tensions of senatorial *adulatio* as a vector of servility in public life, when Maternus challenges the suggestion that he should look to Vibius Crispus and Eprius Marcellus as examples of the kind of successful career which can be attained through *eloquentia*: '*quid habent in hac sua fortuna concupiscendum? ... quod adligati omni adulatione nec imperantibus umquam satis servi videntur nec nobis satis liberi?*' (*Dial.* 13.4–5) 'What do they have in this fortune of theirs that I should desire? ... that, shackled by every sort of flattery, they never seem sufficiently servile to their rulers, or sufficiently free to us?' Because *servitium* is a mode which senatorial speakers do not fully inhabit, because they retain aspects of autonomy, their appearance in the shackles of *adulatio* is more repellent than pitiful.[15]

A closer look at any instance of *adulatio* whether performed by slave, starving parasite, or senator, however, reveals that even the most dependent speech is performed in interactions where agency is shared or divided between the interlocutors. James Scott's by now classic analysis of the production, content, and contexts of resistant speech uncovers a high degree of creativity and flexibility among groups subject to the severest repression and coercion.[16] Meanwhile, texts such as Theophrastus' *Characters* as well as the already mentioned works of ethical philosophy on friendship and flattery by Philodemus, Cicero, and Plutarch present the flatterer as an individual who preys on his wealthier, more powerful victims. Plutarch's title, *How to Tell a Flatterer from a Friend*, implicitly positions his reader – the potential recipient of flattery – as under threat, his social network at risk of infiltration and undermining. Although the flatterer is assumed to occupy a lower social position in these scenarios, he is ascribed the greater agency, continually approaching or intercepting the man whose favours he courts. The context of friendship within which this discourse of flattery (and how to resist it) is elaborated is as relevant to the position of imperial senators as is the paradigm of the slave. The emperor is drawn from the senatorial class, so the language of friendship is most appropriate for speaking of his relations with senators; indeed, he chooses many of his companions from that class. Central to the need to separate friendship from flattery in the ethical texts is that a man expects his friends to advise him appropriately: again, this mirrors some expectations about senatorial or equestrian interactions with the emperor. In this reversal of agency, then, we see that the will of the dominant interlocutor is thwarted by the flatterer's creation of a discourse advantageous to himself but not to his interlocutor. Specifically, the dominant interlocutor suffers in two ways: his social network is damaged or undermined, and his access to true speech and frank opinion is blocked.

The damage to the social network occurs in two ways. First, because flattery disguises itself as friendship, it throws suspicion onto true friendship. So Plutarch directs most of his energy to the flatterer's dangerous similarity to the friend who speaks frankly, since this imitation has the potential to infect all friendships with distrust (Plut., *Mor.* 51c, 50f). Secondly, the flatterer seeks to construct an exclusive relationship with his victim, isolating him from other flatterers or true friends. This is a distinctive and striking feature of Philodemus' flatterer: 'The *kolax* hates all close friends of the men he flatters ... with whom he wages war at banquets. Keeping other flatterers in isolation (*erēmous*), he eats alone and holds them in low esteem' (*PHerc.* 222, col. 7.1–9).[17] Such isolation, in the case of a ruler, is another feature of the tyrant and is usually considered to be the result of the tyrant's own hatred and suspicion of his citizens, as in Tacitus' and Pliny's descriptions of Domitian which we will examine below. When the flatterer deploys his agency, however, solitude becomes something imposed on the victim/ruler, the better to control him. More precisely, as the case of Tiberius shows, the flatterer works on the observable character of his victim. The arch-flatterer Sejanus mobilizes the emperor's known dislike of social interaction and induces him to withdraw to the island of Capri: time and again this situation is referred to by Tacitus as *solitudo*.[18] A retreat of this sort from regular social interaction with imperial subjects has the dangerous consequence of diminishing the ruler's sense of a common humanity. In the case of both Tiberius and Domitian, their reclusiveness is conceptually linked to their cruelty, which – as we have already seen – induces fear and a propensity for flattery in their subjects. Hence the cycle of flattery-isolation-fear becomes a self-perpetuating cycle and obscures the sense of where this destructive interaction was initiated: by the threatening tyrant inducing flattery, or by the self-interested flatterer propelling the ruler into distrustful isolation. The language of animality is deployed again, this time to convey how fundamental human social qualities are perverted and destroyed. Plutarch quotes (and refutes) Bias saying that the fiercest of wild animals is the tyrant, just as the fiercest of domesticated animals is the flatterer (Plut., *Mor.* 61c): once more the shared agency of subject and ruler involved in fostering this vice is implied. And Pliny's memorable account of Domitian as a wild beast concludes with an observation on his perpetual state of isolation: *non adire quisquam non adloqui audebat, tenebras semper secretumque captantem, nec umquam ex solitudine sua prodeuntem, nisi ut solitudinem faceret* (Plin., *Pan.* 48.5). 'No one dared to approach or address him, as he sought out always the darkest and most withdrawn of places and never emerged from his isolation unless he could make another.' Advising the Emperor Trajan on the principles of good rule, Dio Chrysostom declares that 'if solitude (*erēmia*) is miserable, and to be feared above all, we must consider solitude to be not the lack of human company, but the lack of friends' (Dio Chrys., *Or.* 3.101).

The flatterer's attack on his addressee's social circle works towards a state of solitude which, when translated to interactions with the emperor, contributes to the construction of a tyrant. It also illustrates how the shared agency of flattery makes subjects complicit in creating the kind of ruler they then endure. The second deleterious effect of flattery is on truth and frankness; again, translating this problem to imperial interactions demonstrates the extent of its damage to communication even of basic knowledge. The swiftly changing context of civil war in AD 69 brings out in two episodes how unwieldy and obstructive *adulatio* is to the flow of information and processes of decision: the first when Otho has gone to the praetorian camp to be declared emperor; the second after the legions in Moesia have gone over to Vespasian. Relaying such unwelcome news to the Emperors Galba and Vitellius respectively would require a commitment to truth; their subjects instead take refuge in the pleasing speech of flattery and its attendant speech mode, unreliable rumour.

> *affertur rumor rapi in castra incertum quem senatorem, mox Othonem esse qui raperetur, simul ex tota urbe, ut quisque obvius fuerat, alii formidine augentes, quidam minora vero, ne tum quidem obliti adulationis.*
>
> Hist. 1.29.1

> The rumour was brought to the emperor that some senator – it was unclear who – had been taken away to the camp, then that Otho was the one who had been taken away, and then all at once, from all round the city, wherever each man had encountered him, some exaggerating the news from fear, others minimizing the truth, having not even then forgotten the need for flattery.

The impressionistic syntax replicates the gradual acquisition of more precise details, but the eye-witness accounts turn out to be the most unreliable, driven by emotion and the desire to please the emperor. Flattery in this instance consists of diminishing the threat of an imperial pretender who appears to have gained the support of the urban military, and it prefigures a succession of delays and hesitations which have fatal consequences for Galba and the inhabitants of the city (the worst violence is narrated *Hist.* 1.40–44). It is ironic that Galba himself, in his speech of advice to his newly-adopted successor, has identified precisely this problem in ruler–subject interaction: *inrumpet adulatio, blanditiae et pessumum veri affectus venenum, sua cuique utilitas* (*Hist.* 1.15.4). 'Flattery and smooth talk will infect your relations with others, and their own self-interest, which poisons true goodwill.'[19]

The unwelcome news for Vitellius comes from further afield and thus cannot be immediately translated into action: Aponius Saturninus, governor of Moesia, writes to inform the emperor of the third legion's defection. Saturninus himself, like Galba's informants, distorts the truth because of self-interest: he too is defecting to the Flavian side. Hence he minimizes the danger through omissions,[20] while Vitellius' friends elaborate the sparse information into misleading reassurances.

> *sed neque Aponius cuncta, ut trepidans re subita, perscripserat, et amici adulantes mollius interpretabantur: unius legionis eam seditionem, ceteris exercitibus constare fidem.*
>
> *Hist.* 2.96.1

> But Aponius did not tell the whole story, being uncertain because of the sudden turn of events, and the emperor's flattering friends provided a rather favourable interpretation of his tale: they said this was just a mutiny, confined to one legion; the loyalty of the other forces would stand firm.

This is most likely a *consilium* at which Saturninus' letter is read,[21] where information should be processed through deliberation, and advice should be translated into effective action. The contamination of both information and advice has a disastrous effect, though here it chimes in with the emperor's own desires, as evidenced by his attempt to suppress the bad news among the soldiers in the city (*Hist.* 2.96.2). By contrast, Germanicus as commander in AD 16 sought to bypass the problem of his friends' *adulatio* by disguising himself as a common soldier and eavesdropping on his legions (*Ann.* 2.12.3). Tiberius, near the end of his life, and after having realized the extent to which he was circumvented by Sejanus, seems to have sought an equivalent way round *adulatio* when he commands the will of Fulcinius Trio – and the abuse of the emperor contained therein – to be publicly read.

> ... *patientiam libertatis alienae ostentans et contemptor suae infamiae, an scelerum Seiani diu nescius mox quoquo modo dicta vulgari malebat veritatisque, cui adulatio officit, per probra saltem gnarus fieri.*
>
> *Ann.* 6.38.3

> ... vaunting his tolerance for another man's freedom of speech and contemptuous of his own bad reputation, or perhaps, having long been in the dark about Sejanus' crimes, he now began to prefer the speech of others to be publicized whatever its nature, and thus through abusive words to become aware at last of the truth which flattery obstructed.

For an emperor to be *nescius* or *ignarus* is potentially fatal for his rule (as the narratives of Galba and Vitellius in *Histories* attest):[22] hence Tiberius is better known for anxiously reasserting his control of knowledge, as he does at *Annals* 3.69.2 and 4.8.3. As we explore the extent to which the flatterer initiates the terms of *adulatio* or responds to an initiative from their interlocuter, we see that flattery damages both participants in the interaction and that agency is quite frequently shared between the two. Flattery becomes an elaborate exchange within which it is no longer clear where the initiative for the terms of flattery arises, or whether the advantages for each side outweigh the disadvantages. What also emerges is that, despite the flatterer's desire to have his addressee to himself, flattery as a mode of speech acts like an infection, spreading to other speakers seemingly without regard for their desires or intentions. The way flattery spreads across different sites of interaction and different classes of speaker creates a new grouping in the Roman polity. Tacitus is not alone in his resistance to this new group formation; he tracks the spread of flattery from slaves to senators in order to show how *adulatio* is a vector of political alienation. By re-emphasizing the agency of human speakers and expressing moral disgust at their capitulation to *adulatio*, Tacitus resists also the notion that external conditions should determine how one speaks to the emperor.

In the turbulent narrative of *Histories* Tacitus finds the best opportunity to display the behaviour of the populace, who emerge as a significant actor as the position of emperor is rapidly vacated and refilled.[23] Their role is to sustain the culture of *adulatio*, whose emptiness is exposed by the swift changes of addressee. This is a point made by Pliny also, when he differentiates senators from the people who adapt their old acclamations to the new Emperor Trajan with a facile lack of discrimination: *quanto paulo ante concentu formosum alium, hunc fortissimum personat* (Plin., *Pan.* 2.6). 'With the same full throats that they recently acclaimed one as elegant, they now acclaim this ruler as most valiant.' In *Histories*, however, the people are more dangerously indiscriminate: not only do they address all rulers with the same empty words, but they absorb into their collective all social distinctions. The beginning of this new group formation is initiated during Otho's coup, when the people gather outside the Palatine where Galba is holding council.

> *Vniversa iam plebs Palatium implebat, mixtis servitiis et dissono clamore caedem Othonis et coniuratorum exitium poscentium ut si in circo aut theatro ludicrum aliquod postularent: neque illis iudicium aut veritas, quippe eodem die diversa pari certamine postulaturis, sed tradito more quemcumque principem adulandi licentia adclamationum et studiis inanibus.*
>
> Hist. 1.32.1–2

Now the whole plebeian body filled the Palatine, intermingled with servile elements and with the dissonant clamour of those demanding the slaughter of Otho and death to conspirators, as if they were requesting some game or other at the circus or theatre: and in these shouts there was no judgement or sincerity, since in the one day they were going to request opposite things with equal fervour, but it was the tradition of those clamouring in support of whichever *princeps*, marked by licence of flattery and meaningless enthusiasms.[24]

At the end of Book 1, as Otho goes out to war, popular acclaim is characterized with the same collection of terms, bringing together *adulatio*, slavishness, and lack of care for the state.

clamor vocesque vulgi ex more adulandi nimiae et falsae. quasi dictatorem Caesarem aut imperatorem Augustum prosequerentur, ita studiis votisque certabant, nec metu aut amore, sed ex libidine servitii, ut in familiis, privata cuique stimulatio, et vile iam decus publicum.

Hist. 1.90.3

The noise and shouts of the crowd were, as is flattery's custom, excessive and insincere. They competed in enthusiasm and prayers, as if they were sending off Caesar the dictator, or the Emperor Augustus, not motivated by fear or by affection but with the caprice of household slaves, where each is spurred on by his own interest and public honour is held at low account.

The people of Rome are repeatedly aligned with slaves in an alliance of interests already noted by Tacitus at the beginning of the work when he refers to *plebs sordida et circo ac theatris sueta, simul deterrimi servorum* (*Hist.* 1.4.3). 'The filthy plebs, accustomed to the circus and the theatre shows, together with the worst of slaves.'[25] His figuration of this group as debased and morally repugnant overlooks the extent to which their political interaction has been transformed by the Principate: the circus and theatre have replaced the now defunct popular assemblies as the site of exchange between subjects and ruler, and the politics of their exchanges focusses not on *iudicium* and public honour but on grain doles, taxes, and holiday provision.[26] In other words, Tacitus indicts the plebs for failing to engage in a mode of critical judgement and effective communication for which no site has been provided. Part of his point is to observe how senators too can be drawn into the plebeians' practice of empty, collective speech. Just as the people standing outside the Palatine are intermingled with slaves, so too the equestrians and senators will become part of this group when they break into the Palatine in search of Galba: *tum vero non populus tantum et imperita plebs in plausus et immodica studia, sed equitum plerique ac senatorum … nimii verbis, linguae feroces* (*Hist.* 1.35.1). 'And now not just the people and the ignorant plebs, but many of the equestrians and senators joined in the applause and the immoderate enthusiasm … excessive in their words, violent in their speech'. These scenes draw together the different groups through a mode of speech with carefully defined qualities: exaggeration or excess (*nimia, immodica*); an enthusiasm which cannot be relied upon (*studia inania*); a failure to correspond to truth (*falsa, neque veritas*) or to a stable value system (*iudicium, decus publicum*). While the political and rhetorical ignorance of the plebs might excuse their indulgence in this kind of speech, Tacitus' refusal to make allowances even for them points to how inexcusable he finds the capitulation of the well-educated elite.

The juxtaposition of Tacitus' narratives with the ethical works on flattery shows us how he draws on pre-existing discourses which associate *adulatio* with slavishness and the perversion of socially productive relations. As the latter half of this section has shown, Tacitus maps out the political effects of this speech mode: the isolation of the ruler, the enervation of his political council, and the charade of his encounters with the general populace. Yet *adulatio* has its seductions as well as its pitfalls for the senatorial speaker, and section 1.2 turns to the way *adulatio* exercises rhetorical skills and appeals to aesthetic sensibilities.

1.2 The art of *adulatio*

When Otho faces the Vitellian forces in north Italy in AD 69, he calls for a council to decide whether he should go to battle or delay a confrontation. The commanders who make up his council are the consular senators Suetonius Paulinus, Marius Celsus, Annius Gallus, and his own brother L. Salvius Otho Titianus, as well as the Praetorian Prefect Licinius Proculus. The military experience of the first three (Suetonius Paulinus was the general who put down the revolt of Boudicca in Nero's reign) is offset by the ignorance of Titianus and Proculus who are *imperitia properantes*, 'impetuous through inexperience' – yet their advice prevails.[27] While Paulinus' argument focusses on the resources available to each side and the merits of delaying battle for two or three days, Titianus and Proculus declare that *fortunam et deos et numen Othonis adesse consiliis, adfore conatibus*. 'Fortune, the gods, and the divine power of Otho himself stood by his counsels and would stand by his endeavours' (*Hist.* 2.33.1). The move from persuasion to assertion and from advice to fulsome praise leaves no room for Otho to consider delay and precludes any debate from the other council members. As Tacitus comments, *ne quis obviam ire sententiae auderet, in adulationem concesserant*. 'They had retreated into flattery, so nobody would dare to engage with their proposal.' As we have already seen in instances of flattery, Otho's bad advisors take the lead from the emperor himself, who had consulted them on whether he should draw out the war or test his fortune (*fortunam experiri*, *Hist.* 2.31.2).[28] The flatterers pick up the term *fortuna* and then exaggerate the idea of divine favour to an excessive degree so that Otho's own *numen* assists his undertakings.[29] In such a context, opponents who argue on the basis of supply chains and of waiting for reinforcements give the impression of slighting the emperor and doubting his divine right to rule. In the same way, these bad advisors foreclose on Paulinus and the others being able to convince Otho to be present at the battle, and Tacitus closes the council scene with the words *is primus dies Othonianas partes adflixit* (*Hist.* 2.33.3). 'This was the first day of the ruin of Otho's cause.' Four days later the Othonians were defeated at Bedriacum, and Otho took his own life.

This episode illustrates the damage done by *adulatio* in a situation where the emperor urgently needs independent and expert advice; it also demonstrates the difficulty of speaking against or around *adulatio*, a subject to which we will return in chapter three. Finally, it offers a glimpse of the artistry involved in a well-turned piece of flattery, and in this respect it bears a strong resemblance to the bad advice given to Vitellius later in the same book (as we saw in section 1.1): *amici adulantes mollius interpretabantur: unius legionis eam seditionem, ceteris exercitibus constare fidem* (*Hist.* 2.96.1). 'The emperor's flattering friends provided a rather favourable interpretation of Aponius' tale: they said this was just a mutiny, confined to one legion; the loyalty of the other forces would stand firm.' In both instances, optimism is reinforced by invoking quasi-numinous forces supporting the emperor (*fortuna, fides*), opposition is implicitly or explicitly down-played, and alliterative flourishes (*adesse consiliis, adfore conatibus / ceteris exercitibus constare fidem*) provide a high-flown conclusion.[30] The attractiveness of the flattery offsets the unpalatable information which is processed away and finally suppressed.

Education in rhetoric equipped speakers to supply such attractive statements, and Tacitus draws attention repeatedly to the care which senators in particular lavish on their *adulatio*. He refers to the *exquisitae adulationes*, the 'carefully constructed flattery' of senators responding to the Emperor Vitellius (*Hist.* 3.37.1); elsewhere he speaks of *quaesitior adulatio* in the senates of Tiberius (*Ann.* 3.57.1) and Claudius (*Ann.* 12.26.1); a hapless senator falls foul of Tiberius for ill-judged but 'carefully thought out flattery', *meditata adulatio* (*Ann.* 6.3.3); and senators at the inauguration of Vespasian's reign, who have a talent for *adulatio*, speak 'in carefully constructed speeches', *compositis orationibus* (*Hist.* 4.4.3). It is tempting to consider terms like *quaesitior* as negative evaluations – Damon translates it as 'laboured' or 'studied'[31] – but in drawing attention to the careful activity of the senators composing their flatteries Tacitus is placing them on the tightrope of rhetorical style which is encapsulated in both the negative and positive connotations of *quaesitus*: artificial and over-elaborate, or carefully researched and purposeful.[32] Each speaker strives to produce a unique, memorable, and gratifying *adulatio*, but their attempts are always precariously poised between the pitfalls of stylistic blandness and ignominious failure. Tacitus points to this in his account of the *quaesitior adulatio* of Annals 3.57,[33] when he does not even bother to specify the 'unimaginative' proposals but singles out those which attract the emperor's scorn and bring infamy upon the proposers:

> at Q. Haterius, cum eius diei senatus consulta aureis litteris figenda in curia censuisset deridericulo fuit, senex foedissimae adulationis tantum infamia usurus.
>
> Ann. 3.57.2

> As for Quintus Haterius, when he proposed that senatorial decisions of that day be inscribed in gold letters on the senate house, he made a laughing stock of himself, an old man who would gain only infamy from his disgusting flattery.

These senatorial decisions are certainly significant for the governance of Rome – Tiberius has just secured tribunician power for his son Drusus – but the suggestion that this moment should be recorded in gold letters, perhaps to signal a new golden age,[34] is regarded as excessive and therefore tasteless (an evaluation to which I will return). Haterius' aim was clearly to enhance his own *auctoritas* as a senior statesman in bringing forward a proposal which would associate his own name with the senate's honouring of the emperor and his successor.[35] Toppling over into absurdity, he brings out the negative implications of *quaesitior adulatio* and is remembered not as a *senator*, an authoritative elder, but as a *senex*, just a foolish old man.[36] But the risk taken by Haterius in the matter of *adulatio* can be understood as the familiar one taken every day by orators testing the limits of style in the senate house or the declamation hall.

The elder Seneca's assessment of Haterius' declamatory style matches Tacitus' assessment of Haterius' proposal as ambitious over-reaching which brings derision on the speaker.[37]

> nemo erat scholasticis nec aptior nec similior, sed, dum nihil vult nisi culte, nisi splendide dicere, saepe incidebat in ea, quae derisum effugere non possent.
> Sen., *Controv.* 4, pr. 10

> Nobody was better suited to or more like the rhetoricians, but because he wanted to say nothing that was not utterly elegant and brilliant he often fell upon coinages which could not escape ridicule.

The aesthetic boundaries of *adulatio* map themselves onto those of *eloquentia*; the contexts in which either performance is judged are remarkably similar. Hence the pursuit of elite competition in rhetoric can continue more or less unchanged through the medium of *adulatio*, as is evident from several accounts of senatorial business. In the Tiberian narrative a frequent competitor is Cornelius Dolabella, whose interventions are often characterized by Tacitus in terms of a path along which this senator seeks to overtake his peers: *solus Dolabella Cornelius dum antire ceteros parat, absurdam in adulationem progressus* (*Ann.* 3.47.3). 'Dolabella, as he worked to outstrip the other senators, moved on to an inane piece of flattery.' *Cornelius Dolabella, dum adulationem longius sequitur* ... (*Ann.* 3.69.1). 'Cornelius Dolabella, as he went further ahead along the path of flattery ...'[38] The aim of speakers like Haterius and Dolabella, and later Lucius Vitellius, is to produce the equivalent of an epigram in the sphere of *adulatio*: a statement that will be remembered and repeated to the glory of both speaker and recipient. Their statements are indeed repeated – Haterius' unfortunate coinage which everyone turns into a dirty joke in Seneca's account, or Vitellius' prayer that Claudius will live to perform many more secular games in Suetonius'[39] – but not in a way that fulfils each speaker's desire for memorability. As Tacitus remarks of another failed attempt at *adulatio* in the reign of Tiberius, *[adulatio] moribus corruptis proinde anceps si nulla et ubi nimia est* (*Ann.* 4.17.1). 'In a corrupt age, flattery is equally perilous whether it is absent or excessive.'

Who decides what is excessive, and on what grounds? As I've already suggested, the way in which the aesthetic boundaries of *adulatio* map onto those of rhetoric enables well-educated speakers and listeners to inhabit its discourse with only minimal discomfort. Rhetoric provides the rules by which they can evaluate when *adulatio* falls short or goes too far, and the pre-existing congruence between rhetoric and ethics only facilitates the way in which a judgement of *adulatio* is also a judgement of the *adulator*. When Tacitus speaks here of the perils of two extremes of *adulatio*, *nulla* and *nimia*, he echoes strictures on rhetorical and ethical decorum going back to Aristotle's advice to avoid the extremes of *elleipsis* (deficiency) and *huperbole* (excess);[40] this advice has been deployed most recently by Quintilian, who winds up his *Institutiones Oratoriae* with an injunction on the orator to speak *magna non nimia* (Quint., *Inst.* 12.10.80). The stylistic tightrope on which each senatorial speaker balances is set up in a context of collective decision-making on the matter of *honor* for the ruler, which will reflect back upon the senate as a collective. The question of stylistic decorum which structures our estimation of when speech acts tip over into excessive flattery has consequences for the way in which the senate obtrudes upon the city and the empire through honorific objects and ceremonies. Here we return to the question, discussed in the introduction, of how to calibrate honorific proposals in a political domain pervaded by *adulatio*.

1.3 *Adulatio* and *honor*

Decorum is explicitly to the forefront in the narrative of AD 21, when Tiberius reports to the senate on the conclusion of the war against Julius Sacrovir in Gaul. The emperor's communication contains a reproof to the public for their apprehension at the start of the war, when Tiberius was criticized for apparent inertia (*Ann.* 3.44.2–3). Now Tiberius articulates what he considers the appropriate response to threats such as Sacrovir, using the language of decorum in a way that bolsters imperial dignity: *neque decorum principibus, si una alterave civitas turbet, *** omissa urbe* (*Ann.* 3.47.2). 'It is not appropriate for rulers to leave the city, just because one or other community is in revolt.' The senate is represented as echoing Tiberius' language when they respond by proposing civic thanksgiving ceremonies for his safe return *et alia decora*, 'and other honours'.[41] In this context, as we have already seen, Cornelius Dolabella intervenes as the figure of excess, proposing 'an inane piece of flattery' in his bid for memorability. The content of each proposal marks out the distinction between an honour (*decus*) which is also appropriate to its recipient and to the occasion (*decorum*), and an *adulatio* which is *absurdus* – silly, but also out of tune, inappropriate.[42] At the same time, the logic behind each proposal enables us to see what both flattery and honorific speech/action aimed at and what vision of emperor–subject relations they wanted to project to the world.

As I observed in the introduction, the senate's tradition of decreeing honours to the emperor has been identified as one of the distinctive performance practices of imperial politics. It is seen as a way of negotiating the pre-eminent position of the emperor while retaining in some form the value system and status of the senatorial aristocracy.[43] Honorific decrees played a part in the various 'consensus rituals' to which emperor, senate, civic populace and soldiers each contributed, and together these consolidated and reaffirmed the ruler's authority and position.[44] The recording of these decrees, which was also a matter for senatorial deliberation, disseminated the senate's authority throughout the city and into the provinces, making the imperial senate a more significant presence throughout the empire than the Republican senate had ever been.[45] Earlier historians of the imperial senate dismissed honorific decrees as an embarrassment,[46] and even some historians writing today will occasionally divorce such activities from the exercise of 'real power' or 'real decision-making'. But the current focus on consensus and on politics as performance has enabled us to see that these honours are doing the work of imperial politics. In addition to maintaining the inequality of power between the ruler and his subjects, honours provide a discourse which *authorizes* the senate:[47] that authority constitutes a resource for the senator as he seeks to carve out a place for himself.

The content of these honorific decrees – titles, triumphs, ovations, thanksgiving ceremonies, statues, altars, temples, and arches – have been the main focus of scholarly attention, because each produces a symbolically rich 'object' which, moreover, continues to provide direction for civic activity. The *supplicatio* or thanksgiving ceremony causes the community of Rome to visit specified temples (or all temples) and participate in the state sacrifices performed there.[48] The dedications of altars and temples have their own ceremonial quality and become thereafter the focus of further religious activities. Arches and statues project the actions and individuals honoured beyond their immediate person,[49] while new honorific titles are disseminated through coins and inscriptions. All of these create, develop, and cement political status and relations in the public sphere through performance. What is often overlooked is the senatorial discussion out of which the honorific decree is produced. Andrew Wallace-Hadrill reminds us '[i]t matters not just what monuments you put up, but what flowery words you use in the senate to propose them, and what words you use in the official record, which ... is deliberately disseminated across the Empire'.[50] Behind the flowery words, even, lies the senate's procedure, itself a ritualized performance of an exchange.[51] It is not merely an exchange of words and opinions but an exchange as transformation: the senate takes in the reports and requests of commanders, provincials, and the ruler himself, and processes these into objects which generate further actions. The senate is therefore not a passive intermediary – a 'clearing house of honours'[52] – but an active mediator, a necessary participant in the creation of objects and ceremonials which perform imperial politics.[53]

As we saw in the introduction, this perspective on the bestowal of honours recuperates the senate from the charge of mere servility, but it is achieved by modern historians in the teeth of Tacitus' repeated undermining of the practice as mere *adulatio*. In chapter three, we will see how Tacitus represents honorific speech which generates productive political truth. The possibility of such speech underpins the episode with which I conclude this chapter, where Tacitus shows the erosion of meaning in improperly applied honorific discourse, and its role in creating the *sordida plebs* that will do so much damage to truth in the civil wars of AD 69.

After he has recounted the killing and decapitation of Nero's wife Octavia in AD 62, Tacitus apostrophizes on the pointlessness of recording *sententiae* so much at odds with the events that provoke them.

> *dona ob haec templis decreta que<m> ad finem memorabimus? quicumque casus temporum illorum nobis vel aliis auctoribus noscent, praesumptum habeant, quotiens fugas et caedes iussit princeps, totiens grates deis actas, quaeque rerum secundarum olim, tum publicae cladis insignia fuisse. neque tamen silebimus, si quod senatus consultum adulatione novum aut patientia postremum fuit.*
>
> Ann. 14.64.3

To what purpose do I recall the gifts decreed for temples in thanks for this atrocity? Whoever seeks to understand the wreck of that era in my work or in any other's, should take it as read that, every time the ruler ordered exile or murder, the gods would be thanked, and that what had once been a way of marking times of good fortune now was used to celebrate public disaster. But I will not be silent if any senatorial decree is innovative in its flattery or extreme in its passivity.

The thanksgiving ceremony is decreed when the state has been relieved from danger. Initially associated with the triumph and therefore with external danger, it becomes associated with the suppression of internal threats from the time of Augustus.[54] Tacitus juxtaposes this civic expression of relief and return to safety with the pathetic image of the twenty-year-old Octavia pleading for her life and having her veins forcibly opened. To give public thanks for such a killing is the worst extreme of indecorum, so far beyond Dolabella's *absurda adulatio* that it threatens to silence the historian.[55] It presumes, therefore, a context where honorific senatorial activity would be appropriate and would play a part in a productive relationship between the ruler and his most privileged subjects. Even though this ideal context is never fully present in Tacitus' narrative, his representation here of a perversion of the meaning of *supplicatio* seems to associate this perversion with *adulatio* and not with honorific decrees in themselves.[56]

The intervention of competitive *adulatio* into honorific discourse sets its language adrift from the civic experience of those who must perform its rituals. The *supplicatio* decreed on Octavia's death will involve the same citizens who demonstrated in favour of her reinstatement only days before (*Ann.* 14.61.1).[57] This provides a poignant counterpart to Tacitus' censorious representation of the populace under Galba and Otho, examined earlier, whose fickleness appears to be self-generated. But the mobs of *Histories* are the products of the Neronian regime, and perhaps their fickleness arises not so much from cynicism as from compulsory participation in meaningless honours of this sort. As we saw in section 1.1, *adulatio* engenders alienation but also arises from it, so the question of who is the victim and who is the perpetrator is in the end difficult to resolve.[58]

Section 1.1 showed us how flattery mimics social relationships, which it then renders meaningless. Section 1.2 demonstrated that the practice of flattery becomes another site for elite competition in speech and is assessed according to rules of decorum. Section 1.3 maintained that decorum polices the boundaries between flattery and true honorific discourse. The implicit backdrop to Tacitus' condemnation of *adulatio* is the possibility of honorific speech which does not disgrace the senatorial subject or isolate the ruler from the truth.

We have traced *adulatio* from its most private manifestation, poisoning the friendships of a powerful man, to its most public, alienating the Roman people as they stand before the temples of their gods. From its implicit violence we now turn to the explicit violence of another mode of speech, that of predatory accusation.

2

Pro incolumitate principis / ex calamitate civium: The Political World of Predatory Accusation

As Philodemus' flatterer makes war on his rivals at the dinner table, so the senators compete in flattery before the emperor. But this competitiveness is taken to violent extremes in the practice of *delatio*: targeting other citizens and bringing them to trial, often for the crime of *maiestas minuta* (usually glossed as 'treason'). Loránd Dészpa perfectly summarizes this as '[a] toxic dynamic ... [resulting] from ... the eagerness of many members of the elite to inscribe themselves into the imperial discourse and hence to bridge the gap between themselves and a distant princeps'.[1] Activities of this sort go beyond the flatterer's general hostility to other subjects, since the *delator* gains his rewards at the cost of loss of status, property, and life for his victims. Tacitus indicates the differences and similarities between *adulatio* and *delatio* when he introduces one of the major treason trials of the early Tiberian reign (AD 22), that of C. Iunius Silanus: *paulatim dehinc ab indecoris ad infesta transgrediebantur* (*Ann*. 3.66.1). 'Gradually thereafter there was a transition from shameful behaviour (*adulatio*) to dangerous actions (*delatio*).'

How, then, is *delatio* like and unlike *adulatio*? First, it is a mode of speech which mimics forms of social interaction in such a way as to transform them utterly. Just as *adulatio* fastens onto the discourses of friendship, only to pervert that relationship and utterly isolate the interlocutor, so *delatio* originates as a civic responsibility – the duty of reporting and prosecuting crime. This duty becomes increasingly focussed on preserving the safety and dignity of the ruler, in accordance with a political vision which yokes together the condition of the ruler and that of the *res publica*. An early and definitive articulation of this view can be found in Cicero's speech of 46 BC to Julius Caesar, *Pro Marcello*, where gratitude towards and praise of the dictator – which negotiates the boundaries of sincerity and flattery – becomes the vehicle for Cicero's political vision of a restored Republic.[2] A crucial hinge between praise and political vision can be discerned in Cicero's treatment of Caesar's fears for his own safety: although Cicero dismisses these as paranoia, he nevertheless finds them worthy of expression, and in the process he consolidates the ideological lexicon of the imperial *delator*.

> *Sed tamen cum in animis hominum tantae latebrae sint et tanti recessus, augeamus sane suspicionem tuam; simul enim augebimus diligentiam. Nam quis est omnium tam ignarus rerum, tam rudis in re publica, tam nihil umquam nec de sua nec de communi salute cogitans, qui non intellegat tua salute contineri suam, et ex unius tua vita pendere omnium?*
>
> Cic., Marcell. 22

But since there are such hiding-places and retreats [of paranoia] in the human mind, let us amplify this suspicion of yours; for at the same time we will amplify your – our vigilance. For who is there among all the citizens so ignorant of the situation, so inexperienced in public affairs, so utterly thoughtless of his own safety or that of the commonwealth, that he would not recognize that his own safety is encompassed in yours and that the lives of all hang on the life of one man – your life?

David Levene has suggested that this passage presents us with both the mortal Caesar, whose safety is a matter of public concern, and a divine Caesar, who guarantees the safety of others.[3] It is clearly a rhetoric which builds up the concept of a ruler whose status every citizen has an interest in supporting, and which finds its counterpart in such phrases of Tacitus as *nec alia rerum <salute> quam si unus imperitet* (*Ann.* 4.33.2). 'There is no safety for the Roman commonwealth unless it is under the command of one man.' In *Pro Marcello* the same concept is evident from Cicero's emphasis on the need to recognize the continued interdependence of Caesar's safety and that of the state: a citizen who fails to understand this truth lacks essential political understanding. The mode of speech which exaggerates Caesar's suspicions of danger (a mode which will be taken up by the imperial *delator*) thus performs a civic duty: it facilitates recognition of a fundamental political truth, that the citizen's safety is encompassed in the safety of Caesar. Hence the following question arises: whose vigilance is to be cultivated by exaggerating suspicions of danger? I have translated the unattributed *diligentiam* as 'your – our vigilance' to highlight the ambiguity. While both the Loeb and the Budé translators suggest that voicing the suspicions of danger should increase *Caesar*'s attention to his own safety, Cicero's ensuing sentences indicate that this mode of speech is supposed to incite the *citizens* towards vigilant protection of the dictator.[4] Cicero returns to the duty of the senatorial citizen in particular as he approaches his peroration.

> *Nisi te, C. Caesar, salvo et in ista sententia qua cum antea, tum hodie maxime usus es, manente salvi esse non possumus. Quare omnes te qui haec salva esse volumus et hortamur et obsecramus ut vitae, ut saluti tuae consulas, omnesque tibi – ut pro aliis etiam loquar quod de me ipso sentio –, quoniam subesse aliquid putas quod cavendum sit, non modo excubias et custodias, sed etiam laterum nostrorum oppositus et corporum pollicemur.*
>
> Cic., *Marcell.* 32

We cannot be safe unless you, Gaius Caesar, remain safe and maintain that position which you have illustrated by your behaviour both previously and especially today. And so all of us who wish everything to be safe, we exhort you and beseech you to have thought for your own life, for your own safety, and, since you think that some danger lies concealed which must be guarded against, each one of us (I know I speak for the others as I do for myself) pledges to you not only our vigilance and guardianship, but even the interposition of our bodies and our lives between you and any harm.

As Joy Connolly has argued, this acknowledgement of 'the limits on [a senator's] sovereign agency' is a necessary part of Cicero's attempt to create a new political world where collective senatorial activity is pursued in parallel with recognition of a pre-eminent dictator or ruler.[5] Cicero expresses this through the image of a senatorial 'bodyguard' for Caesar because the activity of saving or preserving a fellow citizen is the central theme of the speech. Caesar restores *salus* (Cic., *Marcell.* 4) to Marcellus by allowing him to return, just as he has saved (*conservati*, Cic., *Marcell.* 21) Cicero and other senators in the same way. Now they too share his concern for his own safety as comprising the safety of the state and pledge their mental attention and physical integrity to that cause. Cicero's emphasis is on protection, defence, and reintegration of Roman society after civil war, but his collocation of ideas becomes available for a different political vision.[6] By way of comparison, let us examine a letter to Tiberius in

AD 25, where the Praetorian Prefect Sejanus articulates his gratitude and devotion to the safety of the ruler.

> benevolentia Augusti et mox plurimis Tiberii iudiciis ita insuevisse, ut spes votaque sua non prius ad deos quam ad principum aures conferret. neque fulgorem honorum umquam precatum: excubias ac labores, ut unum e militibus, pro incolumitate imperatoris malle.
>
> Ann. 4.39.2

> [Sejanus wrote that] he had become accustomed, through the benevolence of Augustus and more recently the esteem of Tiberius, to bringing his hopes and prayers to the ears of rulers before approaching the gods. Nor was he asking for any glittering honours: as one of the troops, he preferred vigils and toil to ensure the safety of his commander.

Although the relationship between Sejanus and Tiberius is primarily expressed as a military one,[7] the language also evokes the same congruence of elements as in Cicero's address to Caesar: the quasi-divine ruler as the source of benefits, the repudiation of individual glory (appropriate, given Sejanus' equestrian status), and the activity of the speaker imagined as vigilant protection of the emperor. Whereas Cicero left unspecified the dangers threatening Caesar by referring to an indeterminate 'danger that must be guarded against', Sejanus expresses quite clearly who he considers to be a threat when he expresses his intentions more specifically as *firmari domum adversum iniquas Agrippinae offensiones* (*Ann.* 4.39.4). 'To fortify the imperial house against the harmful attacks of Agrippina.' Thus Sejanus – and the *delatores* before and after him – narrow the focus of Cicero's concern with common safety until it has become concern with the ruler's safety to the detriment of (all) other citizens.

Cicero's figure of the senator as bodyguard,[8] deployed more appropriately by the praetorian prefect, provides only a limited practical understanding of how civic activity might ensure the ruler's safety. When we turn instead to speech, the civic activity par excellence, we can immediately see how this protection works in practice: identifying, reporting, and prosecuting the 'danger which must be guarded against' becomes the custodial duty of the citizen. As Tiberius declares in support of the *delator*, 'it would be better to overturn the laws entirely, than to remove their guardians': *subverterent potius iura, quam custodes amoverent* (*Ann.* 4.30.2). The language of protection and guardianship, however, masks an inherent violence towards fellow citizens, which is endemic to all prosecution speech. As I will explore in section 2.1, this violence is kept within manageable limits by legal procedure, which distributes agency across personal and impersonal elements. This offers a complex and productive site for the kind of subject-ruler interactions we've already observed in the case of flattery, where both the conditions of speech and the world created by that mode of speaking are 'co-produced' by senators and emperors. Precisely this issue of agency is explored when Tacitus claims, and immediately undermines the claim, that Tiberius 'restored the laws of *maiestas*' (*Ann.* 1.72.1). Like *adulatio*, *delatio* – accusations of *maiestas* in particular – create a world where the vigilant activity of the citizen is required to protect an ever-fragile ruler and state. In section 2.2, I will look at how safety is conceptualized through these trials and how ideas of injury and harm are associated with the idea of diminution and fragmentation. The paranoid Tiberius of *Annals* 6 after the fall of Sejanus, communicating with the senate through increasingly acerbic letters, can be seen as the product of such a reconfigured world. This theme continues in section 2.3. In its mimicry of citizenship, *delatio* engenders heightened anxiety about the speech acts through which the state is maintained. Tacitus mostly avoids representing the accusatory speech of the *delator* (the indictments of Thrasea Paetus at *Ann.* 16.22 and 28 are a striking exception), but he does engineer more than one scene in which the *delator* speaks in self-defence. These present an opportunity for debating the accountability of imperial subjects and for the historian to ask what kind of citizen is created by the act of *delatio*.

2.1 *Delatio, maiestas*, and distributed agency

How did *delatio* mimic the actions of a citizen, and what were the features that rendered it *infesta*, creating a hostile and precarious mode of existence? These two questions inform each other, as we shall see. The forms of indirect violence against fellow citizens practised by the *delator* were drawn from the legal procedures of the Republic, where prosecution was the responsibility of the individual citizen.[9] Yet the anxiety about gaining benefit from the prosecution of a fellow citizen was socially embedded from the outset,[10] hence Cicero's strictures against too frequently taking on the role: *sed hoc quidem non est saepe faciendum nec umquam nisi aut rei publicae causa ... aut ulciscendi ... aut patrocinii* (Cic., *Off.* 2.50). 'But you should not prosecute very often and never for any reason except the interest of the state, the avenging of wrong, or the support of the provincials.' Under the Principate, the *delator* would identify a range of actions and words as detrimental to state interest in that they threatened the princeps, as when Cossutianus Capito represents Thrasea Paetus' absence from senate as *secessionem ... et partes et, si idem multi audeant, bellum* (*Ann.* 16.22.2). 'Secession and faction and (if many others imitate his daring) open warfare.' Accusations of this sort justify, in Cicero's terms, the *delator*'s prosecution of a fellow citizen. But another source of anxiety derived from the rewards which a successful prosecutor could gain. These earn him the reproach of having perverted the art of speaking: *nam quid est tam inhumanum quam eloquentiam a natura ad salutem hominum et ad conservationem datam ad bonorum pestem perniciemque convertere?* (Cic., *Off.* 2.51) 'For what is more inhumane than to turn your eloquence, bestowed by nature to preserve the safety of your fellows, towards the ruin and destruction of good men?' To indict the *delatores*, Tacitus emphasizes and even exaggerates the extent of their gains:[11] *nec minus praemia delatorum invisa quam scelera, cum alii sacerdotia et consulatus ut spolia adepti, procurationes alii et interiorem potentiam, agerent verterent cuncta odio et terrore* (*Hist.* 1.2.3). 'The rewards of the *delatores* were no less hated than their crimes: some seized priesthoods and consulships as if they were spoils, others procuratorial posts and private access to power. They impelled and overturned everything, inspiring hatred and terror.' The mimicry of citizenship becomes a horrific parody, as the prestigious stages of the senatorial career – priesthoods and consulships – are described as if they were property seized from a defeated enemy.

The violence of the *delatores*, then, is partly an inherent aspect of prosecution itself, which places the citizen in a delicate position between his relations to the state and to fellow citizens and asks him to consider these two sets of relations as separate and separable.[12] One of the ways that the process of prosecution allays the anxieties arising from this position is to 'depersonalize' the act of the prosecutor to a certain extent, by distributing the agency of prosecution across different actors, some of whom would act in the role of responsible magistrates. Before considering this in further detail, we should briefly acknowledge the precise role of the *delator* as opposed to the *accusator* who delivered the formal speech of prosecution (even though they were sometimes one and the same person, and Tacitus uses these terms quite loosely). *Delatio* comes from the phrase *nomen deferre*, the stage of prosecution where an individual is indicted (originally before the praetor) for a specific crime.[13] While the *delator* who brings the charge can proceed as *accusator*, it is not always the case. Indeed, since the *delator* must first make a request (*postulatio*) to bring an indictment to the relevant magistrate, a space has already been made for other accusers to come forward and contribute to the *delatio*. As a mode of speech and action, then, *delatio* could be relatively simple: it would require some understanding of legal procedure, but would not necessarily have to draw on the persuasive arts of formal rhetoric; it could be highly collaborative or even competitive, as multiple agents shared out parts of an accusation in the early stages of the process.[14] But because the *delator* could also be an *accusator*, the term acquires a productive imprecision, particularly in Tacitus' narratives of treason charges. The imprecision blurs the boundaries between acts of indictment (brought to the magistrates or to the emperor) and formal trials held in the senate house.

Since the system of prosecution explicitly allows for the possibility of multiple accusers, it negotiates the troubling violence against fellow citizens which is inherent to the process. Instead, agency is distributed across different actors so as to create the effect of a civic community engaged in the pursuit and punishment of wrongdoing. Tacitus makes use of this distribution of agency not to alleviate the sense of prosecution as violence, but to explore the complex of accountability under the Principate and to portray *delatio* as a corrosive form of speech which does damage beyond its immediate victims in the treason trials.

The first extended account of a treason trial in Tiberius' reign – that of Scribonius Libo in AD 16 – presents some of the features of distributed agency and accountability inherent in prosecution cases.[15] These cut across the tendency in Tacitus' accounts of these trials to assign blame explicitly to the emperor or to a morally bankrupt *delator*. In the trial of Libo, Tacitus strongly implies malevolence on the part of the emperor by suggesting that he placed Libo under surveillance (*Ann*. 2.28.2), introduced a new procedure to enable interrogation of his slaves (*Ann*. 2.30.3), and refused to intervene with the senate on Libo's behalf (*Ann*. 2.31.1). The first *delator* involved in the case, moreover, is represented almost as an incriminator: *iuvenem improvidum et facilem inanibus ad Chaldaeorum promissa ... impulit ... Vt satis testium ... repperit, aditum ad principem postulat* (*Ann.* 2.27.2–28.1). 'He pushed the young man, thoughtless and prone to such foolishness, to consult the predictions of the Chaldeans. ... When he had found enough witnesses, he sought an audience with the princeps.'[16] Overlaying this, however, is a narrative of legal procedure which involves both depersonalized process and multiple agents. The narrative opens with the charge brought against Libo, where the passive form of the verb *[nomen] deferre* elides agency: *defertur moliri res novas* (*Ann.* 2.27.1). 'Libo was indicted for revolutionary activity.' The *delator*/entrapper, Firmius Catus, seeks to bring the evidence he has accumulated before Tiberius, and his request for an audience – *aditum postulat* – mimics the *postulatio* stage of bringing a prosecution. The fact that he is instead forced to work through an intermediary, the equestrian Flaccus Vescularius, exposes how this *delatio* proceeds through a semi-official and hidden route. The second stage of the Libo case seems to emerge from an entirely independent source: a supposed necromancer presents evidence (*indicium*) to Fulcinius Trio, whom the narrative now introduces as a notorious *accusator*.[17] His actions are characterized as swift and aggressive, yet they also follow the outlines of the prosecution process: *statim corripit reum, adit consules, cognitionem senatus poscit* (*Ann.* 2.28.3). 'At once he took hold of the defendant, approached the consuls, sought an inquiry from the senate.' By the time the case reaches trial, Trio and Catus have been joined by Fonteius Agrippa and Vibius Serenus, among whom there is no agreement about who should get to open the case. This slightly unseemly squabble among the four prosecutors attests to their ambition (this was a high-profile case promising rich rewards, given the nature of the alleged crime and Libo's family connections to the princeps) but also demonstrates that they are not necessarily working together.[18] As Steven Rutledge concludes of this episode, 'despite Tacitus' attempt to use this case to depict Tiberius as a ruthless tyrant, the *delatores* were each rather individualistic characters, working on their own.'[19] Crucially, Tacitus shows us the two initial *delatores*, Catus and Trio, pursuing similar procedural paths but through different sites of authority: the imperial path of Catus' *delatio*, involving intermediaries and secrecy; the senatorial path of Trio's, transparent in its violence and immediacy. The distribution of agency inherent to the prosecution process enables a narrative which explores the complexities of personal ambition negotiating between imperial and senatorial politics.

Tacitus' portrayal of *delatio* for treason in the Tiberian regime has remained one of the most difficult issues for historians of the period and for scholars attempting to assess Tacitus' historical understanding. As Bessie Walker summarizes, '[t]he discrepancy between fact and impression ... is nowhere wider'.[20] The impression conveyed is that Tiberius should be held responsible for the reintroduction of the *maiestas* law, its extension beyond seditious acts to disrespectful words, and the development of a culture of surveillance which permeates both public and private life. But there is a glaringly evident discrepancy between this impression and the truth of *delatio* as a pernicious social phenomenon in Tacitus' introduction of the earliest *maiestas* cases of the reign: the charges brought against the equestrians Faianius and Rubrius, and the senator Granius Marcellus in AD 15 (*Ann*. 1.72–74). In these cases Tacitus highlights the agency of the emperor, first with the explicit statement *nam legem maiestatis reduxerat* (*Ann*. 1.72.2) – 'for he reintroduced the *maiestas* law' – and then with a reference to how the evil of such charges infiltrated Rome *Tiberii arte* (*Ann*. 1.73.1) – 'through the cunning of Tiberius'. Yet as the narration of each case proceeds, we learn that Tiberius himself refuses to admit the charges against Faianius and Rubrius, while Marcellus is acquitted of *maiestas* (but charged with extortion). Readers of these chapters have been troubled not only by the way Tacitus' claims do not fit with the events he narrates, but also by the apparent incompetence of such a discrepancy.[21] In an attempt to resolve this issue, scholars have often identified a sort of 'double-vision' operating in these chapters. Tacitus sees various futures in which *maiestas* charges herald a purge in the state: the final years of Tiberius' reign, marked by a paranoid ruler and desperate intermediaries; the development of *maiestas* trials in the Flavian period, and especially in the reign of Domitian in AD 93, where Tacitus expresses a sense of complicit guilt in the downfall of his contemporaries (*Agr*. 45.1). Indeed, Tacitus invites us to see the trivial cases of the early Tiberian years in the light of their futures: *haud pigebit referre... praetemptata crimina, ut quibus initiis quanta Tiberii arte gravissimum exitium inrepserit, dein repressum sit, postremo arserit cunctaque corripuerit, noscatur* (*Ann*. 1.73.1). 'It will not be any trouble to recount these preliminary charges, so that we can understand how and from what beginnings, through the cunning of Tiberius, the most serious damage crept into the state, later was repressed, and finally flared up and took hold of everything.' The longer historical view within which Tacitus situates the episode suggests that he holds Tiberius accountable for a process which reached its point of highest destructiveness long after the emperor's death.

But there is another way of understanding the disjunction between Tacitus' indictment of Tiberius and his narration of trials involving multiple agents operating almost independently of the emperor. For it is not the case that Tacitus underplays the distribution of agency in these episodes. The features we have already identified, which work to depersonalize the violence of prosecution, are all in evidence here: the unnamed *accusator* who charges Faianius (*Ann.* 1.73.2); the passive voice used for the charge against Rubrius (*Ann.* 1.73.2); and the prosecution of Marcellus shared between Caepio Crispinus and Romanus Hispo (*Ann.* 1.74.1). The distribution of agency is underscored by Tacitus inserting a 'sententious characterization' of either Crispinus or Hispo (it is unclear which), identifying them as the type (*exemplum*) of the *delator*.[22] The ethical sketch which follows presents a glimpse of how the *delator* and the emperor share responsibility for the evil which besets the state.

> ... *qui formam vitae iniit, quam postea celebrem miseriae temporum et audaciae hominum fecerunt. nam egens ignotus inquies, dum occultis libellis saevitiae principis adrepit, mox clarissimo cuique periculum facessit, potentiam apud unum, odium apud omnes adeptus dedit exemplum, quod secuti ex pauperibus divites, ex contemptis metuendi perniciem aliis ac postremum sibi invenere.*
>
> Ann. 1.74.1–2

> ... who entered into that mode of living, which later became well known through the misery of the age and the audacity of its citizens. Needy, unheard-of, restless, as he insinuated himself, with his secret evidence, into the emperor's cruel nature, soon he created danger for all the noblest of men: gaining power with one man, he reaped hatred from all. He served as an example followed by others who attained wealth from poverty, who became feared where they had been despised, who sought out ruin for others and finally found it for themselves.

The parallels between this characterization and the earlier description of how *delatio* has developed enable Tacitus to make some important points about agency. In the earlier description *delatio* 'crept into (*inrepserit*) the state through the cunning of Tiberius', so that partial agency is attributed to the emperor. Similarly here Crispinus/Hispo 'insinuated himself (*adrepit*) into the emperor's cruel nature', so that agency is attributed to the *delator*, but there is a suggestion that the ruler provides the conditions for that agency. The language attributes continuity to the phenomenon of *delatio*, which seems to operate with the impersonality of a contagious disease, but the human agents involved in the phenomenon occupy different positions at different times, sharing accountability for this social evil. The very interchangeability of Crispinus/Hispo reflects this shared accountability. But Tacitus' point is not that shared accountability absolves anyone of guilt, and this may be one reason for his blatantly unsupported indictment of Tiberius in these chapters. If Tacitus refuses to absolve imperial subjects of their complicity in the cruelty of rulers, so too he refuses to absolve the ruler of responsibility for the conduct of his citizens.

The question of accountability, and the sense that *delatio* is co-produced by subjects and ruler, is particularly pressing in the aftermath of particular regimes. In the eighteen months from Galba's short reign to the establishment of the Flavian dynasty, we see periodic attempts by senators to hold *delatores* accountable for their actions under Nero. And the same issues were encountered by Pliny (and presumably by Tacitus as well) in the regimes that followed Domitian's death. These issues bring into focus the central question of my investigation – the extent to which the senators of Tacitus' narratives have any power to shape the political world in which they operate as subjects. A repeated plea by *delatores* is that they were compelled by the ruler to undertake their prosecutions, an argument made most forcefully by Eprius Marcellus, one of the *accusatores* in the case of Thrasea Paetus: *non magis sua oratione Thraseam quam iudicio senatus adflictum; saevitiam Neronis per eius modi imagines inlusisse, nec minus sibi anxiam talem amicitiam quam aliis exilium* (*Hist.* 4.8.3). 'It was not his own speech of accusation that ruined Thrasea, but the judgement of the senate as a whole; and Nero's cruelty made play of such show-trials. Marcellus' own friendship with such a ruler was no less distressing than exile was for others.' Marcellus here responds to fellow senators who would charge him with the destruction of Thrasea by pointing to the distribution of agency involved in that trial. This implicates the senators who seek to bring

Marcellus to justice, but also lays the initiative for such trials at the emperor's door. Tacitus' account of the prosecution of Thrasea in *Annals* provides a partial refutation of this claim, as we will see in a moment. But Marcellus' argument that no single person can be blamed for the evils of *delatio* remains a potent one which resonates with other discussions of subjects' agency and responsibility throughout this book.

Because Thrasea's condemnation and suicide (*Ann.* 16.35) have become the concluding scene of the fragmentary *Annals*, we might make the mistake of not recognizing how much Tacitus shapes this treason trial as the climax of the Neronian regime:[23] *trucidatis tot insignibus viris ad postremum Nero virtutem ipsam excindere concupivit interfecto Thrasea Paeto et Barea Sorano, olim utrisque infensus* (*Ann.* 16.21.1). 'Having slaughtered so many notable men, in the end Nero desired to erase virtue itself by killing Thrasea Paetus and Barea Soranus, having long held them both in enmity.' As with the Tiberian cases, Tacitus begins with a strong ascription of agency to the emperor not only by emphasizing his strong emotional engagement with Thrasea (*concupivit, infensus*) but also by removing all intervening stages of *postulatio*, trial, and condemnation by senatorial vote. This sense of a treason trial generated entirely by the ruler is intensified by the long and precise list of Thrasea's offences which recapitulates episodes from the narrative of *Annals* 14–15: these are, however, represented as 'objective' causes and not merely as existing in the mind of the emperor. This provides a transition to the important agency of the *delator*, Cossutianus Capito, who is introduced as motivated by personal grievances against Thrasea Paetus: *quae obliterari non sinebat Capito Cossutianus, praeter animum ad flagitia praecipitem iniquus Thraseae, quod auctoritate eius concidisset, iuvantis Cilicum legatos, dum Capitonem repetundarum interrogant* (*Ann.* 16.21.3). 'Capito was not going to allow these resentments to be forgotten: as well as having a spirit which relished expressions of outrage, he was hostile to Thrasea because he had been brought down by Thrasea's authoritative intervention, when he was helping the Cilicians as they pursued Capito on an extortion charge.'[24] This contextual explanation reminds us that Tacitus, in his account of that extortion trial, introduced Capito as *maculosum foedumque* (*Ann.* 13.33.2) – 'a tarnished and foul character'. But more significantly, the introduction of Capito's attitude to Thrasea (*iniquus* matching Nero's *infensus*) and the 'offence' which engendered that attitude (*quod* following on from the multiple *quod* and *quia* of Nero's resentments), relieve Nero of sole responsibility for the accusation and destruction of Thrasea. The rhetorical work undertaken by Capito in the ensuing speech, which reconfigures Thrasea's various offences as serious threats to the *res publica*, similarly draws agency away from the ruler. Capito concludes his address with an injunction to the ruler to make this trial entirely a senatorial affair: '*denique nihil ipse de Thrasea scripseris: disceptatorem senatum nobis relinque*' (*Ann.* 16.22.5). 'In short, write nothing yourself about Thrasea: leave the senate to arbitrate between us.' The first scene of *delatio* concludes with the familiar addition of a second accuser, Eprius Marcellus.

The balance of agency between senatorial *delatores* and the hostile emperor is summed up in the metaphor Tacitus uses in his account of the trial itself, which is set in motion by Nero's speech/letter rebuking the senate for not attending to their duties. Although he does not name any senator (thereby obeying Capito's injunction), his rebuke provides the conditions for Capito and Marcellus to commence their attack on Thrasea: *oratio principis... audita est... quod velut telum corripuere accusatores* (*Ann.* 16.27.1–2). 'The emperor's speech was heard, which the accusers snatched up as if it were a weapon.' Nero's speech lacks an explicit victim but maintains a sense of latent hostility despite handing over the explicit agency of violence to the accusers. We can compare Pliny's description of the terrifying *delator* of his and Tacitus' own age, Catullus Messalinus: *qui luminibus orbatus ingenio saevo mala caecitatis addiderat. Non verebatur, non erubescebat, non miserebatur; quo saepius a Domitiano non secus ac tela, quae et ipsa caeca et improvida feruntur, in optimum quemque contorquebatur* (Plin., *Ep.* 4.22.5). 'Deprived of sight, he supplemented the evils of blindness with a brutal nature. He had no fear, no shame, no pity; so he was often used by Domitian as a sort of missile, which is set in motion though blind and lacking direction; thus he was aimed at virtuous men.' The order of agency is reversed here, with Domitian as prime mover, but Messalinus does not escape moral censure.

In this section I have suggested that the prosecution process in Rome, which divides tasks among different agents, can be understood as a way of alleviating the anxiety caused by taking on what is essentially an act of violence against a fellow citizen. When it comes to the imperial prosecutions and the more nebulous charges of *maiestas*, this 'distribution of agency' also becomes useful for negotiating ruler–subject relations. Even if the *delator* believes himself to be acting out the emperor's wishes, the extent to which his private wishes, enmities, and advantages are furthered by his actions makes it difficult to maintain that he has no agency in taking up prosecutions. The political world of *delatio*, then, is one in which more than the ruler's interests are served.[25] Tacitus exploits the ambiguity over whose initiative and whose interest drives the practice of *delatio* in order to reflect on how agency is tied to accountability. Having examined the prosecution process, we now turn to the political world generated by the content and rhetoric of *maiestas* charges.

2.2 Majesty and harm: the world of *maiestas*

Tiberius, more than any other ruler, is transformed by the experience of *maiestas* charges over his reign; after the downfall of Sejanus, his interventions in senate (by letter) are increasingly paranoid and violent.[26] But accusations of *maiestas minuta* affect Roman society more generally, especially with regard to ruler–subject relations and the constitution of the ruler's *maiestas* or supremacy. Looking across different sources which recount accusations from the first two dynasties, we can see the kind of world that is created from the nature and context of the charges. Some of these charges are reported as manifestly absurd and others as immediately unsuccessful, but whether they are 'logical' or 'successful' in a legal context is only one part of their effect. Accusations operate much like rumour: even disbelieving or sceptical engagement helps to disseminate a 'culture of accusation' which shapes the discourse of social and political life. In this section, I will look at these effects of *maiestas* charges without considering whether the charges are founded, coherent, or true. Since charges of *maiestas minuta* concern words or actions which diminish or damage the supremacy of the state and/or the ruler, they develop a rich symbolic vocabulary for expressing the nature of political power and for disseminating it across different modes of existence.

The notorious case of Titus Sabinus in AD 28 illustrates how different modes of existence are implicated in this process. Sabinus' case is the most obvious instance of entrapment in the accounts of the *delatores*: the senator Latinius Latiaris encourages Sabinus' expressions of unhappiness at the emperor's treatment of the elder Agrippina, prompting him by expressing criticism of both Sejanus and Tiberius (*Ann.* 4.68.3). Inviting Sabinus back to the private quarters of his house, Latiaris has other senators hide under the floorboards in order to hear his incriminating speech. This enables an *accusatio*, delivered directly to the emperor, who accuses Sabinus in a letter to the senate; Sabinus is immediately dragged off to prison and executed by senatorial decree but without a formal trial.[27] As is frequently the case with the narration of *maiestas* charges, Tacitus presents both the charge and the likely pretext: he begins the episode by telling us that Sabinus was punished 'because of his friendship with Germanicus' (*Ann.* 4.68.1). The implication of the entrapment scene is that Sabinus has participated in speech similar to that of Latiaris, who 'abused Sejanus for his cruelty, arrogance, and ambition, not without some disapprobation (*convicio*) of Tiberius himself' (*Ann.* 4.68.3). The substance of Tiberius' charge, however, is 'corruption of some imperial freedman, and an attempt on the emperor himself' (*Ann.* 4.70.1). Bauman attempts to rationalize this transition of charges from defamation to conspiracy by postulating an intermediate stage in the proceedings: the initial *accusatio* of abusive speech justifies interrogation of Sabinus' slaves, which uncovers their master's alleged interference with the emperor's freedmen.[28] But we can also put the charges together not to recreate a plausible case against Sabinus but to notice how they enable *maiestas* to infiltrate different spaces and different modes of existence.

Because a *prima facie* case of *maiestas minuta* is revolutionary conspiracy, which proceeds through private/secret networks of political alliance, domestic space and friendship become sites which threaten the security of the state and which require surveillance. Sabinus is introduced as a potential object of surveillance because of one friendship (*ob amicitiam Germanici*) and is brought down by what appears to be a close friendship with Latiaris (*speciem artae amicitiae*). This destructive friendship coerces him into a private space – he is literally dragged (*trahit*) to Latiaris' bedroom just as he will be condemned and dragged (*trahebatur*) to execution, his toga pulled over his head to muffle his voice. Public and private spaces are brought together here as equally subject to the infiltrations of *maiestas* charges: just as Romans avoid private conversations after Sabinus' accusation (*Ann.* 4.69.3), so they desert the public streets and squares as he is taken away (*Ann.* 4.70.2). Tiberius' indictment of Sabinus, similarly, is interleaved between the politico-religious and judicial functions of the senate: the accusation comes mid-letter, after the emperor has offered the traditional prayers for the beginning of the year. In one sense, this is a dramatic change of topic (a characteristic of Tiberius' letters); in another sense, the accusation follows on seamlessly from prayers because it is concerned with the same topic: the safety of the *res publica* or the princeps.[29] Again, this creates a world in which *maiestas* pervades different sites and modes of being. Hence it is experienced as inescapable violence by Tiberius' subjects: *quem enim diem vacuum poena, ubi inter sacra et vota, quo tempore verbis etiam profanis abstineri mos esset, vincla et laqueus inducantur?* (*Ann.* 4.70.3) 'What day will be free of punishment, when chains and noose are thrown on a subject amidst rites and prayers, at a time when it is customary to abstain even from profane words?'

Maiestas charges make this process appear natural, as they tie together physical and symbolic acts which are seen to damage the supremacy of the state or ruler – and supremacy has already been tied to security. Hence the complex of charges presents the state or ruler as simultaneously pre-eminent and fragile and associates supremacy with a wide range of attributes in different aspects of social, political, and religious life. As we've already noted, a security threat such as conspiracy is maintained through networks of *amicitia*, so charges of *maiestas* are directed at these networks, resulting in individuals being charged for maintaining friendship or alliance with other citizens: *Aelii Galli amicitia* or *ut C. Pisonis socium* (*Ann.* 5.8.1; 14.65.2). Charges of sedition will also involve scrutiny of the extent and nature of an individual's interaction with the army or the Praetorian Guard, which constitutes the damning element of the accusations against Cn. Piso in AD 21 (*Ann.* 3.12.3; *SCPP* 52–57) or of the posthumous charges brought against the younger Agrippina in AD 59 (*Ann.* 14.11.1). Hence Valerius Asiaticus is accused before Claudius of planning to use his provincial connections in Gallia Narbonensis to foment mutiny among the legions: *parare iter ad Germanicos exercitus, quando genitus Viennae multisque et validis propinquitatibus subnixus turbare gentiles nationes promptum haberet* (*Ann.* 11.1.2). 'He was preparing a visit to the German armies, since he was born in Vienne and was supported by many firmly established kinship links there, so was ready to stir up disturbance among his native peoples.' Whether the threat posed by Asiaticus is genuine or not,[30] its effect is to merge regular municipal business and political relationships (*propinquitates*) with a seditious attempt upon the military.[31] As with the accusations *ob amicitiam*, such a charge attacks the social basis of senatorial and equestrian life, making it available to be redescribed as behaviour which undermines the *res publica* itself.

The *maiestas* charges which are presented in the sources as patently absurd, therefore, perform the important function of making visible the conceptual work that is being effected. *Maiestas minuta* ties together different spheres of subject existence, identifies the safety of the commonwealth with the pre-eminence of the ruler, and situates that pre-eminence across the different spheres. When the Emperors Gaius and Nero, for instance, ground their status as *principes* in cultural supremacy, the practice of eloquence or of literary excellence becomes reconfigured as a challenge to the ruler. Seneca's prestige in this field becomes part of the case made against him in AD 62: *eloquentiae laudem uni sibi adsciscere et carmina crebrius factitare, postquam Neroni amor eorum venisset* (*Ann.* 14.52.3). 'He aspired to a monopoly on praise for eloquence and had begun to practise poetry more regularly after Nero had begun to cultivate this art.' Dio has Seneca as the object of Gaius' resentment for the same reason, in AD 39:[32] 'Lucius Annaeus Seneca, who surpassed (*huperaras*) all the Romans of his time … in wisdom, was almost ruined not because he committed or appeared to commit a crime but because when he pleaded a case in senate he spoke well' (Dio 59.19.7). Gaius' extreme sensitivity to any appearance of excellence or even sufficiency in his subjects has often been seen as irrational, but it reflects the perverted logic of *maiestas*, as both Suetonius and Dio seem to recognize. Suetonius interrupts his list of the emperor's 'punishments' of subjects with the observation, *nullus denique tam abiectae condicionis tamque extremae sortis fuit, cuius non commodis obtrectaret* (Suet., *Calig.* 35.3). 'In short, there was no man in such an abject state or so far down on his luck, that the emperor did not seek to diminish his advantages.' In a similar vein, Dio remarks that 'he was envious (*baskanos*) and suspicious (*hupoptos*) towards everything in the same way' (Dio 59.20.6). Gaius' vision of his subjects is organized around both vertical relations – they should look up to him as princeps, but instead he finds himself looking askance at their position – and resources – even the lowest order of subject (*abiectae, extremae*) has something which he could take away from them. His desire to whittle away their status and endowments derives from a sense that what they have somehow diminishes his supremacy, because he locates that supremacy across all modes of existence.

Conceptualizing the ruler's supremacy, then, proceeds through imagining different ways in which it can be harmed. Some of the language of *maiestas* yokes together the ruler's supremacy and the state's security by using the language of civil war and Republican political dissent (*seditio, secessio, defectio*),[33] and associated terms of disorder (*turbare* and *turbidum*) are especially frequent.[34] This contributes to the pervasive connection, which the Julio-Claudian regimes inherited from Augustus, between princeps, *pax*, and a stable society.[35] This is usually articulated through a presentation of the state as under threat, and the ruler as both supporter and protector, as in Velleius Paterculus' account of the transition of power from Augustus to Tiberius: *in quam arto salutis exitiique fuerimus confinio . . . tanta unius viri maiestas fuit, ut nec pro bonis neque contra malos opus armis foret* (Vell. Pat. 2.124.1). 'In such a narrow margin between safety and disaster as we were . . . the supremacy of one man was so great that there was no need for warfare either to protect the good or to repel the bad.' Rome's *salus* is quite clearly dependent upon Tiberius' *maiestas* in Velleius' formulation.[36] But the *maiestas minuta* charges characterize the ruler's supremacy as fragile and present the need for vigilant citizens – *delatores* – to detect and expose threats. Sejanus in his letter to Tiberius (examined earlier) refers to his *excubias ac labores . . . pro incolumitate imperatoris*: 'night-watches and exertions on behalf of the emperor's safety from harm' (*Ann.* 4.39.2). Sejanus explicitly likens his activity to that of a soldier, appropriately enough for a praetorian prefect (and his successor Tigellinus will use similar language to represent his devotion to Nero, *Ann.* 14.57.2). But the orator does most of the work in identifying, categorizing, and calling for the suppression of threats. He does so by moving along the chain of metaphors already set up by the spread of *maiestas* into different areas of life, declaring that this action or that is tantamount to civil war.[37] We can observe this by looking more closely at the case against Thrasea Paetus and the light in which his offences are placed by his *accusatores*.

As we've already seen, the account of this trial is unusual for the extensive list of causes for Nero's hatred of Thrasea and the extent to which this list overlaps with episodes already narrated by Tacitus. It is also unusual in that we are presented with a formal speech of *postulatio* (by Capito) as well as an accusation speech (by Marcellus), each of which reworks the initial list of causes as threats to the safety of the ruler and the stability of the *res publica*.[38] First, let us review the causes alongside their appearance earlier in the narrative:

1. That Thrasea left the senate when the death of the younger Agrippina was discussed (*Ann.* 14.12.1);
2. That he had not been sufficiently in evidence at the Juvenalian festival (*Ann.* 14.15 – Thrasea not mentioned);
3. That he had intervened in the case of Antistius and secured a more lenient sentence (*Ann.* 14.48–49);
4. That he had been absent from the senate during the decrees for Poppaea's divination, and had not attended her funeral (*Ann.* 16.6 – Thrasea not mentioned).

Capito's treatment of these charges involves tying them to similar alleged actions which escalate the seriousness of Thrasea's dereliction of duty:[39] failing to participate in the new year oaths to uphold the *acta* of the princeps and his predecessors, or in the priests' prayers for the safety of the state and the princeps – a politico-religious activity which, as we have already noted, is brought into play around *maiestas* charges. Capito spells out the threat with the culminating charge of this sequence: *numquam pro salute principis aut caelesti voce immolavisse* (*Ann.* 16.22.1). 'He has never sacrificed for the safety of the ruler or for his heavenly voice.' In the second part of his speech he effectively repeats this charge: '*huic uni incolumitas tua sine cura, artes sine honore*' (*Ann.* 16.22.3). 'To this man alone your safety is of no concern, your literary talent has no respect.' Nero's resentment at Thrasea's absence from his Juvenalia (a disregard of his cultural supremacy) is now given weight by being associated with *impietas* and a latent desire to harm. Similarly, Thrasea's refusal to participate in the political sphere is escalated by adding accusations which interpret this as a refusal to participate in the protection of the state through the senate's judicial function: *nuperrimeque, cum ad coercendos Silanum et Veterem certatim concurreretur, privatis potius clientium negotiis vacavisse* (*Ann.* 16.22.1). 'Very recently, when all senators collectively strove to suppress Silanus and Vetus, Thrasea rather kept his time free for the private business of his clients.'[40] This continuation of social obligations (which would have involved legal representations) while eschewing political and judicial activities is joined together by Capito under the term *secessio*, suggesting that Thrasea carves out a new political sphere to rival that of the curia. Both metaphorically and historically, *secessio* stands at the beginning of a sequence of actions associated with political independence and with disruption to the state: *secessionem iam id et partes et, si idem multi audeant, bellum esse* (*Ann.* 16.22.2). 'This had become secession and factionalism and, if many were to dare to do the same, it would be war.' The rest of Capito's speech elaborates more explicitly on historical parallels, presenting Thrasea as a new Cato more dangerous than any new Cassius or Brutus, for he threatens both *imperium* and *libertas* (*Ann.* 16.22.4). Hence both Capito as accuser and the senate as arbitrator are presented as vitally necessary in the interest of the state.

When the charges come to senate, the co-accuser Eprius Marcellus is said to speak with greater violence not only because of his vehement style – 'his voice, face, and eyes burning' (*Ann.* 16.29.1) – but because he works the metaphorical significance of Thrasea's actions to an even higher degree. Beginning with the declaration that *summam rem publicam agi* (*Ann.* 16.28.1) – 'the greatest concerns of the commonwealth are at issue' – he treats Thrasea's absence from senate not as civil disobedience but as a declaration of enmity: *requirere se in senatu consularem, in votis sacerdotem, in iure iurando civem, nisi contra instituta et caerimonias maiorum proditorem palam et hostem Thrasea induisset* (*Ann.* 16.28.3). 'He, Marcellus, looked for a consular statesman in the senate house, a priest at the sacrifices, a citizen at the oath-taking, but Thrasea in his opposition to ancestral politics and rituals appeared instead in the guise of a traitor and an open enemy.' Similarly, instead of representing him as unconcerned with the safety of the princeps, Marcellus uses the case of Antistius to characterize Thrasea as actively protecting those who would abuse the ruler: *principis obtrectatores protegere solitus* (*Ann.* 16.28.2). Likening Thrasea to an enemy and the protector of others who wish harm enables Marcellus to conclude with a figure in which he suggests that Thrasea's form of self-exile within the state somehow damages the state for others: *ne ... qui fora theatra templa pro solitudine haberet, qui minitaretur exilium suum, ambitionis pravae compotem facerent* (*Ann.* 16.28.3). 'They should not allow a man who treated the public squares, theatres, and temples as a wasteland, who threatened them with his exile, to be master of his evil ambition.'[41] Thrasea's alleged attitude to the public spaces of the community empties them of political and social significance for himself and, Marcellus implies, for others. From the outset of the speech, Marcellus emphasizes the duty of the senate in this matter, reproaching them for their indulgence of Thrasea and his associates up to this point (*Ann.* 16.28.1); now he enjoins them to restore their commonwealth by cutting off the corrosive presence of Thrasea: *abrumperet vitam ab ea civitate* (*Ann.* 16.28.3). 'Let him sever his life from this community of citizens.'

When assessing accusations of this nature in detail, it is difficult not to take sides: to consider whether there is a case to be made against Thrasea, particularly on the difficult charge of non-participation in the senate, or whether the charges are to be dismissed as entirely unjust. Assessing how much of Capito's or Marcellus' rhetoric is 'metaphorical' involves taking sides to a certain degree: is Capito's reference to *secessio* a metaphorical escalation of Thrasea's absence from senate, or is it a fair description? What we have seen from the examination of the charges so far is how they conform to a pattern found elsewhere in accounts of *maiestas* trials, which present the emperor as subject to threats and interpellate senatorial subjects as his vigilant protectors against fellow citizens. The final category of threats to the safety of the emperor concern verbal abuse, which we will turn to in section 2.3. The idea of language as damaging leads into a consideration of how *maiestas* trials and the practice of *delatio* provide a context for talking about speech and citizenship in imperial Rome.

2.3 The speech of *delatio*

Tacitus presents as another innovation of the Augustan regime the extension of *maiestas* from actions to words:

> *si quis proditione exercitum <a>ut plebem seditionibus, denique male gesta re publica maiestatem populi Romani minuisset: facta arguebatur, dicta impune erant. primus Augustus cognitionem de famosis libellis specie legis eius tractavit, commotus Cassii Severi libidine, qua viros feminasque inlustres procacibus scriptis diffamaverat.*
>
> *Ann.* 1.72.2–3

If anyone damaged the army by treachery, or the plebs by conspiracy, or generally diminished the supremacy of the Roman people by managing the commonwealth badly [he was liable to a *maiestas* charge]: actions were liable, words were exempt. Augustus was the first to bring enquiries into defamatory texts under the heading of this law, having been disturbed by the licence with which Cassius Severus had defamed notable men and women in his brazen invectives.

Two features of verbal insult in *maiestas* charges are worth commenting on: first, the way in which accusations of improper speech extend from speech as conspiracy (e.g. *secreti sermones*, *Ann.* 4.21.2) to writing associated with magical practices (e.g. *atroces vel occultae notae*, *Ann.* 2.30.2). In the middle of this spectrum is the speech of reproach or insult: like Cassius Severus' *procacia scripta*, these insults are presented as a sort of hostile language which involves exposure and face-to-face confrontation. The frequently used term *probrum* (and its adjectival form *probrosus*) is often articulated through variants on the phrase 'to cast a reproach in someone's teeth'.[42] Such verbal violence is imagined as a diminution of the ruler's supremacy because invective has always been considered a form of attack on a fellow citizen and because the performance of invective situates the ruler as no more than a fellow citizen. As Suetonius remarks of Helvidius Priscus' offence against Vespasian, *altercationibus insolentissimis paene in ordinem redactus* (Suet., *Vesp.* 15). 'Arguing with the ruler in the most insolent manner, he practically degraded him in social rank.'

The second feature of interest in accusations of verbal insult is how often they appear to mirror the prosecution process itself: the defendant is accused of having, in effect, indicted the emperor or another notable person. The dividing line between an *accusator* and his victim is barely discernible in these instances, a phenomenon later evident in the way that defendants escape the charge of *maiestas* by 'turning informer' (e.g. *Ann.* 6.3.4; Dio 67.13.6) and in the way that senators pursuing former *delatores* for their crimes seem to replicate their violence. So too the distinction is blurred between the defendant on a charge of verbal insult and the recipient of his alleged abuse, a paradox noted by both Dio and Tacitus in the case of Tiberius. Dio remarks that 'whenever Tiberius carefully inquired (*zētōn*) into a case where a man was accused of speaking disparagingly (*kaka elege*) about him, he ended up uttering all the most evil abuse of himself ... and so everything which he punished (*ekolazen*) other men for as *maiestas* (*asebountas*), he committed as an offence (*plēmmelein*) upon himself' (Dio 57.23.1–3). The impersonal actions of judicial inquiry (*zetein*) and sentencing (*kolazein*) are transformed into evil and inharmonious speech (*kaka legein; plēmmelein*) that damages the judicial speaker himself. In Tacitus' version we are presented with a vision of how the emperor is both assaulted and shaped by the *maiestas* allegations: *nam postulato Votieno ob contumelias in Caesarem dictas... audivit Tiberius probra, quis per occultum lacerabatur adeoque perculsus est, ut se vel statim vel in cognitione purgaturum clamitaret* (*Ann.* 4.42.2). 'When Votienus was brought up for charges of invective against the ruler ... Tiberius heard the reproaches with which he was flagellated in private, and he was so struck that he kept calling out that he would be cleared of this either straight away or through an inquiry.' The formal language of prosecution (*postulare, cognitio*) becomes the frame that both regulates and enables verbal violence upon the ruler, who experiences it as tearing and inflicting blows upon him.[43] This leads him to mistake the *cognitio* as an inquiry into his conduct rather than Votienus': whether Tiberius imagines that he will be cleared of the reproaches in Votienus' trial or in a separate trial is not clear. When Votienus is found guilty, Tacitus remarks of the severity of Tiberius' sentencing that he was *obiectam sibi adversus reos inclementiam eo pervicacius amplexus*; 'embracing even more doggedly the lack of mercy of which he was accused by defendants' (*Ann.* 4.42.3). Tiberius becomes precisely the harsh judge which is the substance of the accusations; here he responds to a reproach cast in his face (*obiectam*) not by clearing his name but by changing his behaviour to match the reproach.[44]

Votienus' trial consolidates Tiberius' belief that the senate is a place to be henceforth avoided: *patrum coetus vocesque, quae plerumque verae et graves coram ingerebantur* (*Ann.* 4.42.1). 'The gatherings of the elders and the words, often true and weighty, with which he was in public assailed.' The context of the trial and the use of *ingero* suggests that the words he seeks to avoid are insults,[45] but it is also clear that the infiltration of *maiestas* threats across different actions, words, and socio-political spheres has created a world in which even ordinary senatorial speech – especially when it displays a commitment to truth – can be represented as unsafe for the emperor. The effect of *maiestas* trials upon the practice of speech is to increase self-consciousness about its capacity to help or to harm the civic community. This reflects back on the practice of *delatio*, which Tacitus has introduced to the narrative as disastrous for the state. The extent to which the *delator* violates the norms of citizenship – or justifies himself by asserting his citizen-like qualities – provides principles for understanding and thinking about civic life for the imperial senator. Here I will examine not what Tacitus says about *delatores* but what is said by speakers in his narratives when suitable opportunities arise for attacking or defending the practice of *delatio*. The opportunities themselves illuminate how the *delatores* come individually or collectively under scrutiny. We will return to these in greater detail in chapter three in order to consider their consequences for those who speak against *delatio*. Here my focus is on how defence of *delatio* projects a view of speech as a civic activity in the Principate.

Regime change provides an ideal opportunity for scrutiny of *delatio* and makes evident how the *delator* is caught up in a quasi-symbiotic relationship with the ruler, as we examined in section 2.1. While the *delatores* collectively risk repudiation and even demands for reparation after Nero's death, first at Galba's accession and then at Vespasian's (*Hist.* 4.7–8, 40–43), an individual *delator*, Suillius Rufus, is targeted early in Nero's reign for his actions under Claudius (*Ann.* 13.42–43). Another opportunity for public debate over *delatio* arises when a senator brings the laws about payment for prosecution or advocacy up for discussion: the senate considers a motion on this matter in Tiberius' reign (*Ann.* 4.30) and again in Claudius' (*Ann.* 11.5–7). These debates touch on one of two central objections to *delatores* articulated throughout Tacitus' works: that they speak for monetary reward. Finally, in Tacitus' *Dialogus*, the opening debate between Marcus Aper and Curiatus Maternus on the value of oratory includes Aper's proposal and Maternus' rejection of two *delatores* (Eprius Marcellus and Vibius Crispus) as examples of successful eloquence. Even here, however, the qualities of the *delatores*' speech have less importance for the debate than their social attributes and civic contributions. If we read across these critiques and the defensive responses of the *delatores* themselves, we see that the primary objections to their practice are that they speak to harm fellow citizens and that they do so for profit. It is the combination of these aims that leaves the speech of *delatores* open to the charge of being 'uncivic'. Hence, early in Vespasian's reign, but before his return from the East, the senate attempts a purge of its members by insisting that each senator utter an oath about their past activities: *deos testes advocabant nihil ope sua factum, quo cuiusquam salus laederetur, neque se praemium aut honorem ex calamitate civium cepisse* (*Hist.* 4.41.1). 'Each man began to call on the gods as witnesses that he had not used his power to damage the safety of any other person, nor had he taken any reward or honour from the ruin of citizens.' The performative nature of the oath forcefully disqualifies *delatores* from membership of the senate: if they cannot utter this declaration, then they have no right to remain senators. The fact that some senators are actually driven from the curia during this 'informal censorship' (*velut censura*, *Hist.* 4.41.2) shows that this is a moment where senatorial citizenship is aggressively represented as the antithesis to the practice of *delatio*.

Underpinning these two central, interlocking charges against the *delator* are assumptions about proper civic relations which are not exclusively grounded in returns of money or status and where violence is regulated by law. We have already seen how prosecution procedures negotiate the civic violence at the heart of the process; the reward for the prosecutor maintains anxiety about this violence. Hence the most highly coloured attacks on the *delatores*, by Curtius Montanus in *Histories* and Curiatus Maternus in *Dialogus*, heighten this anxiety through language which juxtaposes the *delator's* monetary gain with the blood of his victims. Montanus refers to Regulus' *libido sanguinis et hiatus praemiorum* (*Hist.* 4.42.4), 'lust for blood and greed for rewards', while Maternus repudiates *lucrosae huius et sanguinantis eloquentiae usus recens* (*Dial.* 12.2), 'the recent practice of this profitable and bloodstained eloquence'. The term *praemium* encapsulates the problem: it denotes a respectable recompense for services but retains traces of its original meaning as *praeda*, property seized by violence. Helvidius Priscus, recalling the damage done by Eprius Marcellus in Nero's reign, invites him to 'enjoy his rewards (*praemiis*) and his impunity from retribution' in the new regime (*Hist.* 4.7.3). When speakers extrapolate from these central charges, they focus on the unproductive civic relations that *delatores* have created around them, marked by hatred (*Ann.* 11.7.2), fear, and debilitating power imbalances (*Dial.* 13.4).

Against this, a *delator* such as Suillius Rufus who is directly under threat from the senate's renewed attention to the *lex Cincia* (which limits gifts to advocates) redescribes his acquisition of wealth as relatively modest and comparable to other respectable careers. In a composite speech of Suillius, Cossutianus Capito, and other *delatores* in the senate, the pay of a legal advocate is set alongside the other 'traditional occupations for a would-be senator':[46] *multos militia, quosdam exercendo agros tolerare vitam: nihil a quoquam expeti, nisi cuius fructus ante providerit* (*Ann.* 11.7.1). 'Many men keep themselves alive with military service, some by working the fields: no one chooses a career without considering in advance how profitable it will be.' Emphasis on agriculture rather than the military enables the speakers to dwell on their moderate income (they will later refer to themselves as *modicos senatores, Ann.* 11.7.3) and to extrapolate from agriculture the metaphor of fertility (*fructus*) with which to counter accusations that they promote unproductive social relations. Their argument is helped here by the terms of the law under discussion, which enables them to speak as advocates rather than prosecutors[47] and to present themselves as offering protection to paying clients rather than as receiving payment 'at the discretion of the senate or the emperor' from the defendant's confiscated estate.[48] Running through the *delatores*' explicit defence of their pay, then, is an implicit counter to the charges that their speech brings about the ruin of citizens and creates a community based on fear, hatred, and greed. As well as representing themselves as protective of less powerful citizens (*Ann.* 11.7.1), they express support of plebeian exercises in rhetoric, demonstrating their commitment to a culturally active community (*Ann.* 11.7.3). Their moderate desire for well-earned pay is presented as part of their capacity to enjoy and celebrate the state at peace: *se modicos senatores quieta re publica nulla nisi pacis emolumenta petere* (*Ann.* 11.7.3). 'They themselves, senators of modest means, in a tranquil commonwealth, seek only the rewards of peace.'

Perhaps the method of defence most appropriate to the *delator* is a form of attack upon another type of citizen, who acts as a useful contrast to highlight the virtues of the *delator* himself. This is the method used when Suillius and others represent themselves as celebrating the rewards of peace, in contrast to the late Republican orators (evoked as positive exemplars by the consul designate, *Ann.* 11.6.2), who are claimed to have enjoyed the *praemia* of civil war and the *merces* of rabble-rousing (*Ann.* 11.7.2). In Nero's reign, when Suillius comes under fire once more, he turns on Seneca and fashions an invective which serves as a vehicle for repeating the self-justifications of his earlier speech.[49] Seneca's frivolous literary activities are contrasted to Suillius' *vividam et incorruptam eloquentiam tuendis civibus* (*Ann.* 13.42.3) – 'vigorous and incorruptible eloquence, used for the protection of citizens'. More boldly, Suillius again contrasts his support of a litigant and the 'reward for an honest day's work' (*praemium honestae operae, Ann.* 13.42.3) with Seneca's alleged adulteries in the imperial household. Finally, Seneca's immense wealth is ascribed to the predatory activities of will-hunting and usury which drain Italy and the provinces, while Suillius' *pecunia* is moderate and gained by labour. Suillius thus can project onto Seneca associations of corruption, enervation, and decadence, while his own life is described in terms of honesty, moderation, and productivity.

While the criticisms of *delatores* harp on the same theme of destroying fellow citizens for reward, the speeches of self-defence are much more diverse and inventive in fashioning justifications for *delatio*. It is perhaps the best testament to the rhetorical skill of these individuals, and it is ironic that it is most in evidence when they speak to defend themselves rather than to accuse others. Scholars have argued that Roman society was unable to shake off the *delatores* because they were a necessary evil in the state.[50] But this section has shown the different ways in which the speech of *delatio* overlaps with senatorial speech or with speech subject to a *maiestas* charge. This chapter illustrates how *delatio* was inextricable not just from the judicial process but from a complex of issues about speech, civic community, and truth. Because the speech of *delatio* could spread, making the category of the *delator* highly permeable, and because responsibility for the condemnation of defendants was shared across the senate, *delatio* appears as a threat to true senatorial speech. As we will see in chapter three, Tacitus, having delineated a world shaped by shameful flattery and predatory accusations, turns his attention to interventions which rupture this world and show the possibilities for another kind of speech.

3

Servitium rupit: Counter-speech

As we have already seen, the two debilitating modes of speech in the Principate create political relations between subject and ruler which Tacitus characterizes in terms of isolation for the ruler and constraint for the subject. A notable effect of each mode is how it cancels out other modes of political speech, making them difficult or even impossible to employ. In that respect, Tacitus' narrative exposes how they constitute truth regimes which coerce other modes of speech and thought. The case we have already briefly examined in chapter one, Otho's war-council before the Battle of Bedriacum, illustrates this difficulty by juxtaposing military knowledge and advice with *adulatio*. Suetonius Paulinus and Marius Celsus, who have presented tactical reasons for delaying the engagement, are silenced by Salvius Titianus and Licinius Proculus precisely because the latter turn to flattery: *neu quis obviam ire sententiae auderet, in adulationem concesserat* (*Hist.* 2.33.1). 'So that nobody would dare to counter their opinion, they had recourse to flattery.' In the world of military discourse the turn to flattery – *concedere* – betrays the speakers' sense of how weak their argument is: they yield or give way to this mode of speech.[1] In another sense, the withdrawal to *adulatio* itself represents a tactical move, retreating to an unassailable position where the 'objective rationality' of military advice loses its powers of veridiction.[2] If Paulinus and Celsus were to press their arguments against Titianus and Proculus, they would effectively be arguing, in the emperor's presence, against his manifest divinity.

The damage done by *adulatio* and *delatio* to other modes of speech is effected through their parasitic relation to forms of sociability, honour, and law which underpin civic life. Because *adulatio* mimics and perverts practices of friendship, it suffocates deliberative and advisory speech which draws on the same practices. The practice of *delatio*, which is exercised within the agonistic sphere of prosecution, is more permeable to counter-argument, but it is still difficult and potentially dangerous to challenge either the practice or individual *delatores*. Nevertheless, Tacitus shows us a range of interventions into the speech world of the Principate which seek to disrupt the operation of *adulatio* and *delatio* and to neutralize or reverse their effects. The strategies of disruption employed by different speakers range from open attacks upon the practice of these modes of speech to engagement with these modes in order to bypass their most deleterious effects. What emerges from an overview of these strategies is an alternative worldview where senatorial speech, reasserting its truth-value, reinstates a deliberative community around its performance. Many of these interventions, as we will see, draw on already circulating imperial discourses in order to create conditions of meaningful exchange with the ruler.

In section 3.1, we will concentrate on methods of countering or bypassing flattery. Here is the one place in this book where I will look at the emperor as a political speaker, examining how Tiberius' reactions against flattery draw on assumptions about ideal ruler–citizen relations. Tiberius' inability to suppress *adulatio* and its effects demonstrates how his political world is shaped by the interests of the flatterers. This highlights the difficulty, for any subject, of bypassing flattery and regaining the language of true honorific speech. This section concludes with an examination of Helvidius Priscus at the start of Vespasian's reign and shows how his proposal of honours works by responding to and 'authorizing' cues within the emperor's own self-presentation.

3.1 *in adulationem lapsos cohibebat*

As we have already seen in the case of Paulinus and Celsus, a direct challenge to the practice of flattery is near impossible – for an imperial subject. It is tantamount to saying that the princeps does not merit whatever excessive praise or honour is proffered. The princeps himself, however, is in a position to reject or comment critically on such offerings; Tiberius' repeated attempts to regulate the manner in which he is addressed illustrates how insidious and seemingly unstoppable is the discourse of *adulatio*. Of the imperial regimes treated by Tacitus, the Tiberian regime is most densely thronged with episodes of *adulatio*,[3] where it is also treated much more self-consciously as an emergent mode of addressing the ruler. Apart from one episode in Book 4, where Tiberius' agitation at discovering how he is abused in private seems to be soothed to a degree by the *adulatio* of the senate, the ruler's reaction to attempted flattery is invariably critical and frequently hostile. This perhaps arises from Tiberius' awareness of the dangers this mode of speech poses for him as a ruler; it is highly likely that he had read Philodemus' treatise *On Flattery*.[4] Three times Tacitus observes that it is not only free speech that is difficult under Tiberius; flatterers also struggle to escape his disfavour. The first of these is after Tiberius has refused the title *pater patriae* and has sharply rebuked – *acerbe increpuit*, a verb which will recur – those who ascribe divinity to him or address him as *dominus* – again a recurring theme. Tacitus remarks *unde angusta et lubrica oratio sub principe, qui libertatem metuebat, adulationem oderat* (*Ann.* 2.87). 'Hence speech was a narrow and slippery path under a princeps who feared outspokenness but hated flattery.' In Book 3, recounting Tiberius' more general disgust at the senate's subservience, he concludes *scilicet etiam illum, qui libertatem publicam nollet, tam proiectae servientium patientiae taedebat* (*Ann.* 3.65.3). 'Indeed even the ruler, who did not want political outspokenness, was wearied at such abject submissiveness from these servile men.' Finally, in Book 4, after the pontifices have unadvisedly included the sons of Germanicus in the new year prayers for the princeps' safety, Tacitus presents the difficulty of getting the level of flattery right. As I've already observed in chapter one, here he practically posits a rule of decorum for this abject form of speech: *[adulatio] quae moribus corruptis perinde anceps, si nulla et ubi nimia est* (*Ann.* 4.17.1). 'Flattery, which in a corrupt age is equally perilous whether it is absent or excessive.' These authorial comments inaugurate an atmosphere of self-consciousness about the practice of flattery, which is borne out by the ruler's reactions.

What we also see in Tiberius' repeated (and failed) attempts to curb *adulatio* is a recognition of the kind of world it creates. As we've already seen with the first example from *Annals* 2 and with the flattering counsel of Licinius and Proculus to Otho in *Histories* 2, excessive language of praise focusses on elevating the emperor to a quasi-divine status (an elevation formalized in the establishment of ruler cult). Tiberius' reactions over and again stress the human nature of this ruler, establish *moderatio* as a cardinal virtue, and insist that honours offered to him should be both precedent-based and deserved. So, for instance, Cornelius Dolabella's proposal that Tiberius review the characters of senators eligible for provincial commands is countered by the emperor asserting the mortal limits of his view and reasserting the role of the law in curbing provincial maladministration (*Ann.* 3.69.1–5).[5] Tiberius' great programmatic speech, outlining the cardinal virtues for which he wants his reign remembered, is prompted by Spain's request to give him divine honours, which he dismisses as *promiscae adulationes* (*Ann.* 4.37.3).[6] Earlier, the proposals to mark the award of tribunician power to his son Drusus – which we looked at in chapter one – receive an imperial reproof as *insolentia* and *contra patrium morem*, projecting Tiberius' well-known conservatism and deference to precedent (particularly Augustan precedent).[7] In short, Tiberian engagement with *adulatio* constitutes an often explicit debate about what sort of ruler Tiberius wants to be.

Patrick Sinclair, in his analysis of Tiberian *sententiae*, observes that when the emperor responds to specific issues in senate, he often formulates a generalized statement which contributes to his overall 'programmatic view' of the Principate.[8] The criticisms Tiberius levels at flatterers certainly fit with this interpretation and to a degree reflect Sinclair's argument that Tiberius is more interested in establishing the status of the Principate than in promoting his own personal status. We can see how such a project would be inimical to the practice of *adulatio*, which focusses on the individual perhaps to the detriment of the office. This can illuminate another feature of Tiberius' response to flattery which we observe across different episodes: his suggestion that the flatterer in some way degrades the *dignitas* and *maiestas* of the imperial office. For the most part, however, these responses point to a strong sense of Tiberius' personal dignity. The first of these episodes involves Cornelius Dolabella once again and has been examined in chapter one: on the suppression of Sacrovir's revolt, Dolabella proposes a triumph for Tiberius as he returns from Campania.[9] Tiberius' response is among the most ironically witty of his *dicta*, but also contains a statement about how the emptiness of flattering speech drains honour from the recipient as much as from the speaker. And in the same breath he proudly restates the extent of his military glories, standing on his *dignitas* as a seasoned general: *non se tam vacuum gloria praedicabat, ut post ferocissimas gentes perdomitas, tot receptos in iuventa aut spretos triumphos iam senior peregrinationis suburbanae inanae praemium peteret* (*Ann.* 3.47.4). 'He declared that he was not so bankrupt of glory that, after taming the wildest tribes of barbarians, after receiving so many triumphs as a young man, after turning down triumphs now as an older man, he would have to petition for a vain reward after pottering around the suburban estates.' Between the framing ideas of emptiness (*vacuum, inane*), Tacitus has Tiberius pile up weighty and sonorous phrases to express the height of his conquests and honours, before descending sharply in style to the banality of mere travel in nearby Campania. Tiberius' message is that he will not allow such banality to deflate the grandeur of what he has achieved in the past.

The same concern to safeguard his dignity is evident in later episodes, even behind Tiberius' increased suspicion – even paranoia – under Sejanus' influence and thereafter. As we've already seen, the pontifices start the year AD 24 by adding Germanicus' two elder sons to the prayers for the emperor's continued safety: *non tam caritate iuvenum quam adulatione* (*Ann*. 4.17.1). 'Not because they held the young men in particular affection, but out of flattery.' Apart from Tiberius' insistence that this constitutes collusion of some sort with Agrippina, it is clear that once more his reaction draws on the idea of decorum and what is due to the *dignitas* of the elder statesman/ruler. After rebuking the priests, he advises the senate more generally, *ne quis mobiles adulescentium animos praematuris honoribus ad superbiam extolleret* (*Ann*. 4.17.2). 'So that nobody would raise up the impressionable minds of the young men with premature honours: the result would be arrogance.' Suetonius' account of the same episode, which he sees primarily as unveiling to the public Tiberius' hostility to his grandsons, nevertheless makes more explicit the concern with *dignitas* in the emperor's recommendations: *non debere talia praemia tribui nisi expertis et aetate provectis* (Suet., *Tib*. 54.1). 'Such rewards ought not to be bestowed except on those who have experience and are more advanced in age.' A similar combination of paranoia and justifiable concern with the dignity of his position is evident in Tiberius' really savage reaction to Iunius Gallio's *meditata adulatio*, which seeks to honour the Praetorian Guard for their service to the emperor. This is an understandably sensitive area for a senator to intervene in, only months after the Praetorian Prefect Sejanus has been executed on suspicion of engineering a coup.[10] Tiberius' verbal assault repeatedly returns to this central idea of encroachment on the emperor's prerogative: *violenter increpuit, velut coram rogitans, quid illi cum militibus,* *quos nec dicta <nisi> imperatoris neque praemia nisi ab imperatore accipere par esset* (*Ann*. 6.3.1). 'He violently rebuked Gallio, repeatedly asking him, as if there in the flesh, what had he to do with the soldiers? It was not appropriate for them to hear pronouncements from anyone except a commander, nor to receive rewards except from a commander.' The use of *par* to express how Gallio has transgressed suggests a violation of the ruler's *maiestas*,[11] in this instance not so much the personally felt *dignitas* of the individual but the sense of what is due to the position of emperor. Each time Tiberius responds to flattery by standing on his dignity, he challenges the flatterers' implicit position – that the emperor is pleased to inhabit a world where his every action is shadowed by exaggeratedly honorific commentaries and gestures. Instead, he recasts their 'embellishment' of him as offence and debasement. Despite Tacitus' remarks in Book 3 on the emperor's hostility to *libertas* (with which I began this section), in his overview of the first part of Tiberius' reign he concedes that a productive alternative to *adulatio* has been consistently offered to the senate.

> *publica negotia et privatorum maxima apud patres tractabantur, dabaturque primoribus disserere, et in adulationem lapsos cohibebat ipse.*
>
> *Ann*. 4.6.2

> All public business and the most significant private business was handled in the senate, the opportunity was given to the leading men of the state to discuss them, and when they degenerated into flattery, the ruler himself discouraged them.

Tiberius' commitment to maintaining a public discourse in this way sets him at odds with the *adulator*, whose chosen medium is a private conversation where he can foster distrust and seek to isolate his victim from his other friends. By way of riposte, Tiberius makes the rebuke of flatterers part of the public discourse he seeks to uphold. The senators who compete in *adulatio* in the curia are already involved in a more complex network of dynamics than private conversation. In the senate, each speaker strives to trump the previous honorific statement or proposal and is either brilliantly successful or fails spectacularly – the parallel with competitive declamation is evident. Tiberius and Tacitus each plays the part of judge in this competition; just as Tacitus invites his readers to participate in evaluating each senator's *infamia* in the light of history,[12] so Tiberius invites senators of his own time to share in his critique of their peers. This implicit appeal to a collective sphere of judgement (an important theme to which we will return) cuts across the *adulator*'s attempt to create a 'special relationship' with the ruler, reducing him to just another of the throng of senators,[13] or even lower. Tiberius' notorious (and ever-quotable) outburst at *Ann.* 3.65 can thus be read as an expression of frustration not only at the extent of *adulatio*, but at the absence of a critically acute audience for his rebukes.

> *tempora illa adeo infecta et adulatione sordida fuere, ut non modo primores civitatis ... sed omnes consulares, magna pars eorum qui praetura functi multique etiam pedarii senatores certatim exsurgerent foedaque et nimia censerent. memoriae proditur Tiberium, quotiens curia egrederetur, Graecis verbis in hunc modum eloqui solitum 'o homines ad servitutem paratos!'*
>
> *Ann.* 3.65.2–3

> That regime was so infected and soiled with flattery, that not only the highest elite of the state ... but also all men of consular status, a great number of those who had held the praetorship, and even many junior senators would competitively get on their hind legs and make disgraceful and extravagant proposals. It is related that Tiberius, whenever he went out from the curia, habitually exclaimed in Greek, 'oh men self-prepared for slavery!'

The ubiquity of *adulatio* is underscored by the list of participants in descending order of social and political status (the same order that would be used for their actual participation in any debate). But Tiberius still seeks or at least manufactures an evaluative audience to bear witness to his disgust. As he leaves the curia, accompanied certainly by freedmen and personal guard, probably by advisors of senatorial rank,[14] and possibly even by the whole senate, his use of Greek creates a group of educated listeners from among his entourage.[15] Many aspects of the story make Tiberius' statement seem like a marginal gloss: the use of 'non-official language', the timing of the remark as the emperor departs from the space of deliberative speech, the anecdotal quality of the incident itself.[16] But the statement is also crafted for direction back to the centre, being precisely the sort of dictum that would circulate socially back to the senators it indicts. And it makes a performance of Tiberius' routine departure from the curia, turning it almost into an act of protest.

The failure of the ruler himself to check the practice of *adulatio* and its effects in the world tempers any potential critique of a mere subject who tries to divert this debilitating mode of speech. Diversion and refashioning are the only available strategies for subjects, since direct challenge of an *adulator* implies rejecting their praise of the ruler. The one attempt at reintroducing true honorific language narrated by Tacitus which actually seems to succeed is the intervention of Helvidius Priscus in the first senate meeting after Vespasian's accession, late in AD 69. In this crucial regime change, Tacitus presents Helvidius initiating a succession of proposals designed to set the agenda for the new ruler: the first of these is his participation in the senatorial approval of honours for the Flavian generals.

> *eaque omnia Valerius Asiaticus consul designatus censuit; ceteri voltu manuque, pauci, quibus conspicua dignitas aut ingenium adulatione exercitum, compositis orationibus adsentiebantur. ubi ad Helvidium Priscum praetorem designatum ventum, prompsit sententiam ut honorificam in bonum principem *** falsa aberant, et studiis senatus attollebatur.*
>
> Hist. 4.4.3

> All these things Valerius Asiaticus proposed as consul designate; the rest gave their agreement by facial expressions or hand gestures, and a few – who held notable dignity or a well-honed talent for flattery – with carefully constructed speeches. When the turn came for Helvidius Priscus as praetor designate, he brought forward a proposal which not only brought honour to a good ruler but was equally lacking in falseness, and he was carried aloft by the enthusiastic response of the senate.

Tacitus immediately tempers the positive result of this intervention by foreshadowing Helvidius' eventual end (he was exiled under Vespasian, and later executed, apparently without the emperor's knowledge): *isque praecipuus illi dies magnae offensae initium et magnae gloriae fuit* (*Hist.* 4.4.3). 'And this day especially was for him the beginning of his great offence – and his great glory.' But before we concur with Tacitus' longer-term view, let us examine the dynamics of Helvidius' *sententia* in the context of this crucial senate meeting, for the *adulatio* which it interrupts has arisen in particular circumstances, nor is Helvidius' disruption of this *adulatio* quite the doomed act of heroism that Tacitus' afterword suggests. This is the senate meeting which ratifies the Eastern legions' declaration of Vespasian as emperor (six months after the event) and is therefore a deliberative session focussed on establishing a new regime.[17] Helvidius is therefore disrupting or bypassing a mode of speech which is familiar to the senators in addressing other rulers, but is not yet an established mode of communication with *this* ruler. It could be seen as an attempt to set a new tone in how one addresses the emperor, to inaugurate a new mode of speech.[18]

Indeed, Helvidius might well be responding to a prompt given by Vespasian himself, whose words to the senate (by letter) are described in the previous chapter as *civilia de se, de re publica egregia* (*Hist.* 4.3.4): 'citizen-like about himself, exceptional about the commonwealth'. The term *civilis* has, since Augustus, been associated with the practice of *moderatio* in a ruler, with his self-presentation as a citizen among other citizens;[19] Vespasian's juxtaposition of moderate language about himself with grandiloquence on the subject of the state shows the appropriate stylistic level for each topic and implies a programme for his status as ruler. Helvidius' *sententia* might seem an equally appropriate response, avoiding the 'excessive and insincere' qualities of the now-traditional flattery.[20] But Helvidius is not just reacting to Vespasian's initial self-presentation; he is also participating in and attempting to redirect his fellow senators, whose initial, positive response to Vespasian is dissipated by their less positive reaction to Vespasian's second-in-command, Licinius Mucianus.[21]

The senate's general response to Vespasian's civility is described by Tacitus first as *alacritas*, joy or eagerness, and then as *obsequium*, compliance or obedience (*Hist.* 4.3.4). *Alacritas* is a significant term for emotion at this point, as it suggests that the senate's optimism fuels a new political energy. This suggestion is not entirely dispelled by the senate's immediate *obsequium* and their appointment of Vespasian and Titus to the consulate. As Vielberg has demonstrated, *obsequium*, certainly in *Histories*, encompasses senatorial behaviour from opportunistic servility (*Hist.* 1.19.1) to moderate compliance; he sees this episode in Book 4 as entirely representative of Tacitus' more neutral use of the term.[22] The difference between the two forms of *obsequium* can be discerned in the fit between compliance towards the emperor and care for the state, which has already been prompted by Vespasian speaking *de re publica egregia*. In Book 1, in the senatorial response to Galba's adoption of an heir, compliance and public-spiritedness are completely separate: the senators speak *obvio obsequio, privatas spes agitantes sine publica cura* (*Hist.* 1.19.1). 'Meeting Galba halfway with their compliance, deliberating on their secret, individual ambitions without any care for the public good.'[23] By contrast, in Book 4 the senate expresses its compliance to the emperor by discharging its political duties – the most immediate of which was the replacement of consuls for the year.[24] Thus, *obsequium* here constitutes a response to Vespasian's self-presentation on senatorial terms; the bestowal of *consulare imperium* upon Vespasian and Titus constitutes the truth of the new emperor's *civilitas*. More than simply following the lead given by Vespasian's letter (and *obsequium*, derived from *sequor*, implies taking direction from another), senatorial obedience provides the seal or guarantee to the emperor's power and its character.[25]

Mucianus disrupts this productive building of imperial–senatorial relations by taking it on himself to also send a letter to the senate. His arrogance stands in sharp contrast to Vespasian's *civilitas* and is noted by the recipients, who comment *id vero erga rem publicam superbum, erga principem contumeliosum* (*Hist.* 4.4.1). 'But this was hubristic in relation to the state and insulting towards the emperor.' The most damaging effect of Mucianus' letter, however, is in the way it throws the senate back into modes of speech which have been the resort of subjects under a tyranny. Tacitus shows a rift opening between the senators' private speech – the *sermones* in which they complain about Mucianus' *superbia* – and their deliberative speech in the senate: *ceterum invidia in occulto, adulatio in aperto erant: multo cum honore verborum Muciano triumphalia de bello civium data* (*Hist.* 4.4.2). 'But their ill-will was concealed, and their flattery was on display: with much honorific verbiage, triumphal ornaments for the war against citizens were bestowed on Mucianus.' Here is where *adulatio* returns to senatorial discourse, and those who do not have the will to flatter become sunk in inertia, as we've already seen with Tacitus' image of senators delivering their assent by facial expressions or hand gestures.[26] This is precisely the opposite of what Tacitus has described in his preface as the conditions of productive senatorial speech under a ruler – 'when it is permitted to think what you want and say what you think' (*Hist.* 1.1.4) – and these are the conditions that Helvidius seeks to restore when he stands to deliver a different *sententia*. Whatever the long-term effects of his intervention (about which Tacitus immediately warns us), the impact on the senators at that moment is to re-energize their *studia*, their enthusiasm and engagement.[27]

What was it that Helvidius said? Frustratingly, the text is corrupt at this point: we are told that the *sententia* 'brought honour' to a good (or new) emperor, either because Helvidius proposed some form of honour or because he expressed sentiments which honoured Vespasian. We are also told that 'falsehoods were absent', and there seems to be a connection between these two qualities (expressed by *ut* and sometimes by *ita* inserted before *falsum aberant*) which highlights that honorific speech does not have to descend to the emptiness or exaggeration of *adulatio*.[28] The crucial term in the phrase is *bonum*, which guarantees that this statement is 'externally true' (in the sense of 'corresponding to reality'). If the emperor is a good man, Helvidius' honorific words are suited to their addressee, therefore *falsa aberant*.[29] But more than this, Helvidius' words are 'internally true': they reflect his opinion of the emperor as a good man. The guarantee of truth in Helvidius' words rests not just on the external condition of Vespasian's virtue, but on Helvidius' inner judgement and outward articulation of that virtue as the proper object of senatorial assessment.

By choosing a moment where a change of regime is signalled and effecting a separation between *honor* and *adulatio*, Helvidius momentarily breaks through the discourse of flattery and lays claim to a discourse that we could identify as praise or panegyric. As I observed in the introduction and in chapter one, honorific discourses and decrees are often assimilated back into the category of *adulatio* by modern readers who are uncomfortable with the ancient praise of rulers. And, as we have also seen, the delicate balance between *honor* and *adulatio* is a matter of decorum, that self-regulation which produces and maintains the orator throughout his existence.[30] Helvidius' calibration of the necessary conditions in which he speaks (the discourse offered to the senate by the new ruler) with his inner will (his commitment to *constantia*, which we will examine in chapter four) renders his praise a successful rhetorical act, which temporarily creates new conditions for speech.[31] Tacitus' framing of this act by mentioning the future downfall of Helvidius acknowledges, I think, both the provisionality and the future potential of his intervention against *adulatio*.

Against *adulatio*, both Tiberius and Helvidius seek to renew the language of *honor* as an evaluative system which lends authority to subjects even as it enhances the status of the ruler. Evaluation and judgement are important activities which underpin the political world in which a senator's speech has purchase, as we will see in subsequent chapters. In section 3.2, we turn to the different kinds of speech which are mobilized against *delatio*. First, examining the case brought against the Claudian *delator* Suillius Rufus, we see how speakers retrospectively hold prosecutors to account for their predatory actions against fellow citizens. Suillius is also targeted in the second kind of speech against *delatio*: where speakers attempt to limit the future actions of *delatores* by removing the incentives to prosecute. Each of these kinds of speech produce visions of Roman society which place the safety of citizens at its heart. Finally, we turn to the speeches which try to mitigate the harm of individual prosecutions while allowing the practice of *delatio* to continue. This too prioritizes the safety of citizens and has the additional effect of reinforcing the judicial role of the senator. The act of judgement, although it involves participation in predatory accusations, provides an opportunity to promote an alternative political world.

3.2 *de praemiis accusatorum abolendis*

The natural sphere of the *delator* is agonistic discourse, hence attempts to disrupt their mode of speech are particularly difficult. Various speakers verbally attack the *delatores*, attempt to prosecute them for their actions, invoke legal strictures against them, and finally engage with them at the level of individual cases. Each of these counter-modes bears structural similarity to the acts of accusation themselves and, as we have already noted, the *delatores* are as adept at the speech of self-defence as they are at attacking others. In the attempts to hold *delatores* accountable for their actions under previous rulers, we see how speakers try to get past the distributed agency central to the practice of prosecution: the *delator* asserts that he only served the will of the ruler, while his accusers insist that the *delator* was nevertheless responsible for the acts he committed. And behind this debate, however fuelled by self-interest the specific claims are, we see two fundamentally opposed views of the imperial subject and his agency.

This opposition comes out in the substance of charges: while the *delator*, for the most part, ties the safety of the state to that of the ruler and levels accusations against those who harm the ruler's *maiestas*, those bringing charges against the *delator* implicitly associate the state with its citizens. In harming fellow citizens, the *delator* damages the *res publica*: this, not incidentally, restores some of the earlier senses and applications of *maiestas* – one thinks of Cassius Severus, exiled under Augustus for his verbal abuse of *viri feminaeque inlustres* (*Ann.* 1.72.3). So when Suillius Rufus, the exemplar of venality under Claudius, is brought down in AD 58, the charges related to his *delatio* list the notable individuals whom he destroyed in descending order of social importance from consular senators and imperial/senatorial women to anonymous equestrians.[32]

> *ii acerbitate accusationis Q. Pomponium ad necessitatem belli civilis detrusum, Iuliam Drusi filiam Sabinamque Poppaeam ad mortem actas et Valerium Asiaticum, Lusium Saturninum, Cornelium Lupum circumventos, iam equitum Romanorum agmina damnata omnemque Claudii saevitiam Suillio obiectabant.*
>
> Ann. 13.43.2

They alleged against Suillius that, because of the ferocity of his accusations, Q. Pomponius was driven to rebel in self-defence, Julia the daughter of Drusus and Poppaea Sabina were compelled to suicide, Valerius Asiaticus, Lucius Saturninus, and Cornelius Lupus were undermined, and a whole rank of Roman equestrians condemned. In short, that Suillius was responsible for all the brutality of Claudius' reign.

The mounting accusations, first one victim, then two, then three, then a multitude, along with the variety of descriptions for the violence arising from Suillius' speech,[33] shows the care with which the accusers construct their case against the *delator*.[34] But their accusation also functions as an epitaph for the victims, whose names form a sonorous roll-call of the dead: like an epitaph, it serves to rehabilitate as victims those previously discredited as traitors. This accusation is later implicitly justified by Nero as *ultio* or vengeance (*Ann.* 13.43.5) – we recall that 'the avenging of a wrong' was one of the acceptable reasons for undertaking a prosecution. Although the true vengeance of the accusers is on behalf of Seneca, whom Suillius has imprudently attacked, the fiction that they speak to avenge the memory of former victims promotes the protection of fellow citizens, not of the ruler, as the primary focus of civic vigilance.

The same notion prompts the strategy by which the senate, twelve years later at the start of Vespasian's reign, attempts to effect a purge of its members by initiating an oath: *deos testes advocabant nihil ope sua factum, quo cuiusquam salus laederetur, neque se praemium aut honorem ex calamitate civium cepisse* (*Hist.* 4.41.1). 'Each senator began to call on the gods as witness that no deed had been undertaken by his efforts with which the safety of another had been damaged, and that he had not gained any reward or honour from the harm done to citizens.' The language of safety that has been primarily directed towards the ruler, with prayers inaugurating each year *pro salute principis* and *pro incolumitate principis*, is now redirected back towards the citizens (*cuiusquam salus, calamitate civium*) in a gesture that inaugurates the new regime. Once more, the conscious artistry of the oath, with its dominating trochaic rhythms and highly alliterative closure, demonstrates the rhetorical attention the senators bring to their programmatic statement. As we saw in chapter two, the message they carefully construct and attempt to enforce is that harm to other citizens disqualifies a senator from participation in the deliberative community.

Following through on this message is the insistence on the *delator*'s accountability, which goes to the heart of debates about the extent and limits of an imperial subject's agency and influence. As we have just seen, Suillius is accused of 'all the brutality of Claudius' reign', which transfers responsibility for *saevitia* from the emperor to the *delator*. But the Latin more precisely says 'they accused Suillius of all Claudius' brutality', retaining the idea that Suillius is simply the fall guy for the late ruler's crimes. Suillius picks up on this in his defence, where he (like Eprius Marcellus in Vespasian's reign) attempts to present the reign of the previous emperor as a time in which a subject like himself had no choice but to obey orders.[35] Suillius' defence is relatively straightforward: *ille nihil ex his sponte susceptum, sed principi paruisse defendebat . . . tum iussa Messalinae praetendi* (*Ann.* 13.43.3–4). 'He declared that he had not taken on any case on his own initiative, but had been obeying the princeps . . . then he brought out the excuse of orders from Messalina.' Eprius Marcellus, more cannily, evokes the distributed agency which we have already seen as an embedded feature of prosecutions even before the development of imperial *delatio*: he draws attention to the role of the senate in carrying out the judgement that follows from his prosecution speech.[36] Having complicated the picture with this image of collective senatorial violence, Marcellus lays ultimate blame for *delatio* on the emperor, who made senatorial trials into a spectacle robbed of political significance: *non magis sua oratione Thraseam quam iudicio senatus adflictum; saevitiam Neronis per eius modi imagines inlusisse* (*Hist.* 4.8.3). 'It was not his own speech of accusation that ruined Thrasea, but the judgement of the senate as a whole; and Nero's brutality made play of such show-trials.' *Saevitia* is a crucial term in Marcellus' defence, as it places the emperor beyond the reach of reasoned argument and absolves the *delator* of responsibility for not attempting to influence his ruler for the better. In Suillius' case, his accusers have already appropriated the term without absolving the *delator*, and they continue to use it in their demolition of the 'only following orders' defence, resisting the way in which distributed agency can evade issues of accountability.

> *tum iussa Messalinae praetendi et labare defensio: cur enim neminem alium delectum, qui saevienti impudicae vocem praeberet? puniendos rerum atrocium ministros, ubi pretia scelerum adepti scelera ipsa aliis delegent.*
> *Ann.* 13.43.4

> Then Suillius brought out the excuse of orders from Messalina, and his defence began to totter: why, then, had no other man been chosen who could offer his voice to that brutal, shameless woman? The pawns who carry out horrific acts must be punished when they take the fee for their crimes and then attribute those crimes to others.

The accusers cleverly concede certain points – Messalina's *saevitia* which makes her unreasonable, Suillius' subordinate status as a *minister* who lends only a body part, *vox*, to his empress. Nevertheless, they insist on his accountability, implying first that he willingly competed with others to be Messalina's chosen 'voice'. They continue to re-endow his voice with will and agency when they point to his shifting of blame. The potential ambiguity of the last phrase *delegent*, which could mean 'to delegate' as much as 'to attribute', acknowledges the potential number of actors participating in and therefore responsible for the violence of *delatio*. But the point Suillius' accusers make is that no matter how many people were involved, how many were complicit, how powerful and unreasonable were one's superiors: 'the pawns must be punished'. Distributed agency does not absolve Suillius from responsibility. Tacitus takes this position to its logical and painful conclusion when he declares his own part in the collective responsibility for the Domitianic treason trials of AD 93: *nostrae duxere Helvidium in carcerem manus; nos Maurici Rusticique visus ***; nos innocenti sanguine Senecio perfudit* (*Agr.* 45.1). 'Our hands dragged the younger Helvidius to prison; the sight/gaze of Iunius Mauricus and Arulenus Rusticus [assailed] us; Herennius Senecio drenched us with his innocent blood.'[37]

The indictment of Suillius, in short, draws on concepts which reinstate the senatorial citizen as a responsible member of the political community, who must be accountable for his actions and whose safety constitutes one of the supports of the *res publica*. Yet the motivation for this indictment and the status of the anonymous prosecutors themselves does not reflect these high-flown principles. As we have seen, they are mobilized against Suillius on behalf of Seneca, the recipient of Suillius' disgruntled abuse. Tacitus' account of the prelude to the trial multiplies the agents involved and distributes agency across them: *nec deerant qui haec isdem verbis aut versa in deterius Senecae deferrent. repertique accusatores* (*Ann.* 13.43.1). 'Nor was there any lack of people to report Suillius' comments to Seneca, verbatim or considerably embellished. And accusers were found.' Those reporting to Seneca replicate the original act of *delatio, nomen deferre*, while the passive *reperti* leaves open the question of whose malevolent will drives the action. The prosecutors, then, exemplify the process that they expose in their indictment of Suillius. As I've already indicated, this does not nullify the significance of the potential political world evoked by the concepts behind their charge; it does, however, remind the reader that attempts to intervene in the speech of *delatio* are very easily absorbed into this mode of speaking. The anonymity of the prosecutors in this case facilitates such absorption, as they possess no ethical portrait which can be used to counter the suggestion that they are not so very different from the man they accuse.

Attempts to hold *delatores* accountable for their past actions revolve around the interpretation of recent history, in the absence of full knowledge of the past emperor's will.[38] An alternative challenge to *delatio* is posed by senators who seek to change legal or ethical norms so as to limit the actions of future *delatores*. This approach avoids the risk of being undermined as a personal or self-interested attack, while continuing to engage with this mode of speech within its 'proper' sphere, especially when the challenge concerns changing or more rigorously enforcing the law. As we have already seen in chapter two, Suillius is one of the *delatores* at the centre of the most prominent example of this approach, when the consul designate for AD 47, C. Silius, calls for the *lex*

Cincia to be more rigorously enforced.[39] Central to the debate between Silius and the *delatores* is the social impact of being paid for delivering a speech. While the *delatores* paint a picture of this economic exchange as a productive force in Roman society, Silius, drawing on a more conservative senatorial standpoint, presents the *delator*'s pay as a pollution that infects public life. Language of dirt, decay, and disease permeate his speech: *nunc inimicitias accusationes, odia et iniurias foveri, ut quo modo vis morborum pretia medentibus, sic fori tabes pecuniam advocatis ferat* (*Ann.* 11.6.2). 'These days feuds, accusations, hatred and a sense of wrong are allowed to fester, and just as an outbreak of disease brings money to doctors so the corruption of the forum pays the advocate.' The pure and healthy social body which lies behind Silius' rhetoric is both ethical and aesthetic: the senator who avoids the degradation of a fee which makes of him a subordinate keeps both his life and the practice of *eloquentia* free of corruption.[40]

Silius' extrapolation of the ethical connotations of the *lex Cincia* and his use of *exempla* from the Augustan and Tiberian regimes demonstrates the difficulty of maintaining a depersonalized attack on *delatio* as a mode of speech. Indeed, the speech Tacitus gives Silius here goes beyond his original proposal and is presented as a response to either heckling or extended debate at the senate meeting: *deinde obstrepentibus iis, quibus ea contumelia parabatur, discors Suillio Silius acriter incubuit* (*Ann.* 11.6.1). 'Then at the noisy expostulations of those against whom this insult had been set in motion, Silius, being at odds with Suillius, fiercely entered the fray.' Apart the ferocity of Silius' response, its precise aim is placed under question here. Woodman's translation, as Malloch points out, 'seems to make Silius' speech directed narrowly at Suillius', whereas Malloch's own interpretation (which my translation here follows) is that 'Silius launched an attack that affected many more people than Suillius.'[41] Their debate highlights how, in Tacitus' representation, Silius, drawn into an impassioned exchange, momentarily becomes indistinguishable from the *delator* whose damaging actions he seeks to remedy: the juxtaposition of their near-interchangeable names points to the blurring of their identities.[42] Tacitus perhaps facilitates the implicit undermining of Silius' intervention when he interposes a cross-reference to Silius' spectacular downfall in the following year: *Silio ... cuius de potentia et exitio in tempore memorabo* (*Ann.* 11.5.3). 'Silius ... whose power and ruin I will record at the proper time.' Ascribing *potentia* to the consul designate because of his implication with Messalina, Tacitus looks forward to the power struggle between the imperial wife and freedmen narrated later in Book 11 (*Ann.* 11.26–28). Its mention at this point in the narrative juxtaposes the world of palace intrigue with that of senatorial-judicial debate. What Tacitus' blurring techniques illustrate above all is that the principled and objective stance introduced in Silius' initial proposal cannot remain untouched by the discursive world which has come to be associated with the *delator*. Even the usual practice of impassioned debate and violent language – which Steven Rutledge has shown is by no means the exclusive domain of the *delator*[43] – brings Silius and Suillius into uncomfortable alignment.

Is Silius wrong to abandon a depersonalized challenge to *delatio*? Arguably not, since the point of the law is to consider its consequences upon persons. Tacitus has already narrated another attempt to curb *delatio* through enforcement of existing laws, in the reign of Tiberius. Here again, the senate focusses on the rewards given to prosecutors, but, in notable contrast to the individualism and high emotion of the episode in Book 11, proposals and counter-proposals are carried out almost entirely through impersonal passive verbs.

> *actum de praemiis accusatorum abolendis, si quis maiestatis postulatus ante perfectum iudicium se ipse vita privavisset. ibaturque in eam sententiam, ni durius contraque morem suum palam pro accusatoribus Caesar inritas leges, rem publicam in pracipiti conquestus esset: subverterent potius iura quam custodes eorum amoverent. sic delatores, genus hominum publico exitio repertum et <ne> poenis quidem umquam satis coercitum, per praemia eliciebantur.*
>
> *Ann.* 4.30.2–3

Then a motion was brought about the need to abolish rewards for prosecutors if a defendant charged with *maiestas* took his own life before judgement had been reached. And the proposal was about to be passed when Tiberius, speaking rather sternly and more openly than usual, intervened in support of the prosecutors, complaining that legislation would be meaningless and the state would fall into peril: it would be better to overturn the laws entirely than to remove their guardians. Thus the *delatores*, a type of person made for public ruin and never sufficiently checked even by punishments, were attracted by rewards.

The emperor, named and endowed with affective qualities of speech (*durius, conquestus*), stands out in an otherwise depersonalized scene. The *accusatores/ delatores* in defence of whom he speaks are referred to in the conclusion as a *genus hominum*; the senators who challenge them disappear behind the standard terms for senatorial procedure (*actum, ibatur*). And the proposal itself seems to lack engagement with the events which surround it: as Woodman points out, despite Tiberius' intervention, the practice of not rewarding prosecutors in these situations seems to be the norm both before and after this episode.[44] The positioning of this episode, moreover, between the narrative of C. Silius Caecina Largus' *maiestas* trial (*Ann.* 4.18–20) and the introduction of Suillius Rufus for the first time (*Ann.* 4.31.3), suggests that it looks forward to the more impassioned episode in Book 11, where the challenge to *praemia* is reactivated by Silius Caecina's son. Reading across the two episodes enables the reader to critique two contrasting (and equally unsuccessful) ways of articulating the legal challenge to *delatio*.

The final mode of speech which aims to work around *delatio* is engagement with the process of judgement. This mode takes on board the inevitability, for a senator, of being subsumed into the agonistic discourse increasingly dominated by *delatio*. As we have seen, the senate's implication in judgement at *maiestas* trials is a mark of its increased importance under the Principate – and of its potential guilt. Eprius Marcellus defends his actions under Nero by pointing to the *iudicium* of the senate which ultimately caused the destruction of Thrasea Paetus. But engagement in the exercise of *iudicium* as a serious act of deliberation appears in some contexts as the most effective intervention, precisely because it does not interrupt *delatio* but participates in the final stage of the process, when the *delator* or *accusator* falls silent. There are four instances of such engagement: three are from the Tiberian narrative – two performed by M. Lepidus and one by Cn. Lentulus – the final engagement is from the Neronian books and is performed by Thrasea Paetus. The importance of Lepidus and Thrasea and the parallels between their interventions has attracted extensive scholarly attention.[45]

These interventions occur at the point when senators are called upon to agree the proposed penalty. First, Lentulus and Lepidus each uses his *sententia* to modify the proposal so as to secure a portion of the condemned's estate for their heirs. Lentulus intervenes in the case of C. Silanus in AD 22, who is to be exiled and stripped of his property (we have already seen how Cornelius Dolabella uses this case as an opportunity for *adulatio* towards the princeps).

> *eadem ceteri, nisi quod Cn. Lentulus separanda Silani materna bona, quippe Appia parente geniti, reddendaque filio dixit, adnuente Tiberio.*
>
> Ann. 3.68.2

> The other senators agreed to the proposal, except that Cn. Lentulus declared that Silanus' property, inherited from his mother (since he was the son of Appia), should be kept separate and handed over to his son, and Tiberius agreed with this.

Similarly, Lepidus modifies the proposals in the case of C. Silius Caecina in AD 24 (father of the Silius in AD 47 who challenges Suillius and the other *delatores*), where Silius' wife Sosia Galla has also been implicated in the trial. We have already briefly examined this case in the introduction.

> *Sosia in exilium pellitur Asinii Galli sententia, qui partem bonorum publicandam, pars ut liberis relinqueretur censuerat. contra M. Lepidus quartam accusatoribus secundum necessitudinem legis, cetera liberis concessit.*
>
> Ann. 4.20.1–2

> Sosia was driven into exile on the *sententia* of Asinius Gallus, who proposed that half her property should be confiscated and the other half left to her children. Against this Lepidus conceded a quarter to the prosecutors according to the requirement of the law and the rest to the children.

These interventions, as we will see in more detail shortly, avoid challenging the practice of *delatio* and confine themselves to effective action in the margins of each case, with significant consequences for the families concerned. In more extensive episodes, Lepidus and Thrasea use their *sententiae* to propose a different penalty for the condemned. In both cases their speeches are in response to the proposal of a death penalty: I will focus here on the rhetoric of their counter-proposals. Lepidus speaks at the trial of Clutorius Priscus in AD 21, condemned for composing and reciting a poem in anticipation of Drusus' death.

> *... sententiaque Haterii Agrippae consulis designati indictum reo ultimum supplicium. Contra M. Lepidus in hunc modum exorsus est ... 'cedat tamen urbe et bonis amissis aqua et igni arceatur; quod perinde censeo ac si lege maiestatis teneretur.'*
>
> Ann. 3.49.2, 3.50.1, 4

... and by the *sententia* of the consul designate, Haterius Agrippa, the ultimate punishment was declared. Against this, M. Lepidus discoursed in this fashion ... 'Let him depart from the city and, stripped of his property, be denied water and fire, which I give as my verdict as if he were being tried under the law for *maiestas minuta*.'

In a strikingly similar case in AD 62, the praetor Antistius Sosianus is charged with composing and reciting abusive poetry about Nero.

censuitque Iunius Marullus consul designatus adimendam reo praeturam necandumque more maiorum. ceteris inde assentientibus, Paetus Thrasea, multo cum honore Caesaris et acerrime increpito Antistio ... disseruit. ... quin in insula publicatis bonis, quo longius sontem vitam traxisset, eo privatim miserior et publicae clementiae maximum exemplum futurum.

Ann. 14.48.2-3, 4

[A]nd the consul designate Iunius Marullus proposed that the defendant should be stripped of his praetorship and executed according to ancient tradition. While the other senators agreed, Thrasea Paetus spoke with much honour to Caesar and sharply rebuking Antistius ... Rather send him to some island, his property confiscated, so that the longer he dragged out his offensive life, the more he would serve as the best example of a subject's misery and of the state's clemency.

These cases all work around *delatio* by accommodating, even allowing its most offensive feature to operate relatively unchecked: the acquisition of material gain from the ruin of a fellow citizen. Hence Lepidus and Thrasea, proposing exile, pointedly acquiesce to the confiscation of property (*bonis amissis, publicatis bonis*), which routinely accompanies this punishment. Lentulus and Lepidus focus on salvaging some of the property for the children of exiles, but emphasize that there is still property left for rewarding *delatio*: Lentulus does so obliquely by recommending a partition of Silanus' property (*separanda*), while Lepidus explicitly spells out that confiscated wealth goes to the accusers. This concession of *praemia* is in stark contrast to the strategies we have seen earlier, where senators attempt to challenge the *delator* precisely by targeting his access to material gain. Instead, these speakers concentrate on and attempt to mitigate the second offensive feature of the *delator* – his ruin of citizens. One type of intervention is aimed at preserving the life of the defendant, while the other type saves the defendant's family line. In this respect these speakers feed into the concept that the safety of fellow citizens is an important bulwark of the *res publica* and the proper focus of oratorical activity. Yet they touch on such a concept while conceding to the discourse of the *accusator*: each of them speaks in support of punishment and explicitly in condemnation of the defendant. Thrasea, as we see, engages in invective against Antistius, which is described as *acer* (recalling the *acerbitas* of men such as Suillius), while Lepidus excoriates Clutorius' actions as pollution and madness. The speech of condemnation and law together provides each speaker with a vocabulary to work their way round to an accommodation which secures some degree of salvation for the condemned. In this context, even the disagreement between Asinius Gallus and Lepidus acquires a new dimension: Gallus too is concerned to mention allocation of property to Sosia's children. Perhaps the two senators are co-operating as much as disagreeing, using open debate to work their way towards a reduced penalty for the family.

Are these speakers subsumed within the discourse of the *delator*, or do they carve out a judicial space (of limited independence) within that discourse? There is a sense that all three senators, Lentulus, Lepidus, and Thrasea, are keeping alive the notion that participation in the exercise of senatorial judgement has some potential efficacy, even if just for the exercise itself. This sense is conveyed particularly by the contrast between their interventions and the conduct of Clutorius' and Antistius' trials more generally. In each case, part of the charge is that the defendant recited his offensive poetry at a private gathering, and in each case one of the witnesses to that recitation simply denies the fact.

> *id Clutorius in domo P. Petroni socru eius Vitellia coram multisque inlustribus feminis per vaniloquentiam legerat. ut delator extitit, ceteris ad dicendum testimonium exterritis, sola Vitellia nihil se audivisse adseveravit. sed arguentibus ad perniciem plus fidei fuit.*
>
> Ann. 3.49.1–2

Clutorius boastfully recited this poem in the house of P. Petronius in the presence of Petronius' mother-in-law, Vitellia, and many other noble women. When a *delator* came forward, the rest were intimidated into giving their testimony, and Vitellia alone insisted that she had heard nothing. But those denouncing him to ruination had more credibility.

Antistius praetor ... probrosa adversus principem carmina factitavit vulgavitque celebri convivio, dum apud Ostorium Scapulam epulatur. exim a Cossutiano Capitone ... maiestatis delatus est ... et cum Ostorius nihil audivisse pro testimonio dixisset, adversis testibus creditum.

Ann. 14.48.1, 2

The praetor Antistius composed abusive poems about the emperor and publicly disseminated them at a busy dinner party, when he was dining at the house of Ostorius Scapula. Immediately he was charged with *maiestas minuta* by Cossutianus Capito ... and when Ostorius as witness said he had heard nothing, witnesses to the contrary were believed.

The presence of a *delator* or an accusation of *maiestas* is taken as a foregone conclusion, a process seen vividly in the final years of Tiberius' reign when defendants are accused and immediately dragged to execution or forestall their condemnation by drinking poison as their accusers finish their speeches.[46] Here, it contributes to a judicial scene of inertia, where the opportunities offered by the favourable testimonies of Vitellia and Ostorius – and even the opportunities to exploit conflicting reports – do not seem to be taken up.[47] Tacitus narrates the trials in this way, I suggest, to emphasize the difference between partial and total concession to the discourse of the *delator* and to highlight the efficacy and potential productivity of Lepidus' and Thrasea's partial concession.

One aspect of that potential productivity is that these senators actively exercise and thereby revitalize the concept of senatorial *iudicium*. In this way, Lepidus and Thrasea constitute a response to Eprius Marcellus' indictment of senatorial guilt: *non magis sua oratione ... quam iudicio senatus adflictum* (*Hist.* 4.8.3). 'It was not the speech of the *accusator* so much as the judgement of the senate which destroyed the defendant.' Lepidus and Thrasea replace senatorial guilt with senatorial responsibility and counterpose to the *eloquentia* of the *accusator* the care of the *iudex*. To pursue this further, let us examine more closely Lepidus' speech in the trial of Clutorius. This is a significant speech in *Annals*, being the first extensive direct speech delivered by an imperial subject,[48] and Lepidus has been brought to the reader's attention early in the narrative as a man of suitable ability and character to be Augustus' successor (*Ann.* 1.13).[49] His intervention, moreover, is lent further *gravitas* by being filtered through the language of Sallust, in his version of the speeches of

Julius Caesar and Cato the younger on the punishment of the Catilinarian conspirators.[50] Thus Lepidus' authority seems equally potent in the old world of the Republic and the new world of the Principate. In this context, the kind of *iudicium* he projects through his discussion of this particular case can be seen as quasi-programmatic for the role of the efficacious imperial senator.

Lepidus' *sententia* moves beyond the question of what punishment is suitable for the crimes of which Clutorius has been convicted to consider what the inflicting of punishment upon Clutorius says about the *iudices* – that is, the emperor and the senate. His central statement sums up this position: '*est locus sententiae, per quam neque huic delictum impune sit et nos clementiae simul ac severitatis non paeniteat*' (*Ann.* 3.50.2). 'There is space here for a judgement which ensures that this man does not get away with his crimes unpunished and that we do not have cause to regret either our clemency or our severity.' The congruence between *impune* and *non paenitet* draws out the parallel consequences for the condemned man and his judges: as we have already seen, uttering a *sententia* exposes a senator to the judgement not only of his contemporaries but of posterity. Within the space of this *sententia*, Lepidus gathers together the various considerations which must bear upon judgement, from the bodily experiences of punishment which might be inflicted on Clutorius to the affective conditions of moderation, clemency, severity, and mercy which must be consciously accommodated and calibrated in the posture of the *iudex*. The act of judging others necessarily involves assessing and forming the self-as-judge. Once Lepidus has finished the process of articulating the necessary position of the *iudex* between *clementia* and *severitas* and has sketched out the consequences for the commonwealth of avoiding the death penalty, only then does he return to an evaluation of Clutorius' mental condition, which suggests the appropriateness of the punishment which he then proposes. This places the judgement of Clutorius in its 'proper context', rather than the narrow perspective with which Lepidus opened ('*si unum id spectamus*', 'If we were to look at this crime in isolation'). When Lepidus concludes his *sententia* by placing all these considerations under the application of the *lex maiestatis*, he enacts a version of what Clifford Ando has identified as a pervasive strategy in Roman law for regulating phenomena which exceed law's existing vocabulary.[51] After conceptually bringing together bodily, affective, and mental states of being, distributed across various times and shared among the various participants in the trial, Lepidus demonstrates the complexity of thought and imaginative range inherent in the act of judging 'as if liable to the law'.

One important feature of consideration in the speech is, of course, the relationship between the projected senatorial *iudex* and the princeps. Lepidus frames his reference to 'our clemency or our severity' with comments on the emperor's moderation and mercy (*principis moderatio, misericordiam eius*) in a way which suggests that he includes the emperor among the *nos* who are engaged in judgement.[52] In a similar, though more openly politicized vein, Thrasea Paetus argues for a decision to be reached which will stand as an example of *publica clementia*, which he imagines as the product of 'a senate operating under an exceptional ruler, and bound by no constraints' (*Ann.* 14.48.3). The political world projected by these interventions is one where senators restore weight to the exercise of *iudicium* and maintain a relationship with the ruler characterized by shared concerns with the ethical position of the *iudex* and with the condition of subjects.[53] Here each of the speakers picks up on existing cues in imperial discourse to project an image of the ruler which he is likely to accept and assimilate, in a feedback loop similar to that between Vespasian and Helvidius Priscus, examined in section 3.1. Lepidus' reference to *moderatio* chimes with the language of Tiberian self-presentation,[54] while Lentulus' and Lepidus' concern to preserve senatorial family lines by securing property for heirs matches the care displayed by both Augustus and Tiberius in the same regard.[55] Thrasea's speech projects a ruler who promotes senatorial judgement and who practises and exemplifies *clementia*; he thereby feeds back to Nero the behaviours that the young emperor was so anxious to display at the start of his reign.[56] The kind of ruler and ruler–subject relations projected by these speeches, in short, are far from unrealistic; rather they rework elements of imperial discourse in the process of creating a space for senatorial speech which both engages with and holds itself separate from the harmful speech of the *delatores*.

In this section we have seen how those who challenge or engage with *delatio* have to share the discourse of the *delatores* to do so. This is a delicate negotiation which lays these speakers open to the charge of collusion, or of being no different from those they indict. Through these engagements, however, speakers raise significant questions about agency and accountability under autocratic rulers and promote alternative visions of civic responsibility. But how do we judge the efficacy of these speeches, especially when the Tiberian senate – after the execution of Clutorius – is thereafter blocked from the exercise of *clementia*, and Nero responds to Thrasea's proposal not with acceptance but with offence? Just as Tacitus undercuts Helvidius' successful disruption of senatorial *adulatio* by juxtaposing his long-term view of its disastrous outcome, so too he gives decisive directions on how we are to receive Lepidus and Thrasea. These authorial interventions foreground the critical dimension of Tacitus' archive; they suggest that the character of the speaker is crucial to judging political efficacy, and that this will provide one pathway for the transmission of such efficacy to the future. In chapter four, we will explore how a speaker's character is presented and judged, both in the performance of speech and in Tacitus' narration.

Part Two

The Critical Archive

4

Existimatio vitae: The Judgement of Character

As chapter three has shown, it is a delicate business to negotiate a mode of speech which can counter or work around the damaging speech modes of *adulatio* and *delatio*. The speakers often risk having their attempts assimilated to the very modes of speech they seek to escape. What has already emerged from my analyses of very different speakers, such as Suillius Rufus the venal *delator* or Marcus Lepidus the exemplar of senatorial virtues, is the importance of 'ethos'. This is the technique in rhetoric whereby the speaker projects an appropriate and attractive *persona* congruent with the character of his subject and audience.[1] Ethos effectively creates the speaker through his relationship to the audience; the speaker addresses and therefore constitutes his audience as a particular kind of political body, and in the process creates political worlds. This performed self also attempts to conjoin the effects of speech with some concept of value or virtue existing beyond speech (but only attained through speech). Such gestures towards a pre-existent virtue allay the age-old anxiety about rhetoric as an art: how it enables a speaker to persuade others of a position he does not believe himself. The idea that performed ethos does have some connection to the speaker's lived values instead reassures the audience that the speaker's *eloquentia* is well-directed. This idea grounds the difference between a Suillius or Lepidus not so much in their rhetorical ability as in their ethical character. Hence, I think, the popularity from the Tiberian to the Flavian period (and beyond) of the elder Cato's designation of the ideal orator as *vir bonus dicendi peritus* (Sen., *Controv*. 1, *pr*. 9): 'a good man skilled at speaking'.[2] But behind this assertion, the anxiety persists: if the good man is constructed and performed through speech, is his virtue not an effect rather than an independent support of his rhetorical skill?

This anxiety can never be finally laid to rest; indeed, it is part of what fuels the constant regulation of the orator's self throughout his career,[3] just as it prompts many elite Romans and scholars of antiquity to turn to ethical philosophy as a contiguous mode of discourse for addressing these issues. Tacitus, however, continues to work with the problem of ethos as it is constituted through the inter-relation of rhetoric and historical narrative. That is, Tacitus shows us the performance of ethos in speech and supplements it with narrative which displays the speaker's activity of creating and maintaining their ethos across a career of speech interventions and other public actions. I will illustrate this in section 4.1 with the example of Vipstanus Messalla in *Histories*. We will see several layers of representation combine in the portrayal of a speaker's ethos in historical narrative: a sense of what the speaker is imagined to aim at in self-presentation; a sense of contemporary reception and evaluation of the speaker's ethos (which also projects the audience's ethos); a narrative evaluation of the speaker and his audience, which constitutes a historical judgement; in some cases, an explicit authorial judgement in the ethos of the historian. Tacitus thereby promotes a concept of ethos and moral value as contingent rather than absolute: it emerges as an effect of speech and narrative, but it also drives and is mediated through speech and narrative. Hence he reaffirms the centrality and importance of speech but also brings focus to bear on evaluation and community.[4] The ethos of the speaker, the extent to which he succeeds in performing as a good man, rests on the judgement of his audience – but the audience has already been pre-judged by the speaker as he composes a self that will 'address' this particular, desired audience.[5] As Dean Hammer puts it in relation to the politics of the Homeric world, 'Like politics, ethics is both cultural as it is tied to the expectations of society, and critical as it is shaped and reshaped in its performance. The ethical self is an enacted self that must interpret and apply the standards of a community, as well as encounter occasions in which community expectations are ambiguous, contradictory, or unsatisfactory.'[6] Again, contingency rather than absolute value dominates but does not limit the concept of standards underpinning the orator's enacted self. At the same time, the performance of ethos contributes to interactions which form a political community: the stakes of being a *vir bonus* concern both the self and the state.[7]

In section 4.1, I explore how the performance of ethos is presented in Tacitus' narrative as a subsidiary aim of the speech. Here I will focus on the role of emotion in the evaluation of character, a significant aspect of ethos in rhetorical theory as it is inherited by the Roman tradition.[8] The character of the speaker and the emotions he expresses are supposed to provoke affective responses from the audience. Far from this being peripheral to the act of persuasion, emotion is a significant vector of communication and empathy a fundamental aspect of the political collective formed around the speech performance. As James Martin maintains in relation to contemporary democracy, 'emotions help *situate* subjects in relation to their world, orienting them towards its objects with degrees of proximity and urgency, sympathy and concern, aversion or hostility. These orientations are never fixed or complete but part of ongoing practices of contestation and negotiation whose point of mediation is often rhetorical dispute'.[9] The emotions prompted by speech or speakers in Tacitus' narratives provide us with another way of tracing politically effective speech and the kinds of communities it creates. I will explore this by examining the pleasures of oratory in *Dialogus* as well as the complex of emotions around the figure of Eprius Marcellus in *Dialogus, Annals*, and *Histories*. Marcellus' success in both prosecution and self-defence is offset by his failure, in Tacitus' narratives, to engage the affect of the political community he addresses.

The political community, however, is not always a site of productive, mutually affirming recognition; it can be a site where values are perverted and overthrown and subjects alienated from their own participation. In *Agricola*, Tacitus memorably articulates his experience of years in the senate where he and others voted against their judgement (*Agr*. 45.1–2), arriving at a condition where they were estranged from their own affective states:[10] *et ut corpora nostra lente augescunt, cito extinguuntur, sic ingenia studiaque oppresseris facilius quam revocaveris* (*Agr*. 3.1). 'And just as our bodies slowly grow but are snuffed out in an instant, so our inner selves and desires can be crushed more easily than they can be revived.' Against the fragility of the political community, Tacitus sets historical remembrance as the site where judgement can be made again and values renewed. He achieves this by repurposing speech effects in narrative and thereby providing one further support for the process of creating ethos and community, by extending community judgement to present and future audiences. Each audience, in and of the narrative, is differently addressed by the speaker in the narrative and by the narrator himself. In section 4.2, I will look at how Tacitus implicates past, present, and future audiences by interweaving the speech performance of ethos and the narrative presentation of character. Within this rhythm, moments where the narrative 'pauses' to allow the authoritative intervention of the historian's voice – most notably in his judgements of Marcus Lepidus and Helvidius Priscus – acquire a particular resonance and direct the reader to a new assessment of political efficacy.

4.1 Emotion, speech, and moral principle

The first senate meeting of AD 70 is prominent in Tacitus' narrative of *Histories* 4 as a moment where the new Flavian regime is experienced as potential for change. We have already seen how the senators create an inaugural ritual designed to mark out the *delatores* as unsuitable for inclusion in their body. As their enforcement of this new regime turns into a succession of attacks and counter-attacks between individuals, one man's defence provides a moment's respite.

> *Magnam eo die pietatis eloquentiaeque famam Vipstanus Messalla adeptus est, nondum senatoria aetate, ausus pro fratre Aquilio Regulo deprecari.*
>
> Hist. 4.42.1

> On that day Vipstanus Messalla acquired a great reputation for piety and eloquence, though not yet of senatorial age, when he had the courage to plead on behalf of his brother Aquilius Regulus.

Vipstanus Messalla is the second underage speaker at this session; Domitian has already spoken in his first appearance as a praetor, impressing all with his appropriate modesty (*Hist.* 4.40.1). Whereas Domitian's physical appearance (his high colour appearing as a youthful blush) leads to a misunderstanding of his character, Messalla's words and the way in which he takes on the case brought against his brother demonstrate the full deployment of rhetorical ethos. For Regulus has incurred considerable *odium* from his prosecution of noble families, and the surviving relatives are poised to take revenge. Particularly invidious is the charge that Regulus took on these prosecutions *sponte ... nec depellendi periculi sed in spem potentiae* (*Hist.* 4.42.1). 'Of his own free will ... not with the hope of averting danger, but wishing for power'. As we have already seen, accusations against former *delatores* emphasize the issue of agency, and Regulus' case comes up when the plea of Eprius Marcellus is still fresh in everyone's memory: that the *delatores*, and the senate as a whole, were only the pawns of a brutal emperor (*Hist.* 4.8.3). Messalla deals with this situation by making no attempt to argue the justice of the case.

> *igitur Messalla non causam neque reum tueri, sed periculis fratris semet opponens flexerat quosdam.*
>
> Hist. 4.42.2
>
> Therefore Messalla did not address the case or the character of the defendant, but placing himself in the way of his brother's dangers he had started to bring some people round.

Chilver and Townend conjecture that Messalla here introduces a point of general principle, arguing 'against the whole policy of reviving old grievances'.[11] But I suggest that instead Messalla interposes a speaker's ethos to shield the already damaged character of the defendant, as Cicero had enjoined in *De Inventione*.

> *si causae turpitudo contrahit offensionem ... pro eo homine in quo offenditur alium hominem qui diligitur interponi oportet ... ut ab eo quod odit ad id quod diligit auditoris animus traducatur.*
>
> Cic., Inv. rhet. 1.24
>
> If the morally repugnant nature of the case is likely to attract hostility ... instead of speaking in defence of the man who attracts this hostility, one should interpose another man who is likely to attract approval ... so that the mind of the audience is deflected away from the one they hate to the one they approve of.

Messalla follows this rhetorical advice: instead of Regulus, the young speaker who ruined noble citizens when in no danger himself (*iuvenis admodum, nec depellendi periculi*), Messalla presents himself as a young speaker protecting his brother from danger (*nondum senatoria aetate ... periculis fratris semet opponens*). The phrase *semet opponens*, therefore, corresponds to Cicero's *alium hominem ... interponi*. It does not metaphorically denote Messalla throwing himself bodily in front of his brother so much as point to the self that Messalla creates and presents in his plea. He draws the senate's attention to this rhetorical self, thereby deflecting their opprobrium away from Regulus and his crimes.

Messalla's speech of *deprecatio* – another deployment of ethos advised by Cicero (Cic., *Inv. rhet.* 1.22) – distracts, moves, or persuades a few senators but does not gain universal assent. Curtius Montanus rises to speak against him with one of the most aggressive speeches recorded in Tacitus' works. As Montanus apostrophizes Regulus, expatiates on the enormity of his acts, and warns the senate of the consequences of failing to hold the *delatores* accountable, Messalla fades from the narrative: Montanus has taken the argument back to the *causa* and *reus*, and it is he who receives the agreement of most senators (*Hist.* 4.43.1). But Messalla's performance of ethos has achieved something beyond the immediate aim of the speech: he has not entirely shielded his brother from danger but he has gained a great reputation for *pietas* and *eloquentia*. Though not yet of senatorial rank (it is conjectured he is about 24 years old), he has already begun to generate a presence in the senate house on which he can draw in his later career.[12]

As we've already seen, the orator's ethos is a responsive creation, formed to be appropriate to the character of the speaker, the nature of the audience, and the subject of the speech.[13] Cicero in *De Oratore* has Marcus Antonius address the tasks involved in ethos thus:

> *Valet igitur multum ad vincendum probari mores et instituta et facta et vitam eorum, qui agent causas, et eorum, pro quibus, et item improbari adversariorum, animosque eorum, apud quos agetur, conciliari quam maxime ad benevolentiam cum erga oratorem tum erga illum, pro quo dicet orator. Conciliantur autem animi dignitate hominis, rebus gestis, existimatione vitae; quae facilius ornari possunt, si modo sunt, quam fingi, si nulla sunt.*
>
> Cic., *De or.* 2.182

Thus a very strong feature of success entails gaining approval of the behaviour, principles, actions, and way of life either of those arguing the case or of those on whose behalf the case is argued: and similarly, provoking disapproval of the opponents and winning over the minds of those before whom the case is argued, so that they feel goodwill towards both the orator and the man for whom the orator speaks. Sympathy is won by a man's social standing, his deeds, and the general estimation of his life – which can be very easily embellished (if he has these qualities) or invented (if he has not).

We can evaluate Messalla's strategies in relation to Cicero's terms. Messalla is faced with a situation where the behaviour and principles of Regulus are already the object of general *odium*; to invent good qualities before an audience that has witnessed Regulus' acts of aggressive prosecution would be to insult the intelligence and experience of the senate. His decision to pass over the character of his subject, therefore, signals his deference to the senatorial audience and his tailoring of material to their ethos. What he is able to present, meanwhile, is his own behaviour, principles, and social standing: speaking as a young non-senator, he displays courageous behaviour (*ausus*); defending his brother, he displays the principle of *pietas*; his name attests to his standing as a member of a consular family and to his potential *dignitas* as a senator in years to come.[14] When Messalla positions himself between Regulus and the audience and directs their attention to himself, he also redirects their affective response as signalled by the term *flexerat*, which can denote changing mood as well as mind. Previously the senate felt hatred for Regulus. In looking at Messalla, they presumably feel instead various forms of pleasure, as suggested in Cicero's description: approval (*probari*), that is, satisfaction in perceiving and recognizing virtue; goodwill (*benevolentia*) and sympathy (*conciliari*),[15] enhanced by the sense of being united in feeling.[16]

All these features of ethos are 'entechnic', that is, performed in the speech itself. But the immediate and longer-term contexts of a speech performance would also contribute to its ethos and sustain its effects into the future,[17] creating the extensive performance of the self which is the elite man's career. Senators listening to Messalla speak would know of his *res gestae*: as a military tribune he had taken command of a legion in Moesia after the governor had disgracefully undermined its legate.[18] Tacitus introduces Messalla in the narrative of the Flavian campaigns in north Italy with a characterization which reflects Cicero's attention to what attracts sympathy: *dignitas* and *res gestae*. To this Tacitus appends an *existimatio vitae* from the narrator's perspective.

> *legioni tribunus Vipstanus Messalla praeerat, claris maioribus, egregius ipse et qui solus ad id bellum artes bonas attulisset.*
>
> Hist. 3.9.3
>
> In charge of this legion was the military tribune Vipstanus Messalla – a man with distinguished ancestors, outstanding himself, and the only man to exhibit good qualities in this war.

Just as a speech would have drawn on more general performances and estimation of the self, so the narrative presents character through different layers of representation. Messalla's own performance in senate is conveyed in descriptive terms which combine his subjective intention with outward effect: 'pleading on behalf of his brother ... he did not address the case or the defendant's character ... placing himself in the way'. The immediate and longer-term effects of the performed ethos are evident when Tacitus tells us that 'he had started to bring some senators round' and 'he acquired a great reputation'. These effects are extended into narrative characterization, which encompasses the description of actions – 'he was in charge of the legion', 'he had the courage to plead on his brother's behalf' – and overall evaluation from hindsight – 'an outstanding young man', *etc.*[19]

We've now seen ethos/character projected across speech performances and other public activities, and the vectors of emotion along which ethos communicates and engages in community-formation. To consider more extensively the role of shared emotion, I turn to *Dialogus de Oratoribus*, where the interlocutors self-consciously reflect on the meaning of oratory in the imperial world. The first speaker, Marcus Aper, presenting a defence of oratory as the best occupation for well-educated Romans, aims to persuade his listeners by drawing them into the sense of being an orator. Implicitly, therefore, he constructs a community of those who can imagine the pleasures of oratory and of the performance of the orator across the different modes of his existence. Ethos is fundamental to Aper's persuasive technique, but ethos is also the subject of his discourse, both when he speaks generally of pleasure and when he introduces his examples of successful orators. And here is where Aper's own ethos has come under negative scrutiny: because he presents Eprius Marcellus and Vibius Crispus to illustrate the high status to be gained from oratory, Aper's moral character – and therefore the validity of his claims – has often been repudiated.[20] By tracing the role of pleasure and sympathy in his argument, however, I suggest that Aper, while acknowledging the power of Marcellus' *eloquentia*, withholds judgement on his ethos.

Aper turns to the pleasure of oratory (*Dial.* 6–7) having reviewed its usefulness (*Dial.* 5), and presents three exemplary illustrations in succession: first a generalized character type of the orator (*Dial.* 6); then Aper himself (*Dial.* 7); and finally, illustrating objective success rather than pleasure, Marcellus and Crispus (*Dial.* 8). When Aper first introduces the topic of pleasure, we might expect him to focus on the performance of speech and the joy of exercising *eloquentia*. Instead he emphatically declares that the pleasure of good speaking permeates the orator's experience of living.

> *ad voluptatem oratoriae eloquentiae transeo, cuius iucunditas non uno aliquo momento, sed omnibus prope diebus et prope omnibus horis contingit. quid enim dulcius libero et ingenuo animo et ad voluptates honestas nato, quam videre plenam semper et frequentem domum suam concursu splendidissimorum hominum? idque scire non pecuniae, non orbitati, neque officii alicuius administrationi, sed sibi ipsi dari?*
>
> Dial. 6.1–2

Now I turn to the pleasure of the orator's excellence in speaking, the enjoyment of which is not confined to one particular moment but extends almost through every day and almost every hour. For what is sweeter for a free and noble spirit, one born to honourable pleasures, than to see his own house full and thronged with the gathering of the most brilliant men? And to know that this is given to him not because of his wealth, or his potential to leave an inheritance, or his management of some public duty, but because of *his self*.

The listeners, perhaps expecting to be brought to the senate or the courtroom, find themselves in the orator's house at the morning *salutatio*, where his status is affirmed by the number and the quality of those who attend him.[21] The enjoyment of this status derives from the orator knowing that all of this derives from 'himself/his self', *sibi ipsi*. Christopher van den Berg interprets this as a declaration of 'self-sufficiency';[22] more precisely, *sibi ipsi* can be understood (like Messalla's *semet opponens*) as referring to the ethos performed through *eloquentia* and extended outwards from the moment of speech to the days and hours of the orator's life. Aper continues in this vein, taking his orator from the house through the streets to the courtroom, where he delights in observing how he affects his audience, hushing them to silence and inspiring in them emotions (*Dial.* 6.4). As Aper conveys the pleasure of exercising such mastery through *eloquentia* he performs the very act he describes, moving the listeners to partake of this pleasure. Having begun by engaging his listeners in the more easily understood sensation of social popularity, Aper takes them through the experience of a successful speech performance before arriving at *secretiora [gaudia] et tantum ipsis orantibus nota* (*Dial.* 6.5). 'The more private sources of joy, known only to orators themselves.'

Although the trajectory of his description is from *domus* to courtroom and from externally observable signs of pleasure to secret inner gratification, Aper throughout this passage is concerned with how the orator self-consciously inhabits his *ethos*. He begins with the orator looking at (*videre*) and reflecting upon (*scire*) his thronged vestibule, and ends with the orator's self-satisfaction in the more withdrawn and private space of rhetorical judgement which he shares only with other orators. Yet through the medium of emotion he has permitted his listeners to share in the excitement of the orator, precariously balanced between abject failure and glittering success.[23] As T. J. Luce has observed, both the listeners within the dialogue and second-century Roman readers are highly trained orators themselves, practised in keenly assessing and weighing up the efficacy of speech and speaker.[24] They are prime targets for this sort of emotional appeal. In the following chapter, Aper applies the same process of pleasurable self-reflection to his own *dignitas*, observing that the joys of speaking successfully in any public sphere are greater than that of receiving public office.[25] '*Tum mihi supra tribunatus et praeturas et consulatus ascendere videor, tum adire quod, si non in alto oritur, nec codicillis datur nec cum gratia venit*' (*Dial.* 7.2). 'Then I seem to myself to rise above the tribunates or praetorships or consulate, then I seem to approach that state which, if it does not arise from deep within a man, cannot be bestowed by an imperial grant or gained through reciprocal favours.' Once more, he takes the orator into the street, where the attention he gains among all classes of people attests to his glorious reputation (*Dial.* 7.4). This objective evaluation of Aper's status follows on from his conscious self-assessment – *mihi videor* – equivalent to the generalized orator's knowledge that all of his status derives from *sibi ipsi*, his performed self. The sense of pleasure which animates this conscious ethos is not an enclosed loop of self-absorption. It is dramatized within Aper's speech by the way he brings his orators into the street and is also embedded in his act of communicating emotion to his listeners. This communication places trust in the listeners to recognize and approve the truth of his claims.

The difficulty with Aper's sense of ethos, however, is that it appears to have no moral grounding beyond *eloquentia* itself, and this seems to explain his admiration for the skill of Eprius Marcellus, whom he mentions twice in this speech. Marcellus stands for the man who has nothing but *eloquentia*, but with *eloquentia* he can prevail even over the philosophically informed principles of a man like Helvidius (*Dial.* 5.7). Along with Vibius Crispus, Marcellus provides the climax to Aper's succession of examples, but they are introduced as a daring choice of illustration.

> *ausim contendere Marcellum hunc Eprium . . . et Crispum Vibium . . . <notos> esse in extremis partibus terrae . . . ad demonstrandum oratoriae eloquentiae utilitatem inlustriora exempla sunt, quod sine commendatione natalium, sine substantia facultatum, neuter moribus egregius, alter habitu quoque corporis contemptus, per multos iam annos potentissimi sunt civitatis ac, donec libuit, principes fori.*
>
> *Dial.* 8.1, 3

I would venture to claim that Eprius Marcellus and Vibius Crispus are renowned in the furthest reaches of the world . . . They are striking examples of the benefits of an orator's eloquence: without any advantage of birth, without financial support, neither of them exceptional in their behaviour, one of them despicable in his bodily appearance, for many years now they have been the most powerful men in the state and, as long as they wished, leading men in public life.

Aper here seems to pick the 'worst-case example' to demonstrate the brilliance of his argument that eloquence brings with it every benefit of status and power.[26] He denies to these men precisely the ethical underpinnings outlined by Cicero and exemplified by Messalla: dignity of birth and probity of character. With only the 'entechnic' skills of *eloquentia*, then, Marcellus and Crispus become fabulously wealthy and politically influential. Their success, therefore, seems to undermine the case for ethos and to suggest that one can be *dicendi peritus* even if one is not a *vir bonus*. But there is a significant absence of subjective experience in Aper's portrayal of Marcellus and Crispus. There is no reason why he should not convey either man's sense of pleasure in his own social success or even in his exercise of *eloquentia*. When Tacitus represents Marcellus speaking in *Histories* and *Annals*, he manages to convey something of the speaker's rhetorical brilliance.[27] But neither in the historical narratives nor here in the dialogue is Marcellus or Crispus afforded any emotional affect through which might be communicated a *sense* of ethos, such as we have seen in Aper's first two examples. Instead, the two men are presented entirely objectively, as present-day examples that Aper and his listeners can gaze upon (*'oculis spectanda haberemus'*, *Dial.* 8.2) but whose own experience of the world remains opaque. This is most obvious when Aper drives home the point he has already made about the self-sufficiency which *eloquentia* bestows upon the orator (*Dial.* 6.2 and 7.2, quoted above): whereas the generalized orator and Aper himself have reflected upon their own position, Marcellus and Crispus exemplify self-sufficiency for someone else (specifically the emperor) to contemplate.

> *Vespasianus, venerabilis senex et patientissimus veri, bene intellegit et <animadvertit> ceteros quidem amicos suos iis niti, ... Marcellum autem et Crispum attulisse ad amicitiam suam quod non a principe acceperint nec accipi possit.*
>
> *Dial.* 8.3

> Vespasian, that revered old man, so tolerant of the truth, knows well and observes that his other friends may depend on those things which they have received from him, ... but Marcellus and Crispus have brought something to their friendship with him which they have not received, which could not be received from a ruler.

It seems that, however much Aper admires the achievements of these men, he cannot imagine their life from the inside. This is all the more noteworthy given that Marcellus and Crispus, presumably, would be the kind of readers who could comprehend the inner satisfactions of the orator as evoked by Aper in *Dial.* 6. What we are left with, then, is an asymmetrical system of empathy: Marcellus may, like Aper's audience, be able to 'get inside' the generalized orator, but his own emotions and inner thoughts are inaccessible. When Curiatus Maternus responds to Aper's argument and challenges his choice of example, he violently reintroduces the language of affect.

> *nam Crispus iste et Marcellus, ad quorum exempla me vocas, quid habent in hac sua fortuna concupiscendum? quod timent, an quod timentur? quod, cum cotidie aliquid rogentur, ii quibus praestant indignantur? quod adligati cum adulatione nec imperantibus umquam satis servi videntur nec nobis satis liberi? quae haec summa eorum potentia est? tantum posse liberti solent.*
>
> *Dial.* 13.4

> As for that Crispus and Marcellus, whom you present to me as models of behaviour, what do they have in that fortune of theirs which I should desire? That they are afraid or that they are feared? That, when every day someone asks something of them, they are resented by the very recipients of their

favours? That, shackled by every sort of flattery, they never seem sufficiently servile to their rulers or sufficiently free to us? What is this power of theirs, then? Freedmen are accustomed to as much.

At the heart of Maternus' diatribe is a glimpse of the inner life of Marcellus and Crispus: *quod timent*. Otherwise the language of affect all pertains to the 'audience' of these men, not merely in the courts or the curia but across their social interactions. After the initial 'symmetry' of mutual fear, Marcellus and Crispus provoke rather than communicate emotions in others. As a result they barely participate in the affects of the community: their self-sufficiency is recast as social isolation,[28] and their acquisition of status makes them, in Maternus' eyes, not 'leading men in public life' but equivalent to *liberti*.

Rather than simply stating that they are 'bad men' in absolute terms, Tacitus grounds the evaluation of Marcellus and Crispus in rhetorical performance and sensibility. Emotionally apprehended values form the basis of a conception of ethos and community from which these speakers are excluded even as their participation in the field of oratory is recognized. When Tacitus comes to narrate Marcellus' most famous speech – the prosecution of Thrasea (*Ann.* 16.28–29) which earned him five million sesterces (*Ann.* 16.33.2) – he juxtaposes its practical and rhetorical efficacy with its ethical failure. The content of his speech was discussed in chapter two: here I turn to its delivery and reception.

> *Cum per haec atque talia Marcellus, ut erat torvus ac minax, voce voltu oculis ardesceret, non illa nota et crebritate periculorum sueta iam senatus maestitia, sed novus et altior pavor manus et tela militum cernentibus. simul ipsius Thraseae venerabilis species obversabatur; et erant qui Helvidium quoque miserarentur, innoxiae adfinitatis poenas daturum. quid Agrippino obiectum nisi tristem patris fortunam? quando et ille perinde innocens Tiberii saevitia concidisset. enimvero Montanum probae iuventae neque famosi carminis, quia protulerit ingenium, extorrem agi.*
>
> Ann. 16.29

While Marcellus uttered these words and suchlike, his voice, face, and eyes were blazing, severe and intimidating as he was. And a new fear crept upon the senate – not that well-known sorrow, so familiar from the almost daily threats – for now they looked upon soldiers, their arms and weapons. At the same time, the revered image of Thrasea himself rose before their eyes; and there were some who had pity also for Helvidius, given over to punishment for a guiltless association with Thrasea. And what was the charge against Agrippinus, except the sad fate of his father? (For he too, though innocent, had fallen prey to the brutality of Tiberius.) As for Montanus, a young man worthy of approval, whose poetry was not disreputable, he was to be driven into exile because he had demonstrated his ability.

As we saw in chapter two, Marcellus ends his speech with a plea to the senate to restore health to the state by excising Thrasea: *abrumperet vitam ab ea civitate, cuius caritatem olim, nunc et adspectum exuisset* (*Ann.* 16.28.3). 'Let him sever his life from this community of citizens, affection for which he long ago shed and which now he has even banished from his sight.' The ethos he performs is that of a vigilant citizen outraged at the harm done by an enemy of the state, and the *indignatio* he expresses is supposed to be communicated to his audience. As Quintilian observes, the most effective way for an orator to communicate emotion is to feel it himself, and the best way to evoke such feeling is to visualize the offence (Quint., *Inst.* 6.2.27–32). Since Thrasea's crime is above all his absence, Marcellus works hard to concretize this absence as an insult that can be felt. The continued absence of Thrasea from the senate strengthens his claim that *caritas* – a communal and mutual esteem between peers – has been rejected and violated.[29]

Tacitus elaborates on the association of visualization and emotion as he portrays the senate moved to entirely different feelings by Marcellus' display. Instead of *indignatio* they feel fear; instead of sharing the affect communicated by Marcellus' voice, face, and eyes, they visualize the absent Thrasea as one worthy of awe and respect. The common feelings of the senate – sorrow, fear, respect, pity – separate them entirely from the performance of ethos they are witnessing, such that their emotions are transformed into a silent counter-judgement of each defendant in the case. Inwardly, they reaffirm communal acts of approbation and recognition of value – most obviously with their evaluation of the unfortunate Curtius Montanus' lifestyle as *proba iuventa*. Thus they replace the scene of sorrow and terror before their eyes with images of men worthy of approval and esteem, effectively repeating the strategy enjoined by Cicero, which we saw Messalla put into practice at the beginning of this section: 'so that the mind of the audience is deflected away from the one they hate, to the one they approve of'. But they do so only to exacerbate their sense of alienation and awareness that the private scene of judgement in their minds will have no bearing on the formal judgements they agree against Thrasea and his companions. And four years later, most of the same senators will have to hear Marcellus assert *non magis sua oratione Thraseam quam iudicio senatus adflictum* (*Hist.* 4.8.3). 'Thrasea was not brought down by his speech so much as by the judgement of the senate.'

By exploring how ethos is performed throughout the speaker's life, I have introduced a new register through which to gauge the effects of speech. We have seen how the ethical success or failure of speakers such as Messalla and Marcellus offset the immediate effects of their interventions. This may seem a small consolation in a scene such as the trial of Thrasea, where Marcellus gains a substantial monetary reward while Thrasea loses his life. Here is where the historical narrative plays an important compensatory role as it becomes the site for recovering small victories. Only in Tacitus' narrative can the unspoken communal values of the Neronian senate be voiced, and the primary vehicle for recovering such voices is the narrator's understanding and re-enactment of rhetoric, emotion, and the principles they archive. In section 4.2 we take a closer look at how character is recorded and evaluated in Tacitus' narratives, observing how it embeds contemporary experience of a senator's performed self but also pointedly suspends narrative to allow for the historian's intervention. These interventions, expressing judgement of individual characters from hindsight, allow both the historian and his reader to participate in the exercise of collective judgement and the maintenance of communal values.

4.2 The critical archive of character

One of Tacitus' best-known programmatic statements occurs in the third book of Tiberius' reign, a narrative more than usually dense with senatorial business. Just before he remarks on how speakers are progressing from the degrading speech of flattery to the harmful speech of *delatio*, Tacitus interpolates a statement of purpose.

> *Exsequi sententias haud institui nisi insignes per honestum aut notabili dedecore, quod praecipuum munus annalium reor, ne virtutes sileantur utque pravis dictis factisque ex posteritate et infamia metus sit.*
>
> *Ann.* 3.65.1

I have made it my practice not to follow up *sententiae* unless they are remarkable for being honourable or of notable disgrace, which I consider to be the especial duty of the historical record, not to pass over virtue in silence and so that immoral words and deeds are marked by fear of bad reputation in the future.

The reader may be surprised to hear that Tacitus intends not to include many *sententiae* in his narrative, given the frequency of references up to this point, but Tacitus goes on to explain that the disgrace of *adulatio* is now so prevalent that he is overloaded with a wealth of morally repugnant material.[30] In that context, the critical intervention of the historian is vitally necessary as a corrective to the poor judgement collectively evinced by the Tiberian senate. Tacitus' emphasis on the especial duty of history and his concern that, without history, virtues would be passed over in silence, implies that the process of community recognition and approval has been entirely suspended. This is belied somewhat by the conclusion to the chapter where the emperor himself exclaims at the submissiveness of the senatorial body, an outburst which indicates that he at least continues in the practice of assessing both speaker and speech.[31]

But Tacitus' identification of a particular task for history is designed to make a special claim for his own discourse within this programmatic statement.[32] Elsewhere in the narrative Tacitus shows us several acts of judgement performed by individuals or groups in response to speakers in the senate. Indeed, the judgement of the historian overlaps with sound judgements of historical agents as frequently as it corrects or supplements inadequate ones. As we've already seen with the affective reaction to Eprius Marcellus accusing Thrasea Paetus, even in a situation where senators are unable to act upon their judgement, their unspoken sense of injustice is retained and recovered by the historian. It could be argued that Tacitus simply retrojects back into his account of the past the values of his own present by which he is able to make the past meaningful in his own time. But we also discern from Tacitus and other authors the sense of a tradition about Thrasea Paetus which was transmitted and still current in the era of Trajan. In particular, the cultivation of his memory by his family and friends, where attribution of 'sanctity' seems to have been part of the discourse,[33] resonates with Tacitus' reference to the *venerabilis species* of Thrasea in the minds of the senators at his trial. This makes the senators' internal judgement of Thrasea part of a shared discourse which may perhaps already have been generated in the past. If so, Tacitus 'pays back' to the past an inherited value system which shapes his own perspective as both a senator and a historian.

The sharing of judgement is important to the concept of a 'critical archive' as a way of understanding how Tacitus combines representation of the past with ongoing evaluative engagement. This is what makes his work a 'recovery' of the past: it reactivates historical agents' self-presentation and ethical critique, and it supplements that critique with the historian's perspective from hindsight. Both of these aspects are necessary for Tacitus: the first, because it restores agency to the senators of the past and also implicitly acknowledges their role in shaping the political values that Tacitus inherited; the second, because Tacitus, having declared his belief in a new 'happiness of times' (*Hist.* 1.1.4), must demonstrate the truth of that belief through the critical assessment he brings to bear upon the past and transmits to the future.

Jonas Grethlein has identified a similar approach to the double perspective of historiography by situating it between the poles of what he calls 'experience' and 'teleology'. In his analysis, historical narrative posits a vantage point from which events in the past are viewed, which affects the representation and understanding of those events: this he terms the 'teleological' view. At the same time, historical narrative, like other mimetic genres, embeds a sense of 'experience': the embodied, cognitive living of the past by historical agents, their own sense of an earlier past and, crucially, of their future as unrealized possibility. This last 'experiential' effect of narrative, the historical agent's own horizon of expectations, Grethlein has termed 'futures past'.[34] My formulation of the 'critical archive' shares some of Grethlein's approach, particularly the focus on what formal features of the narrative enable the reader to participate in or 're-experience' the historical agent's experience. Grethlein is primarily interested in the temporal and existential questions which arise from the tension between experience and teleology, so that the historical agent's sense of his future as open potential – a future perceived from the historian's vantage point as closed past – is a temporal effect. This illuminates one of the features of Tacitus' narrative I am about to examine. When a senator stands to deliver a speech or *sententia*, the brief narrative description of the speaker replicates the audience's perception of his status, ethos, and ambitions. Both speaker and audience experience the moment as open potential in terms of what the speech will achieve and what it will make of the speaker's career. The narrator, with his view from hindsight, can confirm or undermine the expectations of the historical agents.

What I want to emphasize is how Tacitus' sense of the political inflects this narrative dynamic. As Grethlein acknowledges, the vantage point from which Tacitus looks at the past is political rather than purely temporal;[35] my contention is that this relocates the sense of open potential in the present rather than in the past. Many senators in Tacitus' narratives perceive their future as foreclosed by a repressive regime, while Tacitus at the start of *Histories* and *Agricola* declares a future of political possibility opened up by the Trajanic succession. Whatever we think of Tacitus' praise of the present (a debate we reviewed in the introduction), his characterization of this time creates a contrast with the past that he represents. And its effect is to reverse the temporal effect of an open possibility in the past which is closed off by historical hindsight in the present: instead, Tacitus' historical writings commence with a sense of the present as an expansion of horizons, while he looks back on a more circumscribed past. The relocation of political possibility in the historian's own present, moreover, provides a way of recovering political community in the past. The sense of experience which is embedded in the narrative invites the reader to participate in the political community of the past, but from the less circumscribed vantage point of the present.

Shared critical judgement of senatorial ethos, then, opens up a significant space where values are recovered/maintained and their transmission is secured by the very fact of their being shared across historical agents, historian, and readers. How this works in narrative merits a closer look. In section 4.1, I outlined how speech performance presents an ethos drawn from all aspects of the speaker's life, which is rendered in narrative by a brief characterization either juxtaposed to or separated from the account of the speech performance. This was illustrated by the representation of Vipstanus Messalla but is a recurrent feature of Tacitean (and historiographical) narrative more generally. Suetonius Paulinus, who as we noted in chapters one and three attempted to advise Otho on battle strategy in the face of the *adulationes* of other advisors, is a very clear example of how such representations combine internal focalizations (viewpoints of the speaker and his contemporary audience) with external focalizations (those of the narrator and reader).

Suetonius Paulinus dignum fama sua ratus, qua nemo illa tempestate militaris rei callidior habebatur, de toto genere belli censere, festinationem hostibus, moram ipsis utilem disseruit.

Hist. 2.32.1

Suetonius Paulinus, deeming it appropriate to his reputation (according to which nobody at that time was considered more skilful in military matters) to deliver an opinion on the whole nature of the war, discoursed on how haste was the best strategy for the enemy and delay most expedient for their own side.

The order of phrases is clumsy in English, but it is important to see how the speech of Paulinus is preceded by his own thoughts about his ethos ('deeming it appropriate') and the thoughts of others about his qualities ('according to which ...'). Paulinus is driven to speak not only by the problem at hand, but in order to maintain and build up an ethos which has already emerged between his own performance and his perception of how it is received. The thoughts of the speaker merge with the voice of the narrator when Tacitus tells us objectively what Paulinus' reputation was, but this perception coincides with Paulinus' sense of his reputation and justifies his lecture on strategy. The *fama* of a speaker, brought to bear on a performance, condenses into that performance the speaker's actions and general reputation, which is put on display across the narrative. In Paulinus' case, objective comments on his *auctoritas* (*Hist.* 1.87.2) and *prudentia* (*Hist.* 2.39.1), including one in the explicit voice of the narrator (*Hist.* 2.37.2), are exemplified by references to his previous command in Britain during the revolt of Boudicca (*Hist.* 2.37.2) and by his current successful management of volatile legions (*Hist.* 2.24.1). When Otho disregards his qualities and advice, Tacitus' objective references to these qualities then stands as a corrective to the emperor's poor judgement. At the same time, Paulinus' insistence on delay as the best strategy is seen as characteristic of the commander Tacitus calls *cunctator naturae* (*Hist.* 2.25.2), 'a delayer by nature', and the exemplification of that characteristic in the battle narrative of *Hist.* 2.25–26 suggests to both readers and internal audience that it is not always the best military quality: *apud paucos ea ducis ratio probata* (*Hist.* 2.26.2). 'The commander's rationale gained the approval only of a few.'

The language of reputation, judgement, and approval merges the internal, 'subjective' viewpoint of the historical agents (both speaker and audience) with the external, 'objective' narrative point of view. The reader is thus drawn into the political community of the past, constituted in and through evaluation of speakers. In accounts of senatorial debates, we can discern a similar collocation of viewpoints in the actions which contribute to a speaker's construction of ethos and in the way that ethos is received. Even the minimal action of participating in senatorial debate can provide glimpses of ethical performance: here, the orator can draw on the interplay between procedure (speaking in or out of his allotted place), rank derived from seniority or magisterial status (interwoven with familial status), and moral standing based on previous behaviour or actions. Narrative can reflect these displays of ethos even in relatively simple appositional phrases which appear to be no more than introductory descriptions of a speaker. An example extreme in its simplicity is the denotation of a speaker's rank: *Pallanti ... praetoria insignia et centies quinquagies sestertium censuit consul designatus Barea Soranus* (*Ann.* 12.53.2). 'The consul designate, Barea Soranus, proposed praetorian insignia and an award of fifteen million sesterces for [Claudius' freedman] Pallas.' Soranus' ethical position is not expressed – later, Tacitus will group him with Thrasea Paetus as another embodiment of *virtus* (*Ann.* 16.21.1) – but the reference to his rank points to a self-conscious performance. His position as consul designate, which places his *locus dicendi* early in the order of debate, would likely have been established only a few weeks earlier,[36] so the novelty of his rising to speak at this stage would still be fresh for his audience. Soranus could be exploiting this novelty to make a memorable intervention, though it is unclear whether his proposal is in the spirit of servility or mockery.[37]

A stronger sense of how the speaker's awareness of his rank is internalized and mobilized towards development and projection of his ethos can be seen in the introduction of Domitius Afer as *recens praetura, modicus dignationis et quoquo facinore properus clarescere* (*Ann.* 4.52.1). 'Having newly completed his praetorship, of middling rank, and in a hurry to become famous by any means whatever.' Objective and subjective views of Afer combine, as his consciousness of his own position and status drives his ambition, and his inner sense of urgency is perceived through the activities he undertakes without moral discrimination.[38] The sequence of magisterial rank, family standing, and personal habitus in such a phrase evokes the swift succession of name-recognition, acknowledgement of status, and evaluative judgement which would pass through a listening senator's mind as Afer rose to speak. Later comments about Afer reinforce the sense that his contemporary audience perceives his lack of principle just as much as Tacitus does: at the end of the episode he is said to have a better reputation (*fama*) for eloquence than for morals (*Ann.* 4.52.4), and in a later trial nobody is surprised to see him embarking on an invidious prosecution (*Ann.* 4.66.1). The contemporary reception of Afer is overlaid with the hindsight of the historian and his readers, for whom Afer was a significant figure of the previous generation of orators.[39] But the hindsight here remains implicit.

Evaluative language such as *fama/infamia* enables the elision of the contemporary audience's and the historian's perspectives. We have already seen how Q. Haterius, proposing an excessive honour for Tiberius and Drusus, is received as 'a laughing stock ... an old man who will reap only infamy from his disgusting flattery' (*deridiculo ... senex foedissimae adulationis tantum infamia usurus* (*Ann.* 3.57.2)).[40] In a similar vein, the provincial senator Togonius Gallus, 'when he joined in the debate with such great names, low-born as he was, he was received with mockery' (*dum ignobilitatem suam magnis nominibus inserit, per deridiculum auditur* (*Ann.* 6.2.2)). Ateius Capito, presuming to lecture Tiberius on the nature of a treason charge, earns 'extraordinary infamy ... because he was learned in human and divine law, and yet chose to dishonour his public distinction and his personal accomplishments' (*insignitior infamia ... quod humani divinique iuris sciens egregium publicum et bonas domi artes dehonestavisset* (*Ann.* 3.70.3)). Each of these evaluations takes elements of the speaker's performed self – his age, nobility, and learning – as de-authorizing a particular speech act: in the process, the speaker's ethos is picked apart. Significantly, Tacitus shows this as a process that spans the contemporary reception of the speech act and its recording in his narrative.

The evaluative judgement of the historian does not always coincide with that of the historical agents. Since Tacitus differentiates between the foreclosed political possibilities of the past and the reopened potential of his present, he must illustrate that difference through the ethical perspective he brings to bear. Hence some narrative judgements are presented as correctives or supplements to speakers' self-presentation or to their evaluation by the contemporary audience. This is particularly common in the presentation of *delatores* or prosecutors, where Tacitus frequently prefaces their speech with his evaluations as if to minimize the dangers posed by such speakers were they to speak without introduction. The famous composite character sketch of Crispinus/ Hispo in the earliest *maiestas* episode of *Annals* demonstrates this practice (*Ann.* 1.74.1–2), but there is also the treatment of the prosecutors in the trial of C. Silanus in AD 22, a trial presented by Tacitus as a fundamental shift from dishonourable to harmful speech (*Ann.* 3.66). Again, as if to guard against the dangers of their speech, especially of the powerful Mamercus Scaurus, Tacitus undercuts the prosecutors' self-presentation: *proavum suum obprobrium maiorum Mamercus infami opera dehonestabat* (*Ann.* 3.66.2). 'Mamercus, an offence to his ancestors, dishonoured his great-grandfather with his disreputable practices.'[41] Terms for infamy or disrepute, as we have seen in other instances, provide the opportunity to coalesce past and present perspectives, to unite the Tiberian senate and the Trajanic historian in shared judgement of a speaker's ethos – and thus it could be taken here as well. But if Mamercus' contemporaries fail to judge him correctly, Tacitus' evaluation of his infamy emends the archive and secures future judgement.

The need for such security is especially pressing in the case of subjects whose memory is in need of rehabilitation, where Tacitus' corrective evaluation of their speech and ethos defines the difference between past and present and guarantees the new regime of Nerva and Trajan. Here the formally marked interventions of the historian in his accounts of Helvidius Priscus and Marcus Lepidus are quite distinct from the examples reviewed so far in this section and signal the importance, for future political worlds, of establishing a correct evaluation of these speakers. In both these instances, Tacitus signals the turn to narrative and to the historical perspective as a site for critical judgement, but places this turn, significantly, after the historical agents have spoken, registering perhaps that their speech poses no risk to the reader. When he inserts a biographical digression to contextualize Helvidius' political actions, he refers to his own narrative activity as *paucis repetam*, 'I review in a few words' (*Hist.* 4.6.1). In two scenes of authorial judgement on Marcus Lepidus, Tacitus emphasizes his own historical investigation – *comperior* (*Ann.* 4.20.2) – and narrative ordering – *conlocavi* (*Ann.* 6.27.4). Each of these assessments is delivered from the perspective of later time and gains *gravitas* from its appropriation of the language of funeral oratory (indeed, the final example is from Lepidus' obituary). Tacitus thereby situates himself and his critical judgement in a different sphere from that of the contemporary senatorial audience – orators assessing their peers. The juxtaposition of these contemporary and historical judgements raises questions about each of these characters which cannot be finally resolved but which ensure that Tacitus' critical archive remains a live site. Helvidius, as we will see in a moment, emerges as a controversial and invigorating force for past and present audiences, while the apparent consensus about Lepidus is reconfigured by Tacitus to raise further questions about the transmission of political efficacy.

The biographical digression on Helvidius is introduced between two contemporary diverging judgements of his actions in the senate; at first glance, therefore, it seems that Tacitus introduces this wider context and Helvidius' ethical grounding in philosophy to resolve a difficulty in the correct evaluation of these actions. But Tacitus' intervention only intensifies the controversy around Helvidius, so that this scene – the first senatorial meeting of Vespasian's reign – becomes the kind of occasion identified by Dean Hammer, where 'community expectations are ambiguous, contradictory, or unsatisfactory'.[42] We have already seen in chapter three how Helvidius successfully disrupts the *adulatio* of the senate and potentially reactivates more productive ruler–subject relations by responding to prompts in Vespasian's letter to the senate. This receives the initial approbation of the senate: *studiis senatus attollebatur* (*Hist.* 4.4.3). 'He was carried aloft by the enthusiastic response of the senate.' Tacitus immediately undercuts this success with his view from hindsight, where Helvidius will enjoy the rewards of continued praise but will also lose his standing with the ruler and suffer exile and death: *isque praecipuus illi dies magnae offensae initium et magnae gloriae fuit* (*Hist.* 4.4.3). 'And that day was above all the beginning of great displeasure towards Helvidius, and great glory.' But the controversy around Helvidius began earlier, in the reign of Galba, when he first attempted to bring to justice Eprius Marcellus, the prosecutor of his father-in-law, Thrasea Paetus. Just as his speech intervention in Vespasian's regime counters *adulatio*, this earlier intervention is against *delatio*. Tacitus reserves Helvidius' attack on Marcellus for the biographical digression as a way of introducing the later conflict between the two. The effect on the senate also bears comparison with the intervention we have just examined.

> *ut Galbae principatu rediit, Marcellum Eprium, delatorem Thraseae, accusare adgreditur. ea ultio, incertum maior an iustior, senatum in studia diduxerat: nam*

> *si caderet Marcellus, agmen reorum sternebatur.... mox dubia voluntate Galbae, multis senatorum deprecantibus, omisit Priscus, variis, ut sunt hominum ingenia, sermonibus moderationem laudantium aut constantiam requirentium.*
>
> Hist. 4.6.1–2

When he returned [from exile] in Galba's reign he prepared to bring a case against Eprius Marcellus, the *delator* of Thrasea Paetus. This revenge – it is unclear whether it was more significant or more justified – threw the senate into vigorous debate: for if Marcellus were to fall, a whole rank of defendants would have to be destroyed in turn.... eventually when Galba seemed to be less supportive, and since many senators were pleading with Helvidius, he dropped the charges, with diverse comments – such is human nature – from those praising his moderation or lamenting his lack of constancy.

Helvidius does not, like Valerius Messalla, provide the senate with the pleasure of shared moral recognition, but he does offer a different kind of enjoyment: *studia* – energetic responses of praise, counter-suggestion, and disagreement. Even Marcellus himself in the following narrative, when Helvidius makes a proposal to institute a new system of evaluating senators for the upcoming delegation to the new emperor, has his *studium* aroused by the possibility of disgrace and is drawn into an altercation (*Hist.* 4.7.1). Helvidius, therefore, emerges with a different kind of ethos, invigorating debate rather than inviting the consensus of approval. Tacitus himself engages in this debate through his digression, where he supplements Helvidius' political ethos with an account of his family origins and his pursuit of philosophy. In a summation of Helvidius' character which spans all these modes of existence and in terms reminiscent of a funeral laudation, Tacitus anticipates the criticisms of those senators who accuse Helvidius of lacking *constantia*.

> *civis senator, maritus gener amicus, cunctis vitae officiis aequabilis, opum contemptor, recti pervicax, constans adversus metus.*
>
> Hist. 4.6.2

Citizen, senator, husband, son-in-law, friend, in all the duties of life he was consistent; a despiser of wealth, stubborn in pursuit of the good, standing firm against fear.

The grounding of Helvidius' ethical self in philosophy gestures towards a universal, extra-temporal moral absolute, but Tacitus even in this digression continually reorients the discussion towards the world of politics and rhetoric.[43] He insists that Helvidius turns to philosophy so as to be a more principled statesman (*Hist.* 4.5.1) and that his moral principles did not make him indifferent to the kind of reputation he held among his peers (*Hist.* 4.6.1). After the digression's detour into consideration of the true good, Tacitus returns Helvidius to the world of moral relativism, where even the narrator declares it uncertain whether his prosecution of Marcellus is 'more significant or more justified' (*maior an iustior*) – a pair of evaluative terms which fail to make sense as an opposition. Above all, however, the digression alerts us to how Helvidius' political interventions can be understood as rhetorical-ethical evaluations of his fellow citizens: after praising Vespasian as a good emperor (*Hist.* 4.4.3) and attempting to prosecute Marcellus as a *delator* (*Hist.* 4.6.1), he proposes that the senate assess the characters of those they would send as delegates to the emperor.[44] This enables him, in the ensuing altercation with Marcellus, to outline the value for the state of such a procedure.

> *sorte et urna mores non discerni: suffragia et existimationem senatus reperta, ut in cuiusque vitam famamque penetrarent. pertinere ad utilitatem rei publicae, pertinere ad Vespasiani honorem, occurrere illi, quos innocentissimos senatus habeat, qui honestis sermonibus aures imperatoris imbuant.*
>
> *Hist.* 4.7.1–2

> It is not possible to recognize character through random choice and lots: voting and the general estimation of the senate have been established so that they can fully understand the life and reputation of each man. It is relevant to the interests of the commonwealth and to the honour of Vespasian that he be met by those men whom the senate deems most free of blame, who can fill the emperor's ears with honourable advice.

Jakub Pigoń has insightfully read this episode as a significant move in a series by Helvidius, intended to 'strengthen the authority of the senate in relation to the new princeps'.[45] He focuses on two concepts, *amicitia* and *iudicium senatus*, and traces their interplay in the exchange between Helvidius and Marcellus to show how this seemingly trivial procedural decision serves as the vehicle for a debate about senatorial responsibility as much as authority. I suggest that Helvidius, articulating how important it is for the senate to evaluate its representatives rather than choosing them by lot, attempts to reintroduce the language of ethos into procedural politics. The key word here is *existimatio*, not used elsewhere by Tacitus, but a recurrent term for the communal judgement that effects an individual's public standing – we have seen Cicero's use of this term in his discussion of ethos in *De Oratore*. That this ethos has a rhetorical dimension is evident also in Helvidius' sense of the ultimate aim of evaluative selection: so that the emperor's ears will be filled with honourable speech. To ensure that we understand the significance of Helvidius' various interventions and that we do not overlook them as minor quibbles, Tacitus' digression, with its weighty cadences, presents Helvidius as worthy of our consideration and estimation.

Tacitus' pointed critical judgement is also important because Helvidius' intentions and sense of new political possibilities are not fulfilled: the old practice of selecting legates by lot is maintained, and in the following meeting Helvidius' hopes of bringing down Marcellus are not realized (*Hist.* 4.43.1). The *studia* of the senate is redirected towards a trial which consolidates their dignity as a collective and away from self-regulation through scrutiny of individual senators (*Hist.* 4.45.1). Historical hindsight thus might tempt the reader to conclude that Helvidius' attempts were insignificant because they came to nothing. Against this, Tacitus' digression implicitly appeals to a broader teleology which, I suggest, situates Helvidius within Tacitus' own political horizons. Tacitus' determination to believe in the potential of his own future is mobilized through his recognition and reactivation of Helvidius' experience of the new Vespasianic regime as open possibility. To achieve this, his digression presents Helvidius in terms of ethical values which transcend the particular achievements of Helvidius' own lifetime. This is a theme we will return to in chapter five.

While Helvidius' character and the efficacy of his actions is at the centre of intense debate, Marcus Lepidus is subject to an extraordinary consensus. Everyone in the Tiberian regime holds him in the highest esteem: he is judged by Augustus to be the foremost of the three senators suitable to succeed him as emperor (*Ann.* 1.13.2); with the exception of the loathed Cotta Messalinus (*Ann.* 6.5.1), he incurs no discernible enmity from his fellow senators among whom he shines out in wealth, nobility, and achievement; and he remains in favour with Tiberius until he dies of natural causes (*Ann.* 6.27.4). Similar estimation of Lepidus endures in other sources. Vellius Paterculus, who gave more extensive treatment to Lepidus' creditable military career, introduces him with language that highlights not only the man's virtues but also the pleasure that the community experiences in its recognition and approval of those virtues, a dynamic which we have seen underpinning the performance of public self.

> M. Lepidus... quem in quantum quisque aut cognoscere aut intellegere potuit, in tantum miratur ac diligit tantorumque nominum, quibus ortus est, ornamentum iudicat.
>
> Vell. Pat. 2.114.5

M. Lepidus: anyone with the appropriate perception and intellectual capacity would admire and approve of this man and judge him to be a credit to the great men from whom he is descended.

Instead of providing a corrective to contemporary views, therefore, Tacitus supplements the judgement of the past. The gravity with which he weighs in on the question, however, seems almost too heavy-handed given the high degree of consensus about Lepidus. The delayed timing of his intervention into the narrative is even more pointed than in the case of Helvidius: in the first three books of *Annals*, the reader has already encountered Lepidus in a number of key scenes, not least in his mitigation of the punishment of Clutorius Priscus, which we examined in chapter three. The position and style of the historian's judgement, therefore, merits a closer look. Tacitus delivers his views on Lepidus after he has successfully mitigated the sentence against Sosia Galla (also examined in the introduction and chapter three).

> *hunc ego Lepidum temporibus illis gravem et sapientem virum fuisse comperior: nam pleraque ab saevis adulationibus aliorum in melius flexit. neque tamen temperamenti egebat, cum aequabili auctoritate et gratia apud Tiberium viguerit.*
>
> *Ann.* 4.20.2

This Lepidus, I understand, was a significant and wise man in this era: for in many cases he deflected the cruel flattery of others and brought about a better decision. For all that, he did not lack a sense of balance, since his career flourished through an equal amount of authority and favour with Tiberius.

Comperior, as I've already noted, grounds the speaker's judgement in historical knowledge, which here gains added authority by using the language of Tacitus' illustrious predecessor from the triumviral era, Sallust.[46] We have already seen in chapter three how Lepidus' speech in the case of Clutorius Priscus draws on Sallust's representations of senatorial judgements. Here the echoes of Sallust lend authority to Tacitus' judgement as a historian, as a necessary perspective to counteract either contemporary perspectives or the expectations of the reader. Sallust's assessment of the aristocratic consul Metellus is introduced when the narrative has established a pattern of corrupt or incompetent military commanders, and immediately after a digression on plebeian conflict with the nobility. Metellus' exemplary management of a demoralized army, contrary to the expectations engendered by the narrative, therefore requires pointed notice.

> *Sed in ea difficultate Metellum non minus quam in rebus hostilibus magnum et sapientem virum fuisse conperior; tanta temperantia inter ambitionem saevitiamque moderatum.*
>
> Sall., *Iug.* 45.1

> But I understand that Metellus, facing this challenge no less than when in actual warfare, was a great man and a wise one; with such balance he moderated himself between self-interested indulgence towards the army and brutality.

Lepidus takes Metellus' *temperantia* and exercises it in all aspects of his senatorial career (as well as in his military one, which Tacitus omits): his procedural knowledge, rhetorical skill, and personal *auctoritas* are demonstrated through his reception by other senators and the emperor. Lepidus is able to appeal to his different audiences and, crucially, to influence them for the better. His success hinges on the limits that he sets to his own achievements, and this perhaps accounts for the pointedness with which Tacitus sets out his historical judgement of Lepidus. He is a great and wise man *temporibus illis*, for times like these, when more ambitious aims might be impossible to realize – and, interestingly, he is afforded no more interiority than is Eprius Marcellus, as if his success and virtue set him, too, apart from his community. Tacitus does not expect his readers to accommodate their judgement to that of Lepidus' contemporaries so much as to recognize Lepidus' ethics and efficacy in relation to the conditions with which he works. The broader historical and political question which Lepidus provokes has to do with what general principles – if any – Tacitus can extrapolate from his critical archive. This is the point at which Tacitus poses the question, with which I started in the introduction, of whether there are general principles of senatorial behaviour, or whether Lepidus' success is pure chance. Does Lepidus, Helvidius, or any other senator offer principles and practices which can be adopted for the future?

This chapter has opened up the different angles from which Tacitus presents the performed senatorial self, so that we see the senator's creation and maintenance of his ethos, the community's recognition and approval of that ethos, and the historical reader's participation in that process of evaluation. Crucially, we have seen the politics of this process: ethos in its creation and reception not only serves as the vehicle of specific political interventions, it also expresses the values which define a citizen and a community. But being a 'good man skilled at speaking' is not a simple matter, as the cases of Helvidius and Lepidus show. Tacitus presents the historical judgement of these two figures, not to settle the question of their virtue once and for all, but in order to extend the debate about their efficacy into the present day.

5

Narratus et traditus: The Transmission of *mores*

The final words of Tacitus' *Agricola* defiantly assert the immortality secured for his subject by his narrative: *nam multos veterum velut inglorios et ignobiles oblivio obruit; Agricola posteritati narratus et traditus superstes erit* (*Agr.* 46.4). 'For oblivion envelopes many men of antiquity, as if they were without glory or nobility; Agricola, transmitted to the future in narrative, will survive.' Behind this bold claim lies a complex meditation on the nature and interrelation of representation and transmission:[1] What is it about a person that we want to transmit to the future? To whom do we direct our representation? How do we imagine transmission will be taken up? These questions are important for what I have called Tacitus' 'critical archive': the way in which his historical narratives not only record but also transmit political efficacy to the future. In this chapter, I argue that Tacitus shows us this transmission in practice as well as in potential: section 5.1 examines how social networks formed around groups of senators are seen as carriers of values and practices, which in turn reinforce these very networks. Section 5.2 explores the idea that senators transmit not merely political principles, but specific tactics as well: the figure of Thrasea Paetus, who is usually regarded as an exemplar of (impractical) philosophical or Republican ideals, is re-examined as both an inheritor and transmitter of such functional strategies. Section 5.3 uncovers ways in which Tacitus' narrative points to the longer-term effect of political interventions beyond their immediate success or failure, by narrating events of the past in such a way as to orient them towards his own present. In this light I conclude the chapter by re-examining the parallels between the senate of Tacitus' *Histories* 4, at the beginning of the Flavian regime, and the senate of Pliny's letters, in the new regimes of Nerva and Trajan. But first we return to the end of *Agricola* and the role of narrative in network formation.

5.1 The social network

While face-to-face communities enable networks to be fostered through a range of intersubjective exchanges in different spheres, narrative and exemplarity provide important ways for the values and practices of a network to be disseminated further, especially across generations. What Tacitus shows us in *Agricola* is the process of moving his father-in-law's memory from familial practice to broader social cultivation. Agricola starts out being mourned by his widow and daughter, whom Tacitus advises about the appropriate way to remember him. As he reflects on the proper modes of representation, Tacitus shifts mid-sentence to address an unnamed, generic male reader.

> *id filiae quoque uxorique praeceperim, sic patris, sic mariti memoriam venerari ut omnia facta dictaque eius secum revolvant, formamque ac figuram animi magis quam corporis complectantur, non quia intercedendum putem imaginibus quae marmore aut aere finguntur, sed, ut vultus hominum, ita simulacra vultus imbecilla ac mortalia sunt, forma mentis aeterna, quam tenere et exprimere non per alienam materiam et artem sed tuis ipse moribus possis.*
>
> Agr. 46.3

I would give this advice to his daughter and wife: to revere the memory of her father, her husband, so that they recall all his deeds and words to themselves, so that they inwardly maintain the form and image of his disposition rather than of his body – not because I think we should bar representations which are formed in marble or bronze, but like the faces of men, so the representations of faces are weak and perishable, but the form of the mind is eternal: you can comprehend and express this form of the mind not through any material or technique foreign to it but through your self and your principles/behaviour.

Twice in this passage Tacitus refers to the form of Agricola's (or anyone's) mind (*formam ac figuram animi . . . forma mentis*), so that he concretizes internal modes of being even as he denies the possibility of representing them in material form. The only appropriate medium for rendering the form of the mind in the material world, he concludes, is human behaviour – *tuis moribus*. *Mores* are highly suitable for this because they can themselves be described as a 'form of the mind' – as internalized principles and habits which then manifest as behavioural practices, also called *mores*.[2] The enshrining of Agricola in the mourner's mind shapes it so that it becomes the mourner's self at its best, which is also a true representation of Agricola. Any other medium of representation (with one exception) is alien. I have understood *aliena materia* as 'material foreign to the object of representation' rather than 'material used by others', as many scholars have taken it;[3] this interpretation brings out Tacitus' point that the proper medium for representing a good person's mind and disposition is another person's activity of shaping and directing themselves towards the practice of virtue.[4] Intrinsic to this claim is Tacitus' abstraction of Agricola from an exclusively private context of remembrance so that he is shared among the community of readers.

Narrative, the one exception to Tacitus' bar on 'alien material', aids in this more general transmission and is justified as an appropriate medium for *mores* because it represents both internal thought and external action. *Agricola* begins by situating itself in the tradition of narratives 'transmitting to the future the actions and principles/behaviour of exceptional men': *clarorum virorum facta moresque posteris tradere* (*Agr.* 1.1). *Mores*, appearing here in a phrase which signals the work as a biography,[5] not only denote both inner disposition and outward behaviour, but also encompass subjectively held habits and socially maintained norms, procedural practices and higher principles. All of these dimensions of *mores* reveal the interplay between external forces and inner will which constitutes the individual as well as the complex intersubjectivity that maintains or transforms the collective. If *mores* are a framework within which Romans think and act, they are also a structure which can be consciously modified, and thus the term insists on human agency in society and history. Finally, of course, *mores* often encode a value system which is generated internally as much as externally, and around which communities and genealogies are formed. To speak of the *mores* of exceptional men, then, is already to speak in terms of the collectivities within which they lived and to look forward to the future communities to which their memories will contribute.

Agricola's life remains problematic, however, for a reader in search of practices specifically in the senatorial domain, because his activity in Rome is narrated only minimally. His holding of magistracies up to the position of praetor is characterized as conscious inertia and silence rather than the vocal activity of the Roman senators we have been examining (*Agr.* 6.3–4).[6] But Tacitus juxtaposes his act of transmitting Agricola with another group of senators and their transmissions of Thrasea Paetus and Helvidius Priscus.

> *Legimus, cum Aruleno Rustico Paetus Thrasea, Herennio Senecioni Priscus Helvidius laudati essent, capitale fuisse, neque in ipsos modo auctores sed in libros quoque eorum saevitum.*
>
> Agr. 2.1
>
> We have read that, when Thrasea Paetus was praised by Arulenus Rusticus and Helvidius Priscus by Herennius Senecio, it was a capital crime and that the cruelty of punishment fell not only on the authors, but even on their books.

This alternative, parallel tradition of *mores*, which Tacitus carefully keeps going throughout *Agricola*, provides a different combination of principles and habits which Tacitus does not entirely repudiate.[7] It is useful for Tacitus to place this tradition alongside his memorializing of Agricola because it exemplifies the repression of Domitian's regime which Tacitus and Agricola mostly escaped. But this network of senators, which attests to a trans-generational passing down and reception of political principles, is also useful for Tacitus in his longer narratives to construct a 'genealogy of practice' which reaches beyond the immediate network in the present and the future. For a fuller picture of this network, which reflects Tacitus' consciousness of the group, we should turn briefly to the letters of the younger Pliny. Here we see Pliny's interactions with both these biographers as well as with the families of Thrasea and Helvidius. The kinds of activities which foster their network make visible the modes of senatorial existence along which the network is formed, and how individuals work to extend the network in time and space.[8] Pliny's interactions with Arulenus Rusticus, for instance, involve cultural engagement: he sends some work to Rusticus with pleas for critical forbearance (Plin., *Ep.* 9.29) – and appeals for expert support; he undertakes a civil defence at Rusticus' request (Plin., *Ep.* 1.5.5). More telling are his efforts after the trial and execution: Pliny helps Iunius Mauricus, Rusticus' brother, to find a husband for his friend's daughter (Plin., *Ep.* 1.14) and tutors for his sons (Plin., *Ep.* 2.18).[9] This range of activities, as illustrative of Roman social behaviour, is unremarkable, but it attests to what Neil Bernstein has identified as different forms of 'relatedness' which the letters partly construct and fully sustain.[10]

Pliny takes on father-like roles, in harmonious collaboration with Mauricus, as part of the maintenance and extension of the network they share with Rusticus. The terms on which he recommends a husband for the daughter reveal his awareness of the different modes through which this new community member must align with the group: the prospective husband is assessed by class, municipal origin, morality – and his desire to be formed according to the *mores* of his new associates. *Nam ita a me formari et institui cupit, ut ego a vobis solebam* (Plin., *Ep.* 1.14.4). 'For he desires to be shaped and instructed by me, as I was by you both.' Pliny's interest in extending the network proceeds along familial lines here, just as he expresses a hope that Rusticus' sons 'will be found worthy of their father, and of you their uncle': *ut liberi ... digni illo patre, te patruo reperiantur* (Plin., *Ep.* 2.18.4). Similarly he celebrates Thrasea Paetus' daughter Fannia as most worthy of her husband and father in her *animus et spiritus* (Plin., *Ep.* 7.19.3). In both cases what is suggested is not a passive inheritance of family traits, but a cultivation of principles and practices – a cultivation in which a non-familial associate such as Pliny can also participate. Notably throughout these and other letters Pliny conveys both the skill and the pleasure of engaging with others across the different modes of social interaction.[11]

Epistle 1.5, early in the collection, is programmatic for setting out the diversity of interactions that maintain this network and the links through which it is embedded in the society of Flavian Rome more generally. Analysis of this letter has generally focussed on the altercation between Pliny and Aquilius Regulus at the centumviral court, an exchange which is paradigmatic for modern understanding of imperial 'doublespeak'.[12] But the letter is rich in hostile and friendly exchanges which map out opposing and overlapping groups of senators who express their relationships through political affiliation, commitment to different styles of oratory, philosophical creed, and moral standing.[13] Pliny's quarrel with Regulus, for instance, is fostered not only by Regulus' attempt to trap him in a treasonable utterance but also by his criticism of Pliny's veneration of Cicero.[14] On the other side, Pliny accepts the intercession in the quarrel of the notable Vestricius Spurinna – *optimus vir* (Plin., *Ep.* 1.5.9) – but three times declares his preference for the advice of Mauricus and insists on waiting for his return from exile. The deceased Rusticus, meanwhile, on whose client's behalf Pliny appears in court, is abused by Regulus for his former appearance as an envoy for the Emperor Vitellius and for his Stoicism. The simple polarity of Pliny versus Regulus illuminates all these different modes through which senators find affinity with each other – or grounds for abhorrence.

Regulus' attacks on Rusticus and Pliny also illuminate something about the modes of transmission within a network. Just as he obliquely sneers at Pliny's 'emulation' of Cicero, so he refers to Rusticus as 'the ape of the Stoics': *Stoicorum simiam* (Plin., *Ep.* 1.5.2). Regulus thus cleverly strikes at the heart of the imitative process which Pliny (and Tacitus) find so productive about their communities. Instead of seeing imitation as a careful cultivation of good principles, Regulus suggests that his opponents mimic the superficial trappings of a practice they do not understand, and which is in any case discredited. By identifying Rusticus' philosophical study as a topic for invective, Regulus draws on a common repertoire of attacks on philosophers as hypocritical, lazy, or disruptive.[15] This repertoire is what encourages the *delatores* in particular to focus on philosophy (especially Stoicism) when they seek to represent their victims as a threat to the state. Cossutianus Capito, encouraging Nero to permit a charge against Thrasea, identifies him as simultaneously dissident and promoting superficial imitations.

> *et habet sectatores vel potius satellites, qui nondum contumaciam sententiarum, sed habitum vultumque eius sectantur, rigidi et tristes, quo tibi lasciviam exprobrent.*
>
> Ann. 16.22.2

> And he maintains this sect of followers (or should we say henchmen) who do not yet mimic his truculent opinions, but his bearing and expression, stiff and unsmiling, so as to reproach the frivolity of your pleasures.

This familiar rhetoric of the 'uncivic' philosopher resonates with the image, projected by both Capito and Eprius Marcellus, of Thrasea somehow placing a check on the abundance and joy of the Neronian regime.[16] Capito here, and Marcellus in his altercation with Helvidius in *Histories*, also make much of how Stoicism provides a genealogy for these men which leads back to the younger Cato and Brutus the Tyrannicide, a genealogy which locks them into association not only with political disruption but with opposition to the Caesars.[17] This hostile tradition, in turn, feeds into popular conceptions of Thrasea and Helvidius which tend to see them exclusively as philosophically-inspired opponents of their regimes. As a consequence scholars today, even while using scare quotes, rely too much on the 'misleadingly monolithic' terms 'Stoic opposition' and 'Stoic martyrs' when assessing this social circle.[18] It's worth considering how the hostile representations of Thrasea, Rusticus, and Helvidius used ideas about Stoicism not only to portray their behaviour as unproductive for the state, but also to isolate it from potential imitators by characterizing it as a practice requiring full doctrinal immersion. Against this, Tacitus represents these men as acting and speaking in language which has purchase on several modes of senatorial existence – not least the political[19] – and which thereby has the capacity to attract listeners and imitators from a wider sphere of life.

In chapter four, we saw how Tacitus' digression on Helvidius made the unusual move of situating him across all the modes of his existence: 'citizen senator, husband, son-in-law, friend' (*Hist.* 4.5.2). This is not only to show the consistency of Helvidius' ethos (*constantia* is the major quality under debate in that part of the narrative) but to place him in a network of alliances within which he exercises and extends his virtue. Indeed, Tacitus points to the harmony of the different modes of existence earlier in the same sentence, when he juxtaposes Helvidius' election as quaestor with his selection as son-in-law to Thrasea: *quaestorius adhuc a Paeto Thrasea gener delectus e moribus soceri nihil aeque ac libertatem hausit.* 'He was already a quaestor when he was chosen as son-in-law by Thrasea Paetus, and from his father-in-law's principles/behaviour he drew, above all else, the drink of independence.' Even as the narrative swiftly moves to Helvidius' eager absorption of Thrasea's *mores*, it suggests that Helvidius' own *mores* – both philosophical and political – provided the grounds for Thrasea's selection. And, as we've already seen, Helvidius is said to pursue philosophical studies as a guide to the proper conduct of a political career (*Hist.* 4.5.1). Hence, when we reach the concluding words on Helvidius as citizen, senator, husband, son-in-law, and friend, we could be listening in on Thrasea's judgement of the man as much as the narrator's. This moment of selection, moreover, adumbrates the altercation between Helvidius and Eprius Marcellus in the senate, which is precisely about the *mores* of candidates chosen for a delegation to the emperor (as discussed in chapter four).

The striking reference to Helvidius drinking the spirit of independence from his father-in-law, then, shows the transmission of *mores* through familial connections, shared philosophical interests, and common political commitments, but does not prioritize any one of these conduits over the others. When Tacitus recounts the death of Thrasea in *Annals*, he picks up on some of the principles mentioned in *Histories* as underlying the relationship of the two men, showing us, as it were, the 'source' of Helvidius' practice. But Tacitus also shows us Thrasea deliberately opening the spectacle of his death and the transmission of his principles to someone who is not part of his circle. Thus he signals the relevance and applicability of his message to those who are members of his political community but not of his family or philosophical circle.

Thrasea's death-scene is from the start a social affair: the quaestor detailed by the consul to report the senate's decision finds him with 'a throng of notable men and women' listening to his discourse with Demetrius, a Cynic philosopher. Other named figures present are Helvidius, Thrasea's wife Arria, and the senator Domitius Caecilianus – who pre-empts the quaestor by informally delivering the sentence of death (*Ann.* 16.34).[20] This foregrounds the sense of a community fostered by all the different associations we have already identified, and this sense continues with Thrasea's selection of companions for his final moments: his son-in-law, the philosopher, and the unnamed consul's quaestor. Thrasea's speech, as he severs his veins and sprinkles the blood on the ground, is directed to the quaestor (the text of *Annals* breaks off as he turns to Demetrius).

> 'libamus' inquit 'Iovi liberatori. specta, iuvenis; et omen quidem dii prohibeant, ceterum in ea tempora natus es, quibus firmare animum expediat constantibus exemplis.'
>
> *Ann.* 16.35.1

> He said 'Let us make a drink-offering to Jupiter Liberator. Look on, young man; and may the gods forbid such an omen, but you have been born into these days, when it is needful to fortify your mind with examples of constancy.'

Many phrases echo between this speech and the digression on Helvidius in *Histories*: Helvidius turns to philosophy 'so that he could take up public life fortified (*firmior*) against chance'; the narrator praises him as 'constant (*constans*) in the face of fear'; and above all, the motif associating *libertas* with drinking (*Hist.* 4.5).[21] The narrative of *Annals* thus retrospectively confirms what has been claimed in *Histories* about Thrasea's influence on Helvidius. But just as Thrasea's drink-offering is poured out to Jupiter, not to Helvidius, so his speech is directed not to his son-in-law but to the quaestor. That Thrasea directs the same advice to the quaestor as he presumably directed at other times to Helvidius indicates both the consistency of Thrasea's principles and his willingness to transmit them beyond his immediate network.[22]

When Thrasea invites the quaestor to fortify his mind with *exempla* of constancy,[23] he directs us towards exemplarity, the familiar transmission of values in Roman culture through representations of embodied, temporally situated agents.[24] And there are many ways in which Thrasea constitutes a significant *exemplum* for Tacitus' generation and Tacitus' readers. He stands as a complex ethical model in his moments of both political engagement and refusal to engage; these issues are clearly debated in his own time as well. In the next generation, assessments of Helvidius Priscus are partly bound up in the continued questions of Thrasea as an *exemplum* and whether Helvidius imitates him appropriately.[25] This leads into the more general question of whether Thrasea is a model for imitation at all. Tacitus implicitly presents both sides of the debate, for in *Agricola* he rejects nameless individuals 'who have made a name for themselves through ostentatious death, which is of no use to the state': *plerique . . . in nullum rei publicae usum ambitiosa morte inclaruerunt* (*Agr.* 42.4). Thrasea's final gestures are certainly ostentatious,[26] and his words invite the quaestor (and us) to spectate, but his commentary also implicitly claims that his death is of use to the citizens of his time. Readers have struggled to reconcile these two statements in *Agricola* and *Annals*,[27] but their contradiction helps to build up Thrasea as an *exemplum* by making him a locus of ethical debate.

In thinking about Thrasea as exemplary, scholars have generally focussed on what they can discern of the broader principles underlying his actions and have been divided on whether to ground his principles (and Helvidius') primarily in Stoic philosophy or in political Republicanism (although the two are often conflated as in the *delatores*' discourse).[28] What I have done here, instead, is to concentrate on how Thrasea and Helvidius, like Pliny, build relationships across particular but diverse modes of experience which show the interpenetration of philosophical and political understanding in the way that they live their lives and engage in public debate. This broad-base understanding of their principles or *mores* is important if they are to be seen as persuasive by a diverse audience of senators in their own time, and as fertile models for imitation in the future. Indeed, Thrasea can be placed in a senatorial tradition of effective interventions which goes beyond the Stoic or the 'Republican', and which furthers this sense of him as a non-esoteric *exemplum*. Section 5.2 will consider how some of Thrasea's interventions position him at the heart of a practical political tradition in which any senator can share.

5.2 Genealogies of practice

Thrasea's first appearance in the extant narrative of *Annals* sees him engaged in the debates about when and how to participate in politics which mark his career and afterlife: it also provides an opportunity to supply him with a manifesto on his practice. Given what we have noted already about the performance of ethos and the representation of character in Tacitus' accounts of speech acts, it is surprising, perhaps, that Thrasea is not introduced to the reader through such techniques.[29] Instead, Tacitus uses another formal technique to interrupt the narrative and draw our attention to the episode as significant because of Thrasea's participation.

> *Non referrem vulgarissimum senatus consultum, quo civitati Syracusanorum egredi numerum edendis gladiatoribus finitum permittebatur, nisi Paetus Thrasea contra dixisset praebuissetque materiem obtrectatoribus arguendae sententiae. cur enim, si rem publicam egere libertate senatoria crederet, tam levia consectaretur? quin de bello aut pace, de vectigalibus et legibus, quibusque aliis <res> Romana continetur, suaderet dissuaderetve?*
>
> Ann. 13.49.1–2

I would not have recorded the commonplace decree of senate by which the citizens of Syracuse were permitted to exceed the allotted number of gladiatorial shows, were it not that Thrasea Paetus spoke against the proposal and thereby provided fodder for his detractors to denounce him in their own *sententiae*. So why, they said, if he believed that the commonwealth lacked senatorial independence, did he pursue such trivial matters? Surely he should use his skills of persuasion and dissuasion on subjects such as war and peace, taxes and laws, and everything else which the Roman state comprises?

The year is AD 58, two years after Thrasea's suffect consulship, so his opinion would likely have been delivered quite early in the debate, as is evidenced by the *sententiae* which turn from the issue and attack Thrasea for his attention to trivialities. Tacitus' own reference to the decree as *vulgarissimum* supports this judgement of the issue and recalls Pliny's comment on the senate's discussion of insignificant matters under Domitian: 'so commonplace, so minor ... we consulted on the increase of gladiatorial numbers ... as if speaking on the extension of the empire's borders'. *Tam vulgare tam parvum ... de ampliando numero gladiatorum ... quasi prolatis imperii finibus* (Plin., Pan. 54.3–4).[30] Indeed, Thrasea does not dispute the insignificance of the topic: the debate turns on how the treatment of trivial matters illuminates principles of senatorial behaviour. The speech of the detractors can be imagined as a composite speech or as the development of a succession of scornful asides punctuating the central debate. It presents already some of the motifs of invective against Thrasea which will be used in his final accusation, most particularly the opening comment that he sees a need for senatorial independence and the concluding barb implying that he would enjoy taking over regimen of the empire in place of Nero (*Ann.* 13.49.3). And Cossutianus Capito, collecting the material for the charges against Thrasea in AD 66, recalls this event when calling him 'a man who has ostentatiously spoken in favour or against even the commonplace decrees of the senate': *qui vulgaribus quoque patrum consultis semet fautorem aut adversarium ostenderet* (*Ann.* 16.22.1).[31]

This first half of the 'speech' also implicitly initiates a debate on what politics really is, which is presumed not to include the allotment of gladiatorial games to Syracuse.[32] The detractors imagine state affairs as a set of specific issues, all of which are of the highest significance – war, peace, tax, law – and therefore are generalized to the point almost of abstraction. This is highlighted in the following chapters, where Nero is faced with curbing the abuses of tax collectors, action which necessitates understanding of the complex infrastructure of public tax (*Ann.* 13.50.3) and strategic responses of public information and legal adjustment (*Ann.* 13.51). This narrative seems to undercut the detractors' vague gestures towards 'what comprises the Roman state' and suggests that attention to details is an important feature of political decision-making. This is the line taken also by Thrasea in his response to the criticisms.

> *Thrasea contra, rationem poscentibus amicis, non praesentium ignarum respondebat eius modi consulta corrigere, sed patrum honori dare, ut manifestum fieret magnarum rerum curam non dissimulaturos, qui animum etiam levissimis adverterent.*
>
> Ann. 13.49.4

> Thrasea replied against such points, when his friends asked him for a rationale, saying that when he offered correctives to decrees of this sort he was not unaware of present conditions but that he gave his opinion in honour of the senate, in order to make it quite clear that men who turned their minds even to the most trivial matters would not pass over their concern for important issues.

This 'manifesto', if it is delivered in senate, is prompted by subsequent speakers (*amici*) who support Thrasea by giving him the opportunity to articulate the principles behind his intervention. If it is expressed in private (as *amici* might suggest), it is certainly articulated in terms that would be persuasive to senators, who would most likely hear of it informally.[33] Thrasea defends his *sententia* against the charge that it denotes contempt for public affairs, stating instead that he does honour to the deliberative body by taking all their debates seriously: *patrum honor* – the prestige of an imperial senate – becomes a leitmotif of Thrasea's speeches throughout the narrative. But he most markedly disagrees with his detractors on the subject of the proper response to trivial, small-scale or commonplace issues. He presents the business of politics, instead, as beginning from the fine-grained detail – the *levissima* – as a necessary prelude to addressing big issues. The appropriate attitude of the senator is a practised attentiveness – turning his mind consciously towards small details – so that when important questions of policy are posed, he has already cultivated an appropriate ethos of care and made it habitual. The phrase *magnarum rerum cura* bears slight resonances of the *rei publicae cura* which Tacitus in *Histories* regards as the essential virtue of a statesman.[34] A stronger resonance with this passage is *Annals*' digression on historical writing, where Tacitus advises the reader to take care in dismissing what seem to be trivial episodes in his narrative.[35]

Pleraque eorum quae rettuli quaeque referam parva forsitan et levia memoratu videri non nescius sum ... non tamen sine usu fuerit introspicere illa primo aspectu levia, ex quis magnarum saepe rerum motus oriuntur.

Ann. 4.32.1, 2

Very many of the events which I have recorded and which I will record perhaps seem minor and trivial to recollect, as I am well aware ... but it will be of some use to have scrutinized those things which at first glance are trivial, but from which often the movement of significant events arises.[36]

Precisely this principle determines Tacitus' inclusion of the debate about Syracusan gladiatorial games, which he introduces as a vulgar topic unworthy of record except for Thrasea's intervention. The 'significant event' arising from this episode might be the eventual condemnation and death of Thrasea, but it may also be the manifesto in which the recommended senatorial practice of attention to detail corresponds to the best practice of the historian. But there is a difference: whereas the historian scrutinizes trivial matters in order to discern their place in the emergence of significant historical events, the politician gives his attention to trivial issues in order to shape his own practice of attentiveness and persuasion so as to be ready when more important debates arise. Despite this manifesto, Thrasea does not make many appearances in the Neronian narrative of the *Annals*: Tacitus omits any mention of his suffect consulship in his account of AD 56 (*Ann.* 13.25–30) and leaves out Thrasea's involvement in the 'tenacious accusation' which charged Cossutianus Capito with extortion in AD 57 (*Ann.* 13.33.2).[37] The episodes where Thrasea is mentioned, moreover, are all presented in such a way as to signal the further symbolic significance of his interventions, so that they do not seem trivial to the reader. Tacitus, therefore, tells us about the principle of attention to everyday issues in senate but does not really show it, perhaps because he would have to repeatedly excuse such inclusions, as he does at *Ann.* 13.49. It is also the case that we can look to earlier in the narrative to see the kind of practised attentiveness on which Thrasea might draw.

In the Tiberian narrative a prominent example is the senior consular Asinius Gallus, whose energetic activity as a senator – hinted at in Augustus' assessment of him as *avidus et minor* (*Ann.* 1.13.2), or 'eager, but a lesser man' – is above all indicated by the number of times he intervenes in the accounts of senatorial business.[38] Gallus is the first senator to deliver a *sententia* in *Annals*, proposing notable funeral honours for Augustus (*Ann.* 1.8.3); he is also prominent in the debate after the funeral, at which Tiberius repeatedly refuses to assume the role of emperor (*Ann.* 1.12.2–3). As the narrative progresses, the variety of issues on which Gallus speaks becomes a distinctive feature and makes him a possible illustration of Thrasea's principle that a senator should make all issues his concern. Gallus speaks up on problems with the Tiber flooding, on disorderly theatre-actors, and on the revival of sumptuary laws (*Ann.* 1.76, 77; 2.33).[39] He participates in sentencing those found guilty in the senatorial court: Scribonius Libo Drusus, Sosia Galla, and Vibius Crispus (*Ann.* 2.32; 4.20, 30) Repeatedly, his proposals and questions put Tiberius under pressure to articulate details of how his power impinges on the senate and the elite (*Ann.* 1.12; 2.35, 36; 4.71). The frequency and diversity of Gallus' interventions also point to the different levels at which he engages in his political culture, which cannot be reduced to a simple position of complicity with or opposition to imperial power.[40] In some of these episodes Gallus seems concerned most of all with projecting his own authority, as when he recommends consultation of the Sibylline books, probably advertising his experience as a quindecemvir (*Ann.* 1.76.1).[41] In other episodes, his disagreements with other senators may denote competition, as when Tacitus implies that Gallus' role as the voice of senatorial independence has been usurped by Cn. Piso (*Ann.* 2.35.2). Or such competition might mask senators' behind-the-scenes management of a debate towards a desired agreement, as I have suggested could be the case in the trial of Sosia Galla (*Ann.* 4.20.1).[42] Emphatically Gallus is associated with the principle of safeguarding a senator's right to speak,[43] which he exercises in most areas falling under the purview of the imperial senate: laws; the exercise of justice; religion; civic order and the safety of the state; regulation of the senate and its relationship with the ruler. In the process he too negotiates between deleterious and productive modes of speech: he attempts to balance advice with praise of the ruler (*Ann.* 1.12.3), and twice his proposals for sentencing are associated with flattery (*Ann.* 2.32.2; 4.20.2). When Tacitus provides the poignant obituary for Gallus after three years' imprisonment awaiting trial, his final cadence reflects on the indignity of neglecting this 'elder consular, the parent of so many consulars', *consulari seni, tot consularium parenti* (*Ann.* 6.23.1).[44] Gallus is far from an idealized figure in the narrative, then, but both his restless energy and his final epitaph identify senatorial dignity, its maintenance and its generation, as his central concern. What he exemplifies in practice illustrates what Thrasea outlines in his manifesto: that constant exercise of senatorial speech, even on minor issues, ensures the honour of the imperial senate.

What this brief overview of Gallus illustrates is what can be gained from drawing out repetitions of senatorial practice across the narrative, perhaps to understand how functional imitation might operate below the threshold of exemplary principles or characters. Gallus' principles are not those of Thrasea; indeed, in Dio's history Gallus is likened to Helvidius Priscus because each is seen as crudely or improperly imitating the *parrhesia* of his father or father-in-law.[45] When the narrative presents senatorial action in ways that suggest repetition, it serves as a counterpart to such conscious imitation of predecessors. Narrative repetition can imply that senators explicitly imitated the strategic interventions of contemporaries or predecessors, or it can substitute itself for such imitation, affording to the reader a sense that traditional senatorial skills are being passed on. This places on the reader the responsibility for conjecturing or constructing a genealogy in which they too might participate.

The most pointed narrative repetition which invites us to build a genealogy is Thrasea's next senatorial intervention, where he replays the speech of Marcus Lepidus in the case of Clutorius Priscus. I examined these two speeches in chapter three: Lepidus, in the first extensive senatorial speech of *Annals*, argues (unsuccessfully) against the death penalty for Clutorius, charged with the composition of 'offensive' poetry. As I argued there, Lepidus' speech revitalizes the concept of the senatorial judge, which becomes the basis for a relationship between senator and ruler organized around a shared sense of judicial responsibility. Just as Lepidus' speech opens out a 'space for opinion' (*locus sententiae*, *Ann.* 3.50.1) which allows senatorial clemency to negotiate with imperial pity, so Thrasea lays claim to public clemency as available to a senate operating under an exceptional ruler (*Ann.* 14.48.3–4). Each speech implicitly encourages senatorial initiative and provides sufficient coherence with existing imperial ideology to attract the ruler's approval.

Scholars examining the parallels and divergences between these two accounts have considered what Tacitus intends to convey about changes to the imperial senate and the system of the Principate over time. Roland Mayer sees this purely in terms of a contrast between the two emperors.[46] Judith Ginsburg points to how the narrative of Thrasea's intervention shows the impossibility of behaving like Lepidus in the polarized world of Nero.[47] Thomas Strunk similarly sees this episode as highlighting the extremism of the Neronian regime, but argues that the comparison with Lepidus is designed to build up the sense of Thrasea as both moderate and statesmanlike.[48] Eleanor Cowan sees the two episodes as exploring a long-standing debate about the principles underlying judgement and especially punishment. While Lepidus' arguments are situated between *clementia* and *severitas*, by Thrasea's time the value of *severitas* has become debased as *saevitia*.[49] These insightful analyses for the most part locate the experience of repetition at the level of the narrative, where the reader can reflect on the process of historical change. But we could also see the narrative repetition as a representation of transmission, of practice passed on across the generations. That is to say, while there is nothing in the text to suggest that Thrasea is consciously imitating Lepidus, the way in which the whole episode is narrated as a repetition points to the possibility of such imitation. This invites us to consider, beneath the surface of the narrative, an invisible process of transmitting practices.

Let us turn to the similarities between Lepidus' speech and Thrasea's, to uncover the possible modes of transmission to which the narrative gestures. As we saw in chapter three, Lepidus' speech in this case is accorded considerable prominence by Tacitus, but it would also have been a well-known case for having given rise to the procedure of placing a moratorium of nine days on decrees of capital punishment.[50] It is therefore likely to have been recalled or referred to whenever this precedent was cited. The speech, being a *sententia* in a judicial context, incorporates forensic elements into its deliberative structure, but it is the speech of a *iudex*, not an advocate. Since imperial senators would have needed to master arguments of this sort in their new judicial role, there may well have circulated collections of effective judiciary *sententiae* or even compilations of appropriate *topoi*. Certainly Thrasea's speech appears to follow the formula laid down by Lepidus in such a way that we can practically condense the parallels between the two episodes as a set of topical instructions:

1. Do not express any approbation of the defendant;

> **Lepidus** 'with his impious voice Clutorius Priscus has polluted his own mind, and the ears of others'.
>
> *Ann.* 3.50.1

Thrasea 'very fiercely abusing Antistius ...'.

Ann. 14.48.3

2. Praise the ruler and the senate in such a way as to challenge them to match that praise;

Lepidus 'often I have heard our princeps bemoaning the fact that someone has taken his own life, and pre-empted the ruler's mercy'.

Ann. 3.50.2

Thrasea 'this should be the decision of a senate operating under an exceptional ruler, and bound by no constraints'.

Ann. 4.48.3

3. Insist upon the letter of the law;

Lepidus 'but let him depart from the city, give up his property, and be barred from fire and water; this I propose as if he were being tried under the laws for *maiestas*'.[51]

Ann. 3.50.4

Thrasea 'the executioner and noose have long since been abolished, and punishments have been set down by laws through which punishments can be decreed which do not involve excessive cruelty on the part of the judges'.

Ann. 14.48.4

The narrative repetition from this perspective serves as an oblique representation of senatorial traditions passed on through oral tradition and the *acta senatus*, perhaps through handbooks, certainly through letters, to be redeployed in suitable situations.

Thrasea and Lepidus share points of principle as well: each speech contributes to a political world in which the senate and ruler share the exercise of proper judgement; each speaker builds up the authority of the senate through its judicial role. Ethically they are also congruent: where Lepidus is 'great and wise' (*Ann.* 4.20.2), Thrasea is 'virtue itself' (*Ann.* 16.21.1). The parallel episodes in which they appear, however, also point to a practice of transmission in which the senators may have actively participated. My focus on the tactics with which they operate follows the lead given by Thrasea himself (and Tacitus) at the start of this section, to look closely at the seemingly more trivial details of senatorial practice involved in their political interventions. These details underpin their efficacy just as their principles of senatorial honour and the exercise of justice inform their practice of carefully deploying procedure, citing law, and above all offering their *sententiae* on whatever comes before the senate. The central argument of this section has been that Tacitus' narratives present this sort of 'functional imitation' as an important part of senatorial efficacy. My argument works against readings of Thrasea Paetus which see him as heroically upholding an unrealizable ideal. Instead, we should situate him within a tradition of *mores* where his practices are as significant as his principles.

5.3 Future communities

In chapter four we considered how the performance of ethos merged into the narrative representation of character in such a way as to bring together speaker, audience, and reader. Internal audience and reader are united – or compete – in exercising critical judgement of the speaker and thereby communally reaffirming – or correctively reinstating – civic values. This is part of what I have called Tacitus' 'critical archive', but an archive needs to be accessible to future users and Tacitus' representation of transmission plays an important role in this. His narratives show us the transmission of *mores* – whether values or behavioural practices – across four generations of senators, although the 'great divide' of fifteen years in the reign of Domitian is signalled at the start of *Agricola* as a period in which speech and knowledge were almost lost (*Agr.* 3.2). This lends a sense of urgency to the picture Tacitus gives elsewhere of the networks of senatorial action disseminating principles and tactics through diverse connections. It explains why *Agricola* ends by turning away from Tacitus' family and towards you, the future reader (as we saw in section 5.1). As I've suggested in section 5.2, the narrative's representation of transmission invites the reader's participation and suggests once again that the effects of speech extend beyond the speaker's immediate intention – as the immediate failure but far-reaching influence of Lepidus' speech for Clutorius can illustrate. In this section, I will examine how Tacitus takes the idea of transmission and long-term or delayed efficacy and extends it beyond the boundaries of his narrative into his own time. He achieves this most significantly with *Histories* 4 by exploiting the parallels between the senators' hounding of the *delatores* in AD 70 and Pliny's attempted censure of Publicius Certus for the same reasons in AD 93. I will pursue this further by returning to Pliny's careful self-positioning as a fourth-generation member of Thrasea's circle, as we saw in section 5.1. The resonances between Pliny's account of his own senatorial practice and Tacitus' representation of Helvidius Priscus suggest a shared sense of their pivotal role in condensing past political actions and sending them into the future.

We have examined some of the episodes in *Histories* 4 in previous chapters: the *adulatio* of the new Emperor Vespasian and his generals which is punctured by Helvidius Priscus' performance of true honorific speech (*Hist.* 4.4.3, examined chapter three); Helvidius' proposal at the same meeting for a new ethically grounded method of selecting senatorial delegates to greet the emperor, and the ensuing altercation with Eprius Marcellus (*Hist.* 4.6.3–8.5, chapter four); at the next meeting, the combined initiative of a new oath designed to isolate those who had previously gained from prosecuting fellow citizens (*Hist.* 4.41, chapter three); in the ensuing disorder, Vipstanus Messalla's attempted defence of his half-brother Aquilius Regulus; and Curtius Montanus' furious invective against the same man (*Hist.* 4.42, chapters three and four). In the midst of these interventions are other items of senate business in which Helvidius and other senators are active: at the first meeting, Helvidius' second *sententia* (although it is narrated last) is that the Capitol should be restored at public expense, with the help of the emperor (*Hist.* 4.9.2, deferred from *Hist.* 4.4.2); after the debate on how to choose the delegates, a report on public finances prompts Helvidius to propose that the senate, not the emperor, should decide spending limits, a *sententia* which enables him to promote once more the concept of senatorial judgement (*arbitrium senatus*, *Hist.* 4.9.1); the significance that Tacitus accords to Helvidius' quarrel with Marcellus is contextualized with the final items of business, when Musonius Rufus initiates a charge against Publius Celer for his part in the prosecution of Barea Soranus (*Hist.* 4.10). This is explicitly seen as emblematic of the ongoing feud with Marcellus, especially as Soranus was charged and convicted at the same trial as Thrasea (*Ann.* 16.30–33).[52] At the next meeting, after restoring honours to Galba and removing the more egregious Neronian festivals, the senate tries and convicts Publius Celer, an act seen as appeasing the ghost of Soranus.

Again, this is seen as an emblematic moment and is followed up not by Helvidius this time but by Iunius Mauricus (Pliny's friend and Rusticus' brother), who seeks access to Nero's archives in order to discover who initiated the prosecutions of his reign (*Hist.* 4.40.3). Mauricus is perhaps responding to Eprius Marcellus' attempt in the previous meeting to shift blame for the trials onto the dead emperor. His request certainly probes the question of accountability and of the extent and limits of the *delator*'s agency. Since the princeps is not available (or willing) to release this information, the senate has recourse to an alternative generation of truth in the form of the inaugurating oath. Finally, after Curtius Montanus' attack on Regulus, Helvidius makes a final attempt against Eprius Marcellus by delivering a speech in praise of Cluvius Rufus for having never used his *eloquentia* to put another subject in danger. Gradually Helvidius moves to the subject of Marcellus and comes close to driving him and Vibius Crispus from the senate (*Hist.* 4.43).

This overview of two senate meetings is important because so many of the items are inter-related, illustrating how a single senator or a group of senators repeatedly approach a central issue from different angles and with different strategies, but also build on and respond to previous decisions and declarations. The network of senators affected by the trial of Soranus and Thrasea are prominent in these meetings, giving the impression of collaborating on the issue of the *delatores*, but each contributing according to his strengths and status. Helvidius is by far the most prominent, perhaps because of his status as praetor designate which, as I remarked in chapter three, places him first after all the consulars in the speaking order and thus enables him to initiate new ideas before debates have entirely petered out. Curtius Montanus (if it is the younger of that name)[53] is a junior senator and offers only a single *sententia* before delivering his invective,[54] the ferocity of which may be seen as a sign of relative youth or as congruent with the poetic activity for which he was indicted in AD 66.[55] Mauricus, also probably quite junior, makes the boldest approach by tackling directly the emperor's implication in prosecutions; this is in keeping with the outspokenness with which he is characterized in Pliny's letters.[56] The central and most striking act, however, is given to no individual author: the senate as a collective initiates and administers the oath. It is, nevertheless, an initiative that builds from the preceding successful trial of Celer and from Mauricus' failure to access imperial information about the *delatores*.

The second important point to note about these meetings, however, is how they are framed – and predominantly received – as both practical and moral failures on the part of the senate. Tacitus concludes the narrative of each meeting by referring to proceedings as *discordia*, ironically suggesting a continuation within the curia of the civil war that has just concluded in the empire: *tali rerum statu, cum discordia inter patres* ... (*Hist.* 4.11.1). 'In such a state of affairs, when there was discord in the senate ...'; *cum glisceret certamen, hinc multi bonique, inde pauci et validi pertinacibus odiis tenderent, consumptus per discordiam dies* (*Hist.* 4.43.2). 'As the conflict intensified, on the one side there was a majority of good men, on the other side a minority vigorously defending themselves, each maintaining deep-seated hatred towards the other, and the day was spent in discord.' The negative connotations of *discordia* are taken to denote a generally poor assessment of the senate's activity here, summed up by Elizabeth Keitel as 'futile wrangling'.[57] The sense of futility is supported by Tacitus' comment on the third senate meeting, where calls for amnesty from Domitian and Licinius Mucianus induce the senate to abandon the issue they have so passionately taken up: *patres coeptatam libertatem, postquam obviam itum, omisere* (*Hist.* 4.44.1). 'The senators gave up the independence they had initiated, after it was obstructed.' Together with the comments about discord, this statement is taken to signal a senate which deserves indictment both for the actions they took up and for relinquishing them. Scholarly judgement on the senate here seems to match the judgement on Helvidius Priscus in Galba's reign, when he initiated and then dropped charges against Eprius Marcellus, earning reproaches for lack of *constantia* (*Hist.* 4.6.2).[58]

These episodes therefore press the question of efficacy which has been asked throughout this book: the framing narrative points towards failure and futility, but the accounts are suffused with a sense of energy and of hope for a new future as well as with details which show us the senators' rhetorical skill, collaborative strengths, and tactical canniness. Building on the idea of transmission which I have already explored with the Lepidus–Thrasea parallel in section 5.2, I want to consider how *Histories* 4 is constructed so as to appear as a transmission of the principles, passions, and skills of the speakers into Tacitus' own time. Tacitus achieves this by orienting these episodes towards events in the time of Nerva, which are presented as shaped by these earlier initiatives *and* as redeeming these earlier failures. This becomes evident when we read Tacitus' narrative alongside Pliny's accounts of his political activities: his letter detailing the attempted censure of Publicius Certus, for his part in the downfall of the younger Helvidius, occupies the high point in his final book and is explicitly concerned with redemption. It narrates the events which led him to deliver a speech (alluded to elsewhere in the letters) 'on the vindication of Helvidius' (*de Helvidi ultione*) – this is the son of the Helvidius Priscus in Tacitus' narrative. This speech represents another, perhaps the most significant moment in Pliny's ongoing grafting of himself onto the familial network of the Helvidii and their kin, as we saw in section 5.1. But Pliny makes it clear that he does not simply act as a friend of the family; the case is in the public interest because of the *indignitas* suffered by Helvidius during his trial (Plin., *Ep.* 9.13.3). Pliny is vague about what exactly this *indignitas* comprises, whether Certus was the prosecutor of Helvidius, whether he delivered some stinging invective in the course of the trial or judgement, or even if he physically assaulted the defendant. Instead, he recounts Certus' action so that it appears as an assault upon senatorial dignity, rank, and the judicial process itself: *in senatu senator senatori, praetorius consulari, reo iudex manus intulisset* (Plin., *Ep.* 9.13.2). 'In the senate, a senator towards another senator, one of praetorian rank upon a consular, a judge laid hands upon a defendant.' The redemption of the younger Helvidius is therefore tied from the outset to the redemption of the senate's honour after the debasements it has suffered under Domitian.

Pliny's letter thus foregrounds how his action, like those of the elder Helvidius and his colleagues, is deliberately programmatic; each senator pursues a particular case with an eye to the bigger questions it raises. Both take action at the start of a new regime, but Pliny self-consciously chooses to wait until the second year of Nerva's reign to avoid association with what he represents as the irrational violence and anger (*impetus, ira*) of the earliest retaliatory accusations (Plin., *Ep.* 9.13.4). This may provide another context for Tacitus' references to the *discordia* of the senate in AD 70 and it suggests that Tacitus is raising the question of whether the Flavian senators acted too soon.[59] The roundabout way in which Pliny brings charges against Certus also bears comparison with the different tactics against the *delatores* that we have seen adopted in *Histories* 4. Pliny does not bring an indictment against Certus as a preliminary to the formal accusation, along the lines of the prosecution procedure that we examined in chapter two. Instead he makes use of the senatorial privilege of addressing the senate at the start of the meeting and introduces the charge against Certus without naming him (*crimen attingere*, Plin., *Ep.* 9.13.7). Pliny emphasizes the absence of the name by omitting it also from his narrative until Certus is named by his supporters (a point to which I will return); this highlights the difference between a standard indictment – *nomen deferre* – and Pliny's unorthodox approach. After introducing the charge, Pliny is commanded to defer the rest of his speech until it is his turn for speaking; as he is only of praetorian standing, this takes place after several senior senators have had a chance to make their positions known. The climax of the event, then, is Pliny's *sententia* in its proper place, which he presents as effecting a complete reversal in attitude among the senators who had shouted down his first address, warned him in private of the consequences of his actions, and formally spoken against his proposal. A vote in favour of bringing Certus to trial appears to be passed, but the main outcome of the speech, in Pliny's view and in the senate's, is the restoration of senatorial dignity and integrity. Pliny is congratulated by other senators: *quod intermissum iam diu morem in publicum consulendi ... reduxissem; quod denique senatum invidia liberassem ... quod severus in ceteros senatoribus solis dissimulatione quasi mutua parceret* (Plin., *Ep.* 9.13.21). 'Because I had restored the long-lapsed practice of consulting the senate on matters of public interest ... because I had released the senate from the resentment it earned for its severity against other ranks while it passed over senators in shared collusion.' As at the beginning of the account, Pliny therefore redirects the reader's attention away from the immediate consequences and to the wider communal effects of his speech.

The letter, then, is about redemption, but it also performs a sort of redemption, recasting a limited action as a crowning success by emphasizing symbolic victory. Pliny concedes in the final paragraphs that Nerva did not act on the senate's desire for a trial – another glimpse of the distributed initiative and agency in imperial prosecutions – but nevertheless declares 'I achieved what I had set out to do' (Plin., *Ep.* 9.13.22). Certus loses his chance at the consulship and his place in the treasury, the latter of which Pliny characterizes as a *praemium*, suggesting that Domitian had awarded Certus the position for his part in the trial of the younger Helvidius. Indeed Pliny here provides the only quotation from the concluding part of his speech: '*Reddat praemium sub optimo principe, quod a pessimo accepit'* (Plin., *Ep.* 9.13.23). 'Let him return that reward, which he received from the worst of rulers, to the best of rulers.'

There are, of course, details behind Pliny's letter which we can glimpse or conjecture and which would not cast him in so unequivocally heroic a light. He phrases Certus' demotion from the treasury very delicately and omits to mention that he himself succeeded to the position, which effectively secured his place on the consular list. This matches his professed intention at the outset of the letter to 'advance himself' as well as to vindicate Helvidius (Plin., *Ep.* 9.13.2). It also brings Pliny's actions uncomfortably close to that of a *delator* – one who has gained reward or honour from the harm done to a fellow citizen, as the Flavian senators express it in their oath.[60] One of the ways Pliny gets past this difficult similarity is the genealogy in which he places his action; by representing it as vengeance for the younger Helvidius, he can situate it in a chain of vindications going back to Helvidius Priscus' repeated attempts at *ultio* for Thrasea Paetus. Indeed, his expressed motivations for taking up the case against Certus are reminiscent of Thrasea's advice which Pliny quotes in another letter: *suscipiendas esse causas aut amicorum aut destitutas aut ad exemplum pertinentes* (Plin., *Ep.* 6.29.1). 'Cases should be taken up when they involve our friends, when they have no other support, or when they have an exemplary function.' By seeming to follow Thrasea's advice and by soliciting the association of Helvidius' surviving female relatives, Pliny acquires the support of the past for his project.

The interpenetration of past and present is particularly acute between these two episodes because we access them through two narratives which are produced around the same time, by two authors who not only exchange written work but are engaged in face-to-face collaborations. It is generally assumed that *Histories* was published around AD 110, which is now considered to be about the time that Pliny compiled the ninth book of *Epistles*.[61] But this would not have been the first time each author was aware of what the other was writing. Tacitus almost certainly witnessed Pliny's delivery of *de Helvidi ultione*; it was the year of his suffect consulship (was he even the consul who austerely set Pliny to speak in the usual order?). He would very likely also have read the published speech, perhaps even an early draft of the published version, and possibly also the original letter which becomes *Epistles* 9.13. For his part, Pliny was providing material for Tacitus' historical research and must have been attending recitations of his work, if not reading drafts.[62] The resonances between *Histories* 4 and

Epistles 9.13 thus dialogically work over issues about settling the past and opening up the future. Christopher Whitton has identified the relationship as one of 'reciprocity', since both writers are concerned to project a revitalized role for the senatorial speaker.[63] We could add that Tacitus presents a past which chimes in with Pliny's use of the past, because Pliny's narrative of redemption enables Tacitus to represent the Flavian senate's actions as simultaneously unsuccessful (in their own time) and efficacious (in the future). The repeated failures at the beginning of the Flavian regime are oriented towards their future realization in the era of Nerva and Trajan, prompting the reader to reflect on other potential realizations of what they find in Tacitus' archive.

As we've already seen, Helvidius in Galba's reign abandoned his action against Eprius Marcellus, which is paralleled with the Flavian senate giving up their attempt to expel senators who evade the new oath. Tacitus highlights the parallel with the verb *omitto: ea ultio ... omisit Priscus, variis ... sermonibus moderationem laudantium aut constantiam requirentium* (*Hist.* 4.6.1–2). 'Priscus gave up that vengeance, prompting diverse responses from those who praised his moderation or those who asked where his *constantia* had gone.' *Patres coeptatam libertatem ... omisere* (*Hist.* 4.44.1). 'The senators gave up the independence they had initiated ...' This is answered by the joyous expression of redemption in Pliny's letter, when he is congratulated for restoring a long suspended senatorial practice (*intermissum morem*) and for liberating the senate from its poor public reputation (*invidia liberassem*) (Plin., *Ep.* 9.13.21). The *ultio* that was given up appears, in the light of the present, to have merely been suspended for a time; senatorial *libertas* is regained in a tamer context (though both are concerned with the senate's capacity to regulate itself). The achievement of Pliny's speech, moreover, vindicates the principle of *constantia* which he maintains throughout the episode and which he mentions as a key factor in his persuasiveness with the senate (Plin., *Ep.* 9.13.18). Thus his redemption of the younger Helvidius and of the senate expands to encompass also the elder Helvidius Priscus and the Flavian senate.

But the orientation of *Histories* 4 also implies that the victories of the future cannot come about without the actions of the past. The detailed accounts of senatorial business in that book showcase a wide range of tactics through which to broach the problem of the *delatores*. If we focus simply on Helvidius Priscus, we have already seen how he deploys his position in the order of speaking and opportunistically seizes on the matter of the senatorial delegation to Vespasian in the first meeting. His final attempt against Marcellus, where he begins his speech with praise of Cluvius Rufus, may also illustrate the technique of capitalizing on other successful interventions. Helvidius has just witnessed the very positive hearing given to Vipstanus Messalla as he pleads for Regulus – a scene we examined in chapter four – which is superseded by the enthusiastic reception of Montanus' invective. Helvidius' speech in turn may attempt to replicate that succession of effects, moving the audience to pleasurable shared approbation of Cluvius only to fire them up more vehemently against Marcellus. The primary appeal of Helvidius Priscus as an example to the future continues to rest with his principles, but his tactical approach also repays attention. Pliny demonstrates considerably greater agility with his use of senatorial privilege to introduce his case in a way that attracts the greatest attention. His omission of Certus' name not only avoids the charge of impropriety but also draws the senate collectively into the act of charging Certus when his supporters, seeking to defend him, have to name him as the defendant. Pliny thus also reverses the roles of accuser and advocate by requiring the advocates to initiate the charges, while he, speaking now in his 'proper' place, only has to respond to what has already been said by others. Pliny's successful negotiation of procedure, which enables him to reap the benefits of speaking both first and much later, is highlighted by its contrast with the clumsiness of Fabricius Veiento's speech. He also attempts to speak for a second time, supported by a tribune but ignored by the consul, who calls for a division: Veiento is left still trying to speak, an ignominious situation which underscores Pliny's success.

The consciousness that tactics and procedural technique as well as attentiveness to the changing mood of the senate are valuable skills worth passing on is implicit in the framing of Pliny's letter. An earlier letter (Plin., *Ep.* 8.14) showed Pliny's awareness that many aspects of political life were to be learned from attending and witnessing the senate;[64] where that letter looks back to the recent past and mourns the loss of senatorial skills in Domitian's reign, this letter looks forward and transmits to the future Pliny's dexterous management of the session. That future is the young addressee: Ummidius Quadratus, later to be consul in AD 118 and a kinsman of the Emperor Hadrian.[65] Other letters attest to Quadratus' studious interest in rhetoric and Pliny's care for his education; it is to Quadratus that Pliny passes on Thrasea's injunctions on when to take up a case, thereby also recruiting Quadratus into the fifth generation of this senatorial network. *Epistle* 9.13 demonstrates also, I think, Quadratus' astute recognition that *eloquentia* is only one part of what makes a senatorial speech politically effective.

> *Quanto studiosius intentiusque legisti libros quos de Helvidi ultione composui, tanto impensius postulas, ut perscribam tibi quaeque extra libros quaeque circa libros, totum denique ordinem rei cui per aetatem non interfuisti.*
> Plin., *Ep.* 9.13.1

> The more eagerly and attentively you read my speech on the avenging of Helvidius, the more importunately you demand that I write out in full for you what took place beyond the speech, and around the speech, in short the whole order of events which you did not witness because of your youth.

Pliny refers jokingly to this request at the end of the letter: 'you now have a letter as long as the speech you have read ... but that is your own fault, since you were not content with the speech' (Plin., *Ep.* 9.13.26). But Pliny is as aware as Quadratus that the speech is not the whole story and that what was *extra libros* and *circa libros* – Pliny's performance of ethos, his orchestration of procedure, and the moving of the senate from passionate opposition to enthusiastic support – is a politically significant context and a profitable object lesson in the behavioural practices of an effective imperial senator. It is no coincidence that, in his next letter, he addresses Tacitus one last time,[66] declaring his confidence that both writers will be remembered 'for our engagement, our hard work, and our regard for the future': *studio et labore et reverentia posterorum* (Plin., *Ep.* 9.14).

We began this chapter with Tacitus' declaration that *mores* are the true medium for representing and thereby transmitting virtue. By tracing the social networks of imperial senators in Tacitus' and Pliny's narratives, I have attempted to show the diverse modes through which *mores* are cultivated and shared. Through this it is possible to see how Tacitus' declaration does not simply express an ideal but points to a framework, outlined across his narratives, for imitating and adapting effective practices. While Tacitus' accounts of specific debates press home Thrasea Paetus' message to be fully engaged in the politics of your time, the wider temporal scope of his historical writing reminds us that the effects of political speech may not be fully felt until later times.

Conclusion: *sententia*

It will seem strange to the reader, perhaps, that I have not included some of the most distinctive speech acts of Tacitus' narratives, such as Cremutius Cordus' extended defence of historiography before his work was banned and burned (*Ann.* 4.34–35).[1] Or, at the other end of the scale, Cn. Piso's single question – on the order of speaking – which stopped Tiberius in his tracks (*Ann.* 1.74.5–6). With this selective study of senatorial speech, however, I hope to have uncovered the different levels at which they do political work, whether disseminating conceptual visions of the imperial world or negotiating specific gains at the procedural level. Certainly the process of researching this has opened my eyes to the range of powerplay and gamesmanship that Tacitus' (and Pliny's) senators have at their command. No less has it exposed for me the way even the most functional speech act plays its part in structuring what is thinkable and sayable in imperial politics.

What of the 'real power' which frames and limits all of this senatorial activity? I began this project in a spirit of frustration at the gestures made towards large nebulous concepts such as 'real power', 'freedom', and 'Republicanism' when discussing the world of imperial senators. These seemed to me to disregard both the micro-engagements that we encounter in ancient narratives and the generations of scholars on imperial politics who have carefully excavated the precise applications of such concepts in various Roman discourses. As I investigated where 'real power' might be experienced as constraint by imperial subjects, I became increasingly aware that these constraints often emerged from discourses which were not *exclusively* controlled by emperors and other agents of imperial power. This sense of the power of discourses is what I have tried to convey by speaking of the political worlds which emerge from modes of speech and the distributed agency of flattery, *delatio*, and the discourses which oppose them.

Tacitus' pessimism is notorious, yet his turn to history cannot have been simply a despairing turn away from oratory. Just as the opening of *Agricola* declares its commitment as 'transmitting to posterity': *posteris tradere* (*Agr.* 1.1), so the preface to *Histories* reinstates 'care for posterity' (*cura posteritatis, Hist.* 1.1.1) as a central concern of the historian. The sense that Tacitus' narratives pass on practical political knowledge receives support not only from the traditional concept of ancient historical writing but also from Tacitus' reception in early modern Europe, where his sententious statements were excerpted and repackaged as insights ready for contemporary application.[2] In recent years Roman historiography has recovered some of its standing as serious political thought,[3] and we begin to discern the creativity and interpretative flexibility of the early modern excerpters who were not simply 'quoting Tacitus out of context'.[4] One way forward, as this study suggests, is to return to the Tacitean *sententia* – both Tacitus' epigrammatic interventions and the senatorial expressions of opinion contained in his work – and to explore fully how it constitutes a *sententia*: a way of experiencing the world and conveying that experience so as to shape the experiences of others. While Tacitus celebrates a new era in which 'you can feel what you want, and say what you feel (*sentias*)', his narratives explore the consequences of speech for the political worlds that we pass on to others.

Notes

Introduction

1. The Tacitean texts are from Heinz Heubner, *P. Cornelius Tacitus: Historiarum Libri* (Stuttgart: B. G. Teubner, 1978); Heinz Heubner, *P. Cornelius Tacitus: Dialogus de Oratoribus* (Stuttgart: B. G. Teubner, 1983); and Heinz Heubner, *P. Cornelius Tacitus: Annales* (Stuttgart: B. G. Teubner, 1983); Also from A. J. Woodman, *Agricola* (Cambridge: Cambridge University Press, 2014). All translations, unless indicated otherwise, are my own.
2. I will examine Lepidus' action more closely in chapter four.
3. Michel Foucault, *The Courage of the Truth (The Government of Self and Others II): Lectures at the Collège de France, 1983–1984* (Basingstoke: Palgrave-Macmillan, 2011); Richard Alston, 'Foucault's Empire of the Free', *Foucault Studies* 22 (2017): 94–112.
4. Andrew Wallace-Hadrill, *Rome's Cultural Revolution* (Cambridge: Cambridge University Press, 2008), 213–312; cf. Shreyaa Bhatt, 'The Augustan Principate and the Emergence of Biopolitics: A Comparative Historical Perspective', *Foucault Studies* 22 (2017): 72–93.
5. Michel Foucault, 'Truth and Power', in *Power/Knowledge: Selected Interviews and Other Writings, 1972–1977* (Brighton: Harvester Press, 1980), 131.
6. For irony in Tacitus, see Ellen O'Gorman, *Irony and Misreading in the Annals of Tacitus* (Cambridge: Cambridge University Press, 2000). I am especially grateful to Amy Russell and Andrew Wallace-Hadrill for talking through these issues with me.
7. Bhatt, 'The Augustan Principate and the Emergence of Biopolitics', 88–91; Hannah Cornwell, *Pax and the Politics of Peace: Republic to Principate* (Oxford: Oxford University Press, 2017).
8. Holly Haynes, *The History of Make-Believe: Tacitus on Imperial Rome* (Berkeley, CA: University of California Press, 2003) explores the production of truth in *Histories* from a different theoretical perspective.
9. Cf. Dean Hammer, 'Foucault, Sovereignty, and Governmentality in the Roman Republic', *Foucault Studies* 22 (2017): 49–71, on how 'disciplines of ownership' structure differentials of power in the Republican period. On the princeps as

extra-senatorial, see Andrew Wallace-Hadrill, 'Roman Arches and Greek Honours: The Language of Power at Rome', *Proceedings of the Cambridge Philological Society* 36 (1990): 168.

10 For the early modern development of this idea, see Peter S. Donaldson, *Machiavelli and Mystery of State* (Cambridge: Cambridge University Press, 1988), 111–40. For the modern implications, see Mark Neocleous, *Imagining the State* (Maidenhead: Open University Press, 2003), 61–71. On the consequences of this for Tacitus' historical subjectivity, see Olivier Devillers, 'The Concentration of Power and Writing History: Forms of Historical Persuasion in the *Histories* (1.1–49)', in *A Companion to Tacitus*, ed. Victoria Emma Pagán (Malden, MA: Wiley-Blackwell, 2012).

11 Dio 53.19; cf. Adam Kemezis, *Greek Narratives of the Roman Empire under the Severans: Cassius Dio, Philostratus and Herodian* (Cambridge: Cambridge University Press, 2014), 90–149, esp. 94–104.

12 Cynthia Damon, *Tacitus: Histories, Book I* (Cambridge: Cambridge University Press, 2003), 79–80.

13 A similar point is made in relation to Augustan poetry by Nandini Pandey, *The Poetics of Power in Augustan Rome: Latin Poetic Responses to Early Imperial Iconography* (Cambridge: Cambridge University Press, 2018), 1–29.

14 Compare, for instance, Cicero's limited political engagement during Caesar's dictatorship, which nevertheless includes 'pragmatic lobbying' to secure the restoration of other senators: Ingo Gildenhard, *Creative Eloquence: The Construction of Reality in Cicero's Speeches* (Oxford: Oxford University Press, 2010), 224–26.

15 In my earlier exploration of irony in *Annals*, I identified this moment as Tacitus' gesture towards the end of irony – and therefore the end of Tacitean historiography – in this new regime. See O'Gorman, *Irony and Misreading in the Annals of Tacitus*, 181–82.

16 Frederic Ahl, 'The Art of Safe Criticism in Greece and Rome', *American Journal of Philology* 105, no. 2 (1984): 207.

17 Ahl, 'The Art of Safe Criticism'.

18 Shadi Bartsch, *Actors in the Audience: Theatricality and Doublespeak from Nero to Hadrian* (Cambridge, MA: Harvard University Press, 1994).

19 O'Gorman, *Irony and Misreading in the Annals of Tacitus*.

20 Alex Dressler, 'Poetics of Conspiracy and Hermeneutics of Suspicion in Tacitus's *Dialogus de Oratoribus*', *Classical Antiquity* 32, no. 1 (2013): 1–34.

21 Bartsch, *Actors in the Audience*, 122–24; Christopher Pelling, 'Tacitus' Personal Voice', in *The Cambridge Companion to Tacitus*, ed. A. J. Woodman (Cambridge: Cambridge University Press, 2009), 149–50.

22 S. J. V. Malloch, *The Annals of Tacitus, Book 11* (Cambridge: Cambridge University Press, 2013), 89.
23 Miriam Griffin, 'Claudius in Tacitus', *Classical Quarterly* 40, no. 2 (1980): 499.
24 Joy Connolly, 'Fear and Freedom: A New Interpretation of Pliny's Panegyricus', in *Ordine e sovversione nel mondo greco e romano*, ed. Gianpaolo Urso (Pisa: Edizioni ETS, 2008).
25 As observed by Bartsch, *Actors in the Audience*, 234, n. 4.
26 Pelling, 'Tacitus' Personal Voice', 150.
27 Payment for advocates (*Ann.* 11.5–7, chapter three); provincial temples (*Ann.* 3.60–63).
28 Figured speech may, however, remain an element in these speeches; note Quintilian's comment on the use of *emphasis* to plead a case without offending the powerful (Quint., *Inst.* 9.2.68): cf. Ahl, 'The Art of Safe Criticism', 194–96.
29 Bartsch, *Actors in the Audience*, 181.
30 Bartsch, *Actors in the Audience*, 122.
31 Michel Foucault, *On the Government of the Living: Lectures at the Collège de France, 1979–1980* (Basingstoke: Palgrave-Macmillan, 2014), 96–97 (his emphasis); cf. Daniele Lorenzini, 'Foucault, Regimes of Truth, and the Making of the Subject', in *Foucault and the Making of Subjects*, ed. Laura Cremonesi, Orazio Irrera, Daniele Lorenzini, and Martina Tazzioli (London: Rowman & Littlefield, 2016).
32 Pelling, 'Tacitus' Personal Voice', 150.
33 Thomas Strunk has pointed out to me that Tacitus could commit to the truth of Trajan's regime while reserving the right to strip bare its falsehoods should it fail to meet his expectations.
34 Carlos F. Noreña, *Imperial Ideals in the Roman West: Representation, Circulation, Power* (Cambridge: Cambridge University Press, 2011), 169.
35 Vivasvan Soni, 'A Classical Politics without Happiness? Hannah Arendt and the American Revolution', *Cultural Critique* 74 (2010): 37.
36 It's common to see *licet* as denoting either implicit constraint (permitted only up to a point) or lack of constraint to the point of disorder (*licentia*), but the context of *licet* here, as I will argue, is of disciplined speech and thought, and thus conveys the sense of a domain already the speaker's own.
37 Ellen O'Gorman, 'Conspicuous Absence: Tacitus' Republic', in *Unspoken Rome: Absence in Latin Literature and Its Reception*, eds. Tom Geue and Elena Giusti (Cambridge: Cambridge University Press, forthcoming).
38 C. L. Whitton, 'Pliny, *Epistles* 8.14: Senate, Slavery and the *Agricola*', *Journal of Roman Studies* 100 (2010): 127, n. 56, his italics.
39 Another mode is speech in a military context, which would require a dedicated study of its own. See Rhiannon Ash, *Ordering Anarchy: Armies and Leaders in Tacitus'*

Histories (London: Duckworth, 1999); Jonathan Master, *Provincial Soldiers and Imperial Instability in the Histories of Tacitus* (Ann Arbor, MI: University of Michigan Press, 2016); Thomas E. Strunk, *History after Liberty: Tacitus on Tyrants, Sycophants, and Republicans* (Ann Arbor, MI: University of Michigan Press, 2017), 39–77.

40 Cf. Damon, *Tacitus: Histories, Book I*, 81–82; Woodman, *Agricola*, 84. See also Pliny *Epistles* 10.12.2.

41 Woodman, *Agricola*, 84, refers to Tacitus' 'repeating political slogans', 'used by Nerva himself to describe his new reign'.

42 See, for instance, Nathan T. Elkins, *The Image of Political Power in the Reign of Nerva, AD 96–98* (Oxford: Oxford University Press, 2017), 4–23, on imperial coin imagery.

43 Noreña, *Imperial Ideals in the Roman West*, 314–16.

44 Stephen Oakley, '*Res olim dissociabiles*: Emperors, Senators and Liberty', in *The Cambridge Companion to Tacitus*, ed. A. J. Woodman (Cambridge: Cambridge University Press, 2009), 194.

45 Oakley, '*Res olim dissociabiles*', 186.

46 Cf. Holly Haynes, 'Survival and Memory in the *Agricola*', *Arethusa* 39 (2006): 149–70; Myles Lavan, *Slaves to Rome: Paradigms of Empire in Roman Culture* (Cambridge: Cambridge University Press, 2013), 129–32; Aske Damtoft Poulsen, 'The Language of Freedom and Slavery in Tacitus' *Agricola*', *Mnemosyne* 70, no. 5 (2017): 846–49; O'Gorman, 'Conspicuous Absence'.

47 On speech as action in historiography, see Andrew Laird, *Powers of Expression, Expressions of Power: Speech Presentation and Latin Literature* (Oxford: Oxford University Press, 1999), 116–52.

48 But see Matthew Roller, 'The Rise of the Centumviral Court in the Augustan Age', in *The Alternative Augustan Age*, ed. Josiah Osgood, Kit Morrell, and Kathryn Welch (Oxford: Oxford University Press, 2019).

49 Erik Gunderson, *Staging Masculinity: The Rhetoric of Performance in the Roman World* (Ann Arbor, MI: University of Michigan Press, 2000); Erik Gunderson, *Declamation, Paternity, and Roman Identity: Authority and the Rhetorical Self* (Cambridge: Cambridge University Press, 2003); Anthony Corbeill, 'Rhetorical Education and Social Reproduction in the Republic and Early Empire', in *A Companion to Roman Rhetoric*, ed. William Dominik and Jon Hall (Malden, MA: Wiley-Blackwell, 2007); W. Martin Bloomer, *The School of Rome: Latin Studies and the Origins of Liberal Education* (Berkeley, CA: University of California Press, 2011), 170–91; Neil W. Bernstein, *Ethics, Identity, and Community in Later Roman Declamation* (Oxford: Oxford University Press, 2013).

50 Joy Connolly, *The State of Speech: Rhetoric and Political Thought in Ancient Rome* (Princeton, NJ: Princeton University Press, 2007), 237–61.

51 Many of Tacitus' judgements of individual speakers, however, are in dialogue with assessments of the same men by the elder Seneca, or Quintilian.
52 Matthew Roller, 'The Difference an Emperor Makes: Notes on the Reception of the Republican Senate in the Imperial Age', *Classical Receptions Journal* 7, no. 1 (2015): 26, my emphases.
53 Amy Russell, 'The Augustan Senate and the Reconfiguration of Time on the Fasti Capitolini', in *Augustus and the Destruction of History: The Politics of the Past in Early Imperial Rome*, ed. Ingo Gildenhard, Ulrich Gotter, Wolfgang Havener, and Louise Hodgson (London: Oxbow Books, 2019); Amy Russell, 'Inventing the Imperial Senate', in *The Alternative Augustan Age*, ed. Josiah Osgood, Kit Morrell, and Kathryn Welch (Oxford: Oxford University Press, 2019).
54 Cf. Kristina Milnor, 'Augustus, History, and the Landscape of the Law', *Arethusa* 40 (2007): 7–23; J. S. Richardson, 'The Senate, the Courts, and the *SC de Cn. Pisone Patre*', *Classical Quarterly* 47, no. 2 (1997): 510–18.
55 Rees, 'Panegyric', in *A Companion to Roman Rhetoric*, ed. William Dominik and Jon Hall (Malden, MA: Wiley-Blackwell, 2007), 141–43; Daniel J. Kapust, *Flattery and the History of Political Thought: That Glib and Oily Art* (Cambridge: Cambridge University Press, 2018), 1–29 and *passim*.
56 On Pliny's *Panegyricus*, see Bartsch, *Actors in the Audience*, 148–87; Connolly, 'Fear and Freedom'; Paul Roche, 'Pliny's Thanksgiving: An Introduction to the *Panegyricus*', in *Pliny's Praise: The* Panegyricus *in the Roman World*, ed. Paul Roche (Cambridge: Cambridge University Press, 2011); Christopher Whitton, *The Arts of Imitation in Latin Prose: Pliny's* Epistles/*Quintilian in Brief* (Cambridge: Cambridge University Press, 2019), 413–22.
57 Compare Tacitus' reference to the calendar 'tainted by flattery' in the reign of Nero, which the senate under Vespasian 'unburdens' of these untimely honours (*Hist.* 4.40.2).
58 Egon Flaig, 'How the Emperor Nero Lost Acceptance in Rome', in *The Emperor and Rome: Space, Representation, and Ritual*, ed. Christian Ewald Bjorn and Carlos F. Noreña (Cambridge: Cambridge University Press, 2011); effectively repeated with a different case study in Egon Flaig, 'A Coherent Model to Understand the Roman Principate: "Acceptance" instead of "Legitimacy" and the Problem of Usurpation', in *Il princeps romano: Autocrate o magistrato? Fattori giuridici e fattori sociali del potere imperiale da Augusto a Commodo*, ed. Jean-Louis Ferrary and John Scheid (Pavia: IUSS Press, 2015). John Rich, 'Consensus Rituals and the Origins of the Principate', in *Il princeps romano: Autocrate o magistrato? Fattori giuridici e fattori sociali del potere imperiale da Augusto a Commodo*, ed. Jean-Louis Ferrary and John Scheid (Pavia: IUSS Press, 2015), provides a careful evaluation of Flaig's claims and their limitations.

59 Flaig, 'How the Emperor Nero Lost Acceptance in Rome', 281; repeated in Flaig, 'A Coherent Model to Understand the Roman Principate', 89.
60 Clifford Ando, *Imperial Ideology and Provincial Loyalty in the Roman Empire* (Berkeley, CA: University of California Press, 2000); Greg Rowe, *Princes and Political Cultures: The New Tiberian Senatorial Decrees* (Ann Arbor, MI: University of Michigan Press, 2002); John Lobur, *Consensus, Concordia, and the Formation of Roman Imperial Ideology* (New York: Routledge, 2008).
61 Egon Flaig, *Den Kaiser herausfordern: Die Usurpation im Römischen Reich* (Frankfurt: Campus Verlag, 1992), 199.
62 Wallace-Hadrill, 'Roman Arches and Greek Honours', 144.
63 Russell, 'The Augustan Senate and the Reconfiguration of Time on the Fasti Capitolini'.
64 Peter Burgers, 'The Role and Function of Senatorial Debate: The Case of the Reign of Tiberius AD 14–37', *Latomus* 58 (1999): 564–73.
65 For a similarly exaggerated proposal to mark one of Tiberius' campaigns, see *Ann.* 3.47.3, discussed in chapter one.
66 *Hist.* 4.3.3; see also Michael Peachin, 'Exemplary Government in the Early Roman Empire', in *Crises and the Roman Empire*, ed. Olivier Hekster, Gerda de Kleijn, and Daniëlle Slootjes (Leiden: Brill, 2007); *Ann.* 3.57.1; cf. chapter one.
67 For the proposals themselves, see Julián González, 'Tacitus, Germanicus, Piso, and the Tabula Siarensis', *American Journal of Philology* 120, no. 1 (1999): 123–42.
68 The *Tabula Siarensis*, recording the decisions of precisely this debate, refers to the 'collection of proposals' which was submitted to Germanicus' family for approval. See Beth Severy, 'Family and State in the Early Imperial Monarchy: The Senatus Consultum de Pisone Patre, Tabula Siarensis, and Tabula Hebana', *Classical Philology* 95, no. 3 (2000): 318–37.
69 Cf. González, 'Tacitus, Germanicus, Piso, and the Tabula Siarensis', 123.
70 Rees, 'Panegyric', 136–37.
71 E.g. Roche, 'Pliny's Thanksgiving', 5.
72 A similar prioritizing of the senate is visible in the conclusion to the *Panegyricus*; cf. Carlos F. Noreña, 'Self-Fashioning in the *Panegyricus*', in *Pliny's Praise: The Panegyricus in the Roman World*, ed. Paul Roche (Cambridge: Cambridge University Press, 2011), 43–44.
73 Scott Consigny, 'Rhetoric and Its Situations', *Philosophy & Rhetoric* 7, no. 3 (1974): 175–86.
74 Henriette van der Blom, *Oratory and Political Career in the Late Roman Republic* (Cambridge: Cambridge University Press, 2016), 39.
75 Richard J. A. Talbert, *The Senate of Imperial Rome* (Princeton, NJ: Princeton University Press, 1984), 308–23; David Potter, 'Tacitus' Sources', in *A Companion to Tacitus*, ed. Victoria Emma Pagán (Malden, MA: Wiley-Blackwell, 2012).

76 John Matthews, 'Tacitus, *Acta Senatus*, and the Inauguration of Tiberius', in *Roman Perspectives: Studies in the Social, Political and Cultural History of the First to Fifth Centuries* (Swansea: Classical Press of Wales, 2008), reading *Annals* 1.11–12, 14–15.
77 A sensible position on so-called Republicanism is articulated by Andrew B. Gallia, *Remembering the Roman Republic: Culture, Politics and History under the Principate* (Cambridge: Cambridge University Press, 2012), 175.
78 Thrasea's political efficacy will be examined further in chapter five.
79 Matthew Roller, *Constructing Autocracy: Aristocrats and Emperors in Julio-Claudian Rome* (Princeton, NJ: Princeton University Press, 2001), 129–287.
80 Strunk, *History after Liberty*, 21.
81 On the digression, see John Moles, 'Cry Freedom: Tacitus *Annals* 4.32–35', *Histos* 2 (1998): 95–184; Dylan Sailor, *Writing and Empire in Tacitus* (Cambridge: Cambridge University Press, 2008), 261–68; A. J. Woodman, *The Annals of Tacitus, Book 4* (Cambridge: Cambridge University Press, 2018), 171–73.
82 O'Gorman, *Irony and Misreading in the Annals of Tacitus*, 99–100.
83 The conjecture <*salute*> adopted by Heubner brings this passage into alignment with the concept that the Principate ensures peace in the state. For an overview of the emendations and an alternative reading, see Woodman, *The Annals of Tacitus, Book 4*, 181–82.
84 Christopher van den Berg, 'Deliberative Oratory in the *Annals* and the *Dialogus*', in *A Companion to Tacitus*, ed. Victoria Emma Pagán (Malden, MA: Wiley-Blackwell, 2012), 204–5; cf. David S. Levene, 'Tacitus' *Histories* and the Theory of Deliberative Oratory', in *The Limits of Historiography: Genre and Narrative in Ancient Historical Texts*, ed. Christina Shuttleworth Kraus (Leiden: Brill, 1999).
85 T. J. Luce, 'Tacitus' Conception of Historical Change: The Problem of Discovering the Historian's Opinions', in *Oxford Readings in Tacitus*, ed. Rhiannon Ash (Oxford: Oxford University Press, 2012 [1983]), 349–50, discusses this passage as enjoining attention to detail.

Chapter 1

1 A. J. Woodman, *The Annals of Tacitus, Books 5 and 6* (Cambridge: Cambridge University Press, 2017), 223–24.
2 Patrick Sinclair, *Tacitus the Sententious Historian: A Sociology of Rhetoric in Annales 1–6* (University Park, PA: Pennsylvania State University Press, 1995), 7–15.
3 Sinclair, *Tacitus the Sententious Historian*, 24–25, on *-tor* nouns as 'classifying ... actions or behavior within a generally acknowledged set of social categories'.

4 Woodman, *The Annals of Tacitus, Books 5 and 6*, 230.
5 Kapust, *Flattery and the History of Political Thought*, 13.
6 Some examples of Vitellius' flattery to Claudius and his household are at Suet., *Vit.* 2.5; see also Tac., *Ann.* 11.34.1, examined in the introduction.
7 Kapust, *Flattery and the History of Political Thought*, 1–26, provides an in-depth and indispensable analysis of different aspects of falsehood in flattery, as well as insincerity and bullshit.
8 See Holly Haynes, 'Tacitus' Dangerous Word', *Classical Antiquity* 23, no. 1 (2004): 33–61, for a very different take on 'emptyspeak' in Tacitus' Principate.
9 J. Roger Dunkle, 'The Rhetorical Tyrant in Roman Historiography: Sallust, Livy and Tacitus', *Classical World* 65, no. 1 (1971): 12–20.
10 Lucretius 5, 1063–72; cf. Meinolf Vielberg, *Pflichten, Werte, Ideale: Eine Untersuchung zu den Wertvorstellungen des Tacitus* (Stuttgart: Franz Steiner Verlag, 1987), 81.
11 Monkey or ape (Plut., *Mor.* 52b, 64e). Plutarch also likens the flatterer to a cuttlefish and a chameleon because of his changeability (Plut., *Mor.* 51d, 52f, 53d), to a gadfly because of his persistence (Plut., *Mor.* 55e), and to woodworms and lice because of his preference for high-quality victims (Plut., *Mor.* 49b–c).
12 *PHerc.* 222, col. 9.14–16; cf. Voula Tsouna, *The Ethics of Philodemus* (Oxford: Oxford University Press, 2007), 129. See also Plut., *Mor.* 61c–d.
13 Here I am loosely drawing on the insights of Debra Hawhee, *Rhetoric in Tooth and Claw: Animals, Language, Sensation* (Chicago, IL: University of Chicago Press, 2016).
14 This episode is discussed further in chapter three.
15 It is interesting that the speech of freedmen, who are so often defined in terms of their enslaved past, is never characterized in terms of *adulatio*. Tacitus registers his distaste at the freedman's excessive power by configuring his language as either servile (Euodus at the death of Messalina, *Ann.*11.37.4) or arrogant (Pallas defying his accusers, *Ann.*13.23.2).
16 James C. Scott, *Domination and the Arts of Resistance: Hidden Transcripts* (New Haven, CT: Yale University Press, 1990), 132–33.
17 Tsouna, *The Ethics of Philodemus*, 128; Jerome Kemp, 'Flattery and Frankness in Horace and Philodemus', *Greece & Rome* 57 (2010): 69–70. See also Theophr., *Char.* 2.10, with reference to the *kolax* whispering in his victim's ear and watching him while he speaks to others, out of a desire for exclusive access.
18 Sejanus recommends solitude, *Ann.* 4.41.3; Tiberius' love of solitude, *Ann.* 4.67.2; Tiberius retreats into solitude, *Ann.* 6.1.1; solitude cannot protect his reputation, *Ann.* 6.6.2.

19 Elizabeth Keitel, 'The Structure and Function of Speeches in Tacitus *Histories* I–III', *ANRW* II 33, no. 4 (1991): 2775–76; Elizabeth Keitel, '*Sententia* and Structure in Tacitus *Histories* 1.12–49', *Arethusa* 39 (2006): 220–27.

20 All three Moesian legions have already rejected Vitellius' image, and have been joined by the army in Pannonia, *Hist.* 2.85–86.

21 Thus Rhiannon Ash, *Tacitus: Histories, Book II* (Cambridge: Cambridge University Press, 2007), 368.

22 The same thematic lack of knowledge is seen in the narrative of Claudius' relationship with Messalina; see O'Gorman, *Irony and Misreading in the Annals of Tacitus*, 115–17; Malloch, *The Annals of Tacitus, Book 11*, 391–92.

23 Philip Hardie, 'Crowds and Leaders in Imperial Historiography and in Epic', in *Latin Historiography and Poetry in the Early Empire: Generic Interactions*, ed. John F. Miller and A. J. Woodman (Leiden: Brill, 2010), 24–27.

24 See Ellen O'Gorman, 'The Noise, and the *People*: Popular *Clamor* and Political Discourse in Roman Historiography', in *Complex Inferiorities: The Poetics of the Weaker Voice in Latin Literature*, ed. Stephen Harrison and Sebastian Matzner (Oxford: Oxford University Press, 2018).

25 Robert Morstein-Marx, *Mass Oratory and Political Power in the Late Roman Republic* (Cambridge: Cambridge University Press, 2004), 149–50, on the Republican association of the 'wrong sort' of *populus* with slaves.

26 Gregory Aldrete, *Gestures and Acclamations in Ancient Rome* (Baltimore, MD: Johns Hopkins University Press, 1999), 124–25; Lobur, *Consensus, Concordia*, 52–54; Zvi Yavetz, *Plebs and Princeps* (Oxford: Oxford University Press, 1969), 3–6. As Cynthia Damon, *The Mask of the Parasite: A Pathology of Roman Patronage* (Ann Arbor, MI: University of Michigan Press, 1997), 4, has commented of the figure of the parasite (a cognate of the flatterer), '[at] its barest essentials, we find a system in which words and services are exchanged for food'.

27 Ash, *Tacitus: Histories, Book II*, 168. Tacitus introduces Licinius at the start of the campaign as 'unaccustomed to war' (*Hist.* 1.87.2).

28 Gwyn Morgan, *69 AD: The Year of Four Emperors* (Oxford: Oxford University Press, 2006), 130.

29 Ash, *Tacitus: Histories, Book II*, 168, reviews the possible meanings of *numen* here, commenting that it 'may also have a hybristic undercurrent'.

30 Observed by Ash, *Tacitus: Histories, Book II*, 168, 368.

31 Cynthia Damon, *Tacitus: Annals* (London: Penguin Books, 2012), 114, 225.

32 Compare the *quaesiti honores* devised to reflect Tiberius' civic generosity, discussed in the introduction.

33 Noted by A. J. Woodman and R. H. Martin, *The Annals of Tacitus, Book 3* (Cambridge: Cambridge University Press, 1996), 420.

34 G. Alföldy, 'Augustus und die Inschriften: Tradition und Innovation', *Gymnasium* 98 (1991): 299. See *Ann.* 16.3.2 for explicit use of golden age imagery in poetic flattery of Nero (see also Rhiannon Ash, 'At the End of the Rainbow: Nero and Dido's Gold (*Ann.* 16.1–3)', in *Fame and Infamy: Essays on Characterization in Greek and Roman Biography and Historiography*, ed. Rhiannon Ash, Judith Mossman, and Frances B. Titchener (Oxford: Oxford University Press, 2015).

35 Cf. the work done by Vibius Serenus to position himself in relation to senate and emperor in some surviving versions of the *Senatus Consultum de Cn. Pisone Patre* (Alison E. Cooley, 'Paratextual Perspectives upon the *SC de Pisone Patre*', in *The Roman Paratext: Frame, Texts, Readers*, ed. Laura Jansen (Cambridge: Cambridge University Press, 2014), 148–49).

36 Cf. the concluding remarks of Andrea Balbo, *I frammenti degli oratori romani dell'età augustea e tiberiana. Parte seconda: Età tiberiana*, 2 vols (Alessandria: Edizioni dell'Orso, 2007), 22, who points out that Haterius would likely have spoken early in the session because of his seniority, while the reaction to his words demonstrates his negligible influence.

37 Gunderson, *Declamation, Paternity, and Roman Identity*, 97–101; Ellen O'Gorman, 'Intertextuality and Historiography', in *The Cambridge Companion to the Roman Historians*, ed. Andrew Feldherr (Cambridge: Cambridge University Press, 2009), 239–40; Matthew Perry, 'Quintus Haterius and the "Dutiful" Freedman', *The Ancient History Bulletin* 25, no. 3–4 (2011): 133–48.

38 Woodman and Martin (*The Annals of Tacitus, Book 3*, 468) draw out the link between these two passages. They take *longius* as referring to the lengths to which Dolabella goes, relative to his preceding acts of *adulatio*. I take it as suggesting the extent of his *adulatio* relative to other senatorial proposals in the same session.

39 Sen., *Controv.* 4, pr. 10; Suet., *Vit.* 2.5.

40 For the overview of these extremes in rhetoric, see Heinrich Lausberg, *Handbook of Literary Rhetoric* (Leiden: Brill, 1998), 464–68.

41 For *supplicationes*, see Gérard Freyburger, 'La supplication d'action de grâces sous le Haut-Empire', *ANRW* II 16, no. 2 (1978): 1418–39; Talbert, *The Senate of Imperial Rome*, 388–90.

42 Woodman and Martin (*The Annals of Tacitus, Book 3*, 355) note the *traductio* in this passage.

43 Wallace-Hadrill, 'Roman Arches and Greek Honours', 166–69.

44 Rich, 'Consensus Rituals and the Origins of the Principate'; Geoffrey S. Sumi, *Ceremony and Power: Performing Politics in Rome between Republic and Empire* (Ann Arbor, MI: University of Michigan Press, 2005); Trevor S. Luke, *Ushering in a New Republic: Theologies of Arrival at Rome in the First Century BCE* (Ann Arbor, MI: University of Michigan Press, 2014).

45 Rowe, *Princes and Political Cultures*, 59–66.
46 Most notoriously Talbert, *The Senate of Imperial Rome*, taken to task by Wallace-Hadrill, 'Roman Arches and Greek Honours', 148; Rowe, *Princes and Political Cultures*, 64.
47 Russell, 'The Augustan Senate and the Reconfiguration of Time on the Fasti Capitolini'.
48 Freyburger, 'La supplication d'action de grâces sous le Haut-Empire'.
49 Wallace-Hadrill, 'Roman Arches and Greek Honours', for arches. On the imperial statue as an extension of the imperial presence, see Peter Herz, 'Emperors: Caring for the Empire and their Successors', in *A Companion to Roman Religion*, ed. Jörg Rüpke (Malden, MA: Wiley-Blackwell, 2007), 311–12.
50 Wallace-Hadrill, 'Roman Arches and Greek Honours', 147.
51 The procedure for managing senatorial debates is 'traditional' though enshrined in the Augustan *lex Iulia de senatu habendo*. I take it as read that Augustus' legal innovation either canonizes existing traditional procedures in senate or at least presents them as if they were traditional.
52 Rowe, *Princes and Political Cultures*, 60.
53 The terms of my analysis here are drawn from Latour's account of groups (Bruno Latour, *Reassembling the Social: An Introduction to Actor-Network-Theory* (Oxford: Oxford University Press, 2005)).
54 Freyburger, 'La supplication d'action de grâces sous le Haut-Empire', 1423–26. Examples of internal threats whose elimination prompts *supplicatio* includes Scribonius Libo (*Ann.* 2.32.1) and the younger Agrippina (*Ann.* 14.12.1).
55 O'Gorman, *Irony and Misreading in the Annals of Tacitus*, 153–54.
56 Compare Sailor's (*Writing and Empire in Tacitus*, 183–205) argument about the perversion of evaluative language in Tacitus' account of civil war.
57 Yavetz, *Plebs and Princeps*, 125, identifies this event as the cause of popular disillusionment with Nero.
58 On the mutual and cyclical production of *adulatio* and sovereignty, see Shreyaa Bhatt, 'Useful Vices: Tacitus's Critique of Corruption', *Arethusa* 50, no. 3 (2017): 322.

Chapter 2

1 Loránd Dészpa, 'The Flavians and the Senate', in *A Companion to the Flavian Age of Imperial Rome*, ed. Andrew Zissos (Malden, MA: Wiley-Blackwell, 2016), 182–83.

2   See especially Gildenhard, *Creative Eloquence*, 223–33, 358–64; Kathryn Tempest, 'An Ethos of Sincerity: Echoes of *de Re Publica* in Cicero's *Pro Marcello*', *Greece & Rome* 60, no. 2 (2013): 262–80; Joy Connolly, *The Life of Roman Republicanism* (Princeton, NJ: Princeton University Press, 2015), 173–94.
3   David S. Levene, 'God and Man in the Classical Latin Panegyric', *Proceedings of the Cambridge Philological Society* 43, no. 1 (1997): 75, noting also Weinstock's argument that Cicero alludes to an emergent cult of *Salus Caesaris*. See Stefan Weinstock, *Divus Julius* (Oxford: Clarendon Press, 1971), 217–20, for public vows to Caesar's safety.
4   This is implicitly the position of Michel Ruch, *M. T. Ciceronis Pro Marcello Oratio* (Paris: Presses Universitaires de France, 1965), 66, and explicitly the interpretation of Antonella Tedeschi, *Lezione di buon governo per un dittatore. Cicerone,* Pro Marcello*: Saggio di commento* (Bari: Edipuglia, 2005), 117–18.
5   Connolly, *The Life of Roman Republicanism*, 190–94.
6   Pliny in *Panegyricus* refers to the established tradition of praying 'for the safety of the ruler, on which depends the eternity of the empire' (Plin., *Pan.* 67.3) and celebrates a new prayer instigated by Trajan: 'that the gods will keep you healthy and unharmed, if you similarly preserve your subjects' (Plin., *Pan.* 67.5). On 'salutary ideology' in the Neronian period, see Trevor S. Luke, 'From Crisis to Consensus: Salutary Ideology and the Murder of Agrippina', *Illinois Classical Studies* 38 (2013): 207–28.
7   Woodman, *The Annals of Tacitus, Book 4*, 217.
8   Unless we see this as a formal proposal for a senatorial bodyguard: Harold Gotoff, 'Cicero's Caesarian Orations', in *Brill's Companion to Cicero: Oratory and Rhetoric*, ed. J. M. May (Leiden: Brill, 2002), 234.
9   A. H. M. Jones, *The Criminal Courts of the Roman Republic and Principate* (Oxford: Basil Blackwell, 1972), 116–17.
10 Jill Harries, *Law and Crime in the Roman World* (Cambridge: Cambridge University Press, 2007), 21.
11 Rutledge, *Imperial Inquisitions: Prosecutors and Informants from Tiberius to Domitian* (London: Routledge, 2001), presents the evidence that most *delatores* received quite modest benefits from their activities.
12 On the implication of law and violence in *delatio*, see Bhatt, 'Useful Vices: Tacitus's Critique of Corruption'.
13 Jones, *The Criminal Courts of the Roman Republic and Principate*, 62–66, for the Republican procedure; Rutledge, *Imperial Inquisitions*, 16–18, for the early imperial template; Michael Peachin, 'Augustus' Emergent Judicial Powers, the "Crimen Maiestatis", and the Second Cyrene Edict', in *Il princeps romano: Autocrate o magistrato? Fattori giuridici e fattori sociali del potere imperiale da*

Augusto a Commodo, ed. Jean-Louis Ferrary and John Scheid (Pavia: IUSS Press, 2015), for the crucial (and nebulous) development of *maiestas* under Augustus.

14 See, for instance, the struggle for control of Cn. Piso's case between Fulcinius Trio and the associates of Germanicus (*Ann.* 3.10).

15 On this trial, see Richard A. Bauman, *Impietas in Principem: A Study of Treason against the Roman Emperor with Special Reference to the First Century AD* (Munich: C. H. Beck, 1974), 60–61; Andrew Pettinger, *The Republic in Danger: Drusus Libo and the Succession of Tiberius* (Oxford: Oxford University Press, 2012), 5–27.

16 B. Walker, *The Annals of Tacitus*, rev. ed. (Manchester: Manchester University Press, 1960), 92–95, insightfully dissects Tacitus' creation of impressions in this episode.

17 Victoria Emma Pagán, *Tacitus* (London and New York: I.B. Tauris, 2017), 39–41, provides a thoughtful overview of Trio's career.

18 *Ann.* 2.32.1 outlines the rewards for the *accusatores*; Vibius Serenus later falls foul of Tiberius for complaining that his reward was insufficient (*Ann.* 4.29.3).

19 Rutledge, *Imperial Inquisitions*, 160.

20 Walker, *The Annals of Tacitus*, 82; cf. O'Gorman, *Irony and Misreading in the Annals of Tacitus*, 85–86.

21 Sir Ronald Syme, *Tacitus*, 2 vols (Oxford: Clarendon Press, 1958), 418–22; Barbara Levick, 'Tacitus in the Twenty-First Century: The Struggle for Truth in *Annals* 1–6', in *A Companion to Tacitus*, ed. Victoria Emma Pagán (Malden, MA: Wiley-Blackwell, 2012), 269–72.

22 Sinclair, *Tacitus the Sententious Historian*, 13.

23 Clifford Ando, 'Tacitus, *Annales* VI: Beginning and End', *American Journal of Philology* 118, no. 2 (1997): 297–98, discusses the role of imperial deaths in structuring the first six books of *Annals*; Elizabeth Keitel, '"Is Dying so Very Terrible?": The Neronian *Annals*', in *The Cambridge Companion to Tacitus*, ed. A. J. Woodman (Cambridge: Cambridge University Press, 2009), on the Neronian *Annals*' focus on death. On the likely number of books in *Annals*, see Syme, *Tacitus*, 263–66.

24 Roland Mayer, 'Oratory in Tacitus' *Annals*', in *Form and Function in Roman Oratory*, ed. D. H. Berry and Andrew Erskine (Cambridge: Cambridge University Press, 2010), 287.

25 See especially Rutledge, *Imperial Inquisitions*, and Peachin, 'Augustus' Emergent Judicial Powers', for a compelling account of early Augustan *maiestas* cases which emphasizes the initiative of private individuals.

26 Ruth Morello, 'A Correspondence Course in Tyranny: The *Cruentae Litterae* of Tiberius', *Arethusa* 39, no. 2 (2006): 344–47, for the letters of *Annals* 6; See A. J. Woodman, *Tacitus Reviewed* (Oxford: Oxford University Press, 1998), 155–67, for changes in Tiberius' character.

27 Cf. Dio 58.1b.
28 Bauman, *Impietas in Principem*, 121–22.
29 For prayers *pro incolumitate principis*, *Ann.* 4.17.1, 12.68.1; *pro salute principis*, 16.22.1.
30 Tacitus thinks it is a false charge, but Barbara Levick, *Tiberius the Politician*, rev. ed. (London: Routledge, 1999), 62–63, and Rutledge, *Imperial Inquisitions*, 107–8, present well-thought-out revisions of Asiaticus' provincial activity.
31 Compare the allegations brought against Rubellius Plautus and Cornelius Sulla: *propinquos huic Orientis, illi Germaniae exercitus* (*Ann.*14.57.1).
32 Griffin, *Seneca: A Philosopher in Politics* (Oxford: Clarendon Press, 1976), 53–57, on the likelihood of this anecdote.
33 *Seditio* (*Ann.* 3.12.3; 16.30.1); *secessio* (*Ann.* 16.22.2); *defectio* (*Ann.* 16.7.2).
34 *Turbare* (*Ann.* 4.29.1; 12.65.1); *turbidus* (*Ann.* 3.12.3, 3.38.2; 14.57.3, 14.59.4).
35 Lobur, *Consensus, Concordia*; Cornwell, *Pax and the Politics of Peace*; see also the introduction.
36 Compare the opening declaration of the *Senatus Consultum de Cn. Pisone Patre* (*SCPP* 12–15).
37 Sejanus' furious reaction to an unco-operative senate and people in the case of the elder Agrippina provides the basic template for this procedure (*Ann.* 5.4.4).
38 Mayer, 'Oratory in Tacitus' *Annals*', 287–90, provides a comprehensive reading of both speeches.
39 Rutledge (*Imperial Inquisitions*, 115–17) provides an even-handed assessment of the case against Thrasea.
40 Silanus (*Ann.* 16.7–9); Vetus (*Ann.* 16.10–11).
41 Compare the *solitudo* which is produced by flattery, the isolation of the ruler from social contact (discussed in chapter one); cf. also the social/ecological devastation of Roman imperialist conquest (*Agr.* 30.6).
42 *Probrum* derives from the Greek *propherein*, which has the sense of 'to cast a reproach'. *Probrum/probrosus* in *maiestas* charges: *Ann.* 2.50.1, 4.31.1, 14.48.1; Suet., *Tib.* 61.3.
43 Tacitus later uses the same concept of lashing or tearing to denote how the soul of the tyrant bears the mark of his vices (*Ann.* 6.6.2; see also Woodman, *The Annals of Tacitus, Books 5 and 6*, 113–14).
44 On Tiberius' earlier *clementia*, *Ann.* 4.31.2; see also R. H. Martin and A. J. Woodman, *Tacitus: Annals Book IV* (Cambridge: Cambridge University Press, 1989), 201.
45 Martin and Woodman, *Tacitus: Annals Book IV*, 200.
46 Malloch, *The Annals of Tacitus, Book 11*, 108.

47 Sander Goldberg, 'Appreciating Aper: The Defence of Modernity in Tacitus' *Dialogus de Oratoribus*', in *Oxford Readings in Tacitus*, ed. Rhiannon Ash (Oxford: Oxford University Press, 2012 [1999]), 160–63, points out that many *delatores* pursued careers in defence as much as prosecution.
48 Rutledge, *Imperial Inquisitions*, 36.
49 Mayer, 'Oratory in Tacitus' *Annals*', 285–87.
50 E.g. Winterbottom, 'Quintilian and the *Vir Bonus*', *Journal of Roman Studies* 54 (1964): 92–93.

Chapter 3

1 Ash, *Tacitus: Histories, Book II*, 169, nicely renders this as 'they had sunk to flattery'. Heinz Heubner, *P. Cornelius Tacitus: Die Historien, Band II* (Heidelberg: Carl Winter Universitätsverlag, 1968), 127, notes the unusual nature of Tacitus' usage. Morgan, *69 AD: The Year of Four Emperors*, 123–30, carefully articulates the weakness of both sides of the argument in the council.
2 In Plutarch's account (*Otho* 8), Titianus and Proculus provide reasoned arguments for their position.
3 The short reign of Galba statistically receives a higher percentage of references to *adulatio*, but the brevity of the narrative (slightly over half a book) does not make it such a clear comparator with the Tiberian narrative. The Neronian narrative, closer in length, has fewer than half the references to *adulatio*, and the phenomenon is not consciously observed by ruler and subjects.
4 On Tiberius' cultural interests, including his 'study leave' on Rhodes in 20 BC, see Levick, *Tiberius the Politician*, 16–18; on the likely shared cultural interests of Sejanus and Tiberius, see Edward Champlin, 'Seianus Augustus', *Chiron* 42 (2012): 374–78.
5 Sinclair, *Tacitus the Sententious Historian*, 100–15.
6 Christopher Pelling, 'The Spur of Fame: Annals 4.37-8', in *Ancient Historiography and Its Contexts: Studies in Honour of A. J. Woodman*, ed. Christina Shuttleworth Kraus, John Marincola, and Christopher Pelling (Oxford: Oxford University Press, 2010), 369.
7 Eleanor Cowan, 'Tacitus, Tiberius, and Augustus', *Classical Antiquity* 28, no. 2 (2009): 179–210. One of the final scornful remarks Tiberius addresses to a hapless flatterer – his friend Iunius Gallio – is *reperisse prorsus quod divus Augustus non providerit* (*Ann.* 6.3.2). 'For sure, he had discovered a practice which the divine Augustus had not foreseen.'

8   Sinclair, *Tacitus the Sententious Historian*, 96–97.
9   Technically a lesser triumph: *ut ovans e Campania urbem introiret* (*Ann.* 3.49.3).
10 Dio 58.9.2–6 gives a sense of how carefully Tiberius ensured that the Praetorian Guard would remain under his control as he moved against Sejanus. The narrative of *Histories* 1.21–28, thirty-odd years after Gallio's proposal, shows what an ambitious senator such as Otho could achieve by courting praetorian favour.
11 Woodman, *The Annals of Tacitus, Books 5 and 6*, 102.
12 This point is built up through Woodman and Martin's (*The Annals of Tacitus, Book 3*, 352–57) careful reading of *Ann.* 3.47.
13 Russell's analysis of senatorial honorific monuments emphasizes how they project the senate as a collective (see Russell, 'The Augustan Senate and the Reconfiguration of Time on the Fasti Capitolini').
14 Fergus Millar, *The Emperor in the Roman World* (London: Duckworth, 1977), 59–101, for the various ranks within the emperor's entourage. Frédéric Hurlet, 'Les Sénateurs dans l'entourage d'Auguste et de Tibère: Un complément à plusieurs synthèses récentes sur la cour impériale', *Revue de philologie* 74 (2000): 123–50, for the topography of interaction between emperor and senatorial entourage.
15 Woodman and Martin, *The Annals of Tacitus, Book 3*, 457, are surely correct that Tiberius' use of Greek here also makes ironic use of the Greek reputation for *adulatio*, but I am primarily interested in the communicative function of the language.
16 Woodman and Martin, *The Annals of Tacitus, Book 3*, 457.
17 The surviving senatorial *lex de imperio Vespasiani* is alluded to in Tacitus' account of this meeting: *cuncta principibus solita Vespasiano decernit* (*Hist.* 4.3.3), and *eo senatus die, quo de imperio Vespasiani censebant* (*Hist.* 4.6.3). Peachin, 'Exemplary Government in the Early Roman Empire'.
18 This would be congruent with Halm's emendation of the phrase *honorificam in bonum principem* to *honorificam in **novum** principem* (see apparatus criticus). I do not, however, accept this emendation, for reasons explained at the end of this section.
19 Andrew Wallace-Hadrill, 'Civilis Princeps: Between Citizen and King', *Journal of Roman Studies* 72 (1982): 32–48.
20 *Hist.* 1.90.3, discussed in chapter one.
21 Ash, *Tacitus: Histories, Book II*, 283–85, comments perceptively on Mucianus' portrayal as Vespasian's *socius imperii* in *Histories* 2.
22 Vielberg, *Pflichten, Werte, Ideale*, 131.
23 On the dominant theme of care for the state, see Devillers, 'The Concentration of Power and Writing History', and Strunk, *History after Liberty*, 7–37.

24 The consuls had been Vitellius Caesar (killed *Hist.* 3.85) and his brother Lucius (killed *Hist.* 4.2): cf. Gavin Townend, 'The Consuls of AD 69–70', *American Journal of Philology* 83, no. 2 (1962): 125.

25 Here too the co-dependence of emperor and senate, outlined by Paul Plass, *Wit and the Writing of History: The Rhetoric of Historiography in Imperial Rome* (Madison, WI: University of Wisconsin Press, 1988), 104–10, is evident: the power of the emperor is significant – or worthless – in direct correlation to the attitude of the senate who confers that power. Cf. J. E. Lendon, *Empire of Honour: The Art of Government in the Roman World* (Oxford: Clarendon Press, 1997), 114, on Dio 59.23 (honours to Gaius).

26 I am not convinced by Talbert's claim in passing that this represents the usual practice in the imperial senate (Talbert, *The Senate of Imperial Rome*, 255). The parallel usages of *voltu adsentiri* cited by Heinz Heubner, *P. Cornelius Tacitus: Die Historien, Band IV* (Heidelberg: Carl Winter Universitätsverlag, 1976), 22, are set in various sites of communication: the only senatorial example (Cic., *Phil.* 1.14) suggests extraordinary rather than usual practice.

27 The effect of *studia* will be discussed further in chapter four.

28 Proposed supplements are: [just as the speech was honorific to a good emperor...] 'so it was free of flattery, and falsehoods were absent'; 'so it was appropriate to the commonwealth. The falsehoods of flattery were absent...'; 'so it was appropriate to the speaker, since falsehoods were absent'.

29 Thus far my argument follows similar lines to Kapust, *Flattery and the History of Political Thought*, 55–63. Reading across Cicero and Pliny, he sees the problems of flattery transcended by the virtue of the dictator/emperor, which bridges differences of status and power between ruler and subject.

30 Connolly, *The State of Speech*, 169–75.

31 On panegyric (in Cicero) as sustaining a productive irony between will and necessity, see Connolly, *The Life of Roman Republicanism*, 173–201.

32 Rutledge, *Imperial Inquisitions*, 112, comments that this trial was likely brought under the *lex Cornelia de sicariis*, but we have no firm evidence. My argument is that the charge against Suillius, by its similarity to forms of *maiestas*, serves as a commentary on and partial redefinition of the concept of the state which lies behind charges of *maiestas*. All Suillius' alleged victims are consuls *suffecti*: Pomponius AD 45 (on Gaius' death); Valerius AD 35; Saturninus undated; Cornelius AD 42; Poppaea's father was consul in AD 9, and her husband Scipio in AD 24; Julia's father was the heir of Tiberius until his death; her husband Rubellius Blandus was consul in AD 18.

33 Erich Koestermann, *Cornelius Tacitus: Annalen, Band III, Buch 11–13* (Heidelberg: Carl Winter Universitätsverlag, 1967), 320.

34 Here, as elsewhere, I treat the reported speech as if it were unproblematically the words of the speakers. But even if we concede that the artistry is Tacitus', the point remains that he presents us with a (mediated) speech which is demonstrably carefully constructed.

35 A third figure whose indictment raises these issues of agency is Aquilius Regulus, attacked by Curtius Montanus in the first senatorial meeting of AD 70 (*Hist.* 4.42). Heubner, *P. Cornelius Tacitus: Die Historien, Band IV*, 100–103, reviews the echoes of the Suillius case. The opportunity for accusing Regulus, however, is not an act of *delatio* but of disrespect to the dead: he bites the cheek of Piso Caesar's decapitated head.

36 Jakub Pigoń, 'Helvidius Priscus, Eprius Marcellus, and *Iudicium Senatus*: Observations on Tacitus, *Histories* 4.7–8', *Classical Quarterly* 42, no. 1 (1992): 241.

37 Woodman, *Agricola*, 317, argues that Tacitus may not have been in Rome for these trials.

38 Nero refutes Suillius' claim to be acting on orders by consulting the *commentarii* of his predecessor (*Ann.* 13.43.3); an attempt in AD 70 to access Nero's own *commentarii*, to uncover the extent of the *delatores*' agency, is blocked by the new Flavian regime (*Hist.* 4.40.3). See also chapter five.

39 On the original institute of the *lex*, and its ideological implications, see Neil Coffee, *Gift and Gain: How Money Transformed Ancient Rome* (Oxford: Oxford University Press, 2017), 40–43; for this episode, see Malloch, *The Annals of Tacitus, Book 11*, 90–114.

40 Tellingly Silius uses the term *ministerium* for the service an orator provides for pay. Compare with the designation of Suillius as *minister* in Book 13. Malloch, *The Annals of Tacitus, Book 11*, 95, 106–7, rightly observes how easy it is to refute Silius' historical overview of good oratorical practice.

41 Malloch, *The Annals of Tacitus, Book 11*, 96.

42 Woodman, *Tacitus Reviewed*, 218–29.

43 Steven Rutledge, 'Delatores and the Tradition of Violence in Roman Oratory', *American Journal of Philology* 120, no. 4 (1999): 555–73.

44 Woodman, *The Annals of Tacitus, Book 4*, 141, 167.

45 R. S. Rogers, 'The Tacitean Account of a Neronian Trial', in *Studies Presented to Daniel Moore Robinson on His Seventieth Birthday*, ed. George E. Mylonas and Doris Raymond (St Louis, MO: Washington University Press, 1953); Judith Ginsburg, 'Speech and Allusion in Tacitus, *Annals* 3.49–51 and 14.48–49', *American Journal of Philology* 107 (1986): 525–41; Eleanor Cowan, 'Contesting Clementia: The Rhetoric of Severitas in Tiberian Rome before and after the Trial of Clutorius Priscus', *Journal of Roman Studies* 106 (2016): 77–101; Strunk, *History after Liberty*, 99–113. See also chapter five.

46 Titus Sabinus (*Ann.* 4.70) and Considius Proculus (*Ann.* 6.18.1) are taken straight to execution: Dio's narrative of Sejanus' fall recounts a similar compression of process. Vibullius Agrippa (*Ann.* 6.40.1) drinks poison during his accuser's speech; Suetonius refers to this as happening in more than one trial (Suet., *Tib.* 61.4).
47 For traditions of interrogating, interrupting, and otherwise appropriating testimony of witnesses, see Charles Guérin, *La voix de la vérité: Témoin et témoignage dans les tribunaux romains du 1er siècle avant J.-C* (Paris: Les Belles Lettres, 2015), 194–236.
48 Woodman and Martin, *The Annals of Tacitus, Book 3*, 365.
49 Sir Ronald Syme, 'Marcus Lepidus, *Capax Imperii*', in *Ten Studies in Tacitus* (Oxford: Clarendon Press, 1970); Strunk, *History after Liberty*, 97–103.
50 Ginsburg, 'Speech and Allusion in Tacitus'.
51 Clifford Ando, *Roman Social Imaginaries: Language and Thought in Contexts of Empire* (Toronto: University of Toronto Press, 2015), 29–40, 51; on the flexibility of the *maiestas* law which allows its 'extension' to various cases, see Bauman, *Impietas in Principem*, 63–64.
52 Cf. Cowan, 'Contesting Clementia', 93. She argues persuasively that *clementia*, which is 'co-owned' by senate and princeps in the *SCPP*, becomes formalized as the princeps' domain in the aftermath of Clutorius' trial.
53 On the character assessment of candidates for the judiciary list, see Leanne Bablitz, *Actors and Audience in the Roman Courtroom* (Abingdon and New York: Routledge, 2007), 92–93.
54 Woodman and Martin, *The Annals of Tacitus, Book 3*, 367–68.
55 We could point here to Tiberius' actions in the trial against Piso to transmit property to Piso's sons and daughter: *SCPP* 93–106; cf. Severy, 'Family and State in the Early Imperial Monarchy'.
56 *Ann.* 13.4.2–5.1 on Nero conceding *arbitrium* to the senate; *Ann.* 13.11.2 for Neronian *clementia*.

Chapter 4

1 William Batstone, 'The Drama of Rhetoric at Rome', in *The Cambridge Companion to Ancient Rhetoric*, ed. Erik Gunderson (Cambridge: Cambridge University Press, 2009). See also Quint. *Inst.* 6.2.8 on the lack of a Latin equivalent for *ethos*.
2 Winterbottom, 'Quintilian and the *Vir Bonus*'.
3 Gunderson, *Staging Masculinity*; Connolly, *The State of Speech*.

4 Susan Miller, *Trust in Texts: A Different History of Rhetoric* (Carbondale, IL: Southern Illinois University Press, 2008); Joy Connolly, 'The Politics of Rhetorical Education', in *The Cambridge Companion to Ancient Rhetoric*, ed. Erik Gunderson (Cambridge: Cambridge University Press, 2009).
5 James S. Baumlin and Craig A. Meyer, 'Positioning Ethos in/for the Twenty-First Century: An Introduction to Histories of Ethos', *Humanities* 7, no. 78 (2018): 10.
6 Dean Hammer, *The Iliad as Politics: The Performance of Political Thought* (Norman, OK: University of Oklahoma Press, 2002), 172.
7 Thomas N. Habinek, *The Politics of Latin Literature: Writing, Identity, and Empire in Ancient Rome* (Princeton, NJ: Princeton University Press, 1998), 45–59, on *existimatio* and the formation of the Roman aristocracy in the middle Republic.
8 Jakob Wisse, *Ethos and Pathos: From Aristotle to Cicero* (Amsterdam: Adolf M. Hakkert, 1989).
9 James Martin, 'A Feeling for Democracy? Rhetoric, Power and the Emotions', *Journal of Political Power* 6 (2013): 472.
10 O'Gorman, 'Conspicuous Absence'.
11 G. E. F. Chilver and G. B. Townend, *A Historical Commentary on Tacitus' Histories IV and V* (Oxford: Clarendon Press, 1985), 55.
12 See Syme, *Tacitus*, 108, on the absence of Messalla's career from the documentary record and the supposition that he died early.
13 See, generally, James M. May, *Trials of Character: The Eloquence of Ciceronian Ethos* (Chapel Hill, NC: University of North Carolina Press, 1988); Wisse, *Ethos and Pathos*; Richard Leo Enos and Karen Rossi Schnakenberg, 'Cicero Latinizes Hellenic Ethos', in *Ethos: New Essays in Rhetorical and Critical Theory*, ed. James S. Baumlin and Tita French Baumlin (Dallas, TX: Southern Methodist University Press, 1994).
14 Syme, *Tacitus*, 615, *n.* 1.
15 Wisse, *Ethos and Pathos*, 234, on *benevolentia* also involving a sense of sympathy.
16 Miller, *Trust in Texts*, 44–51.
17 May, *Trials of Character*, 9–12; Marshall W. Alcorn, 'Self-Structure as a Rhetorical Device: Modern *Ethos* and the Divisiveness of the Self', in *Ethos: New Essays in Rhetorical and Critical Theory*, ed. James S. Baumlin and Tita French Baumlin (Dallas, TX: Southern Methodist University Press, 1994), 14–16.
18 *Hist.* 2.85.2 for the treatment of the legate. Ash, *Tacitus: Histories, Book II*, 333, remarks that the source for this story is likely Messalla himself.
19 In this judgement, Tacitus also gives his seal of approval, presumably, to Messalla's self-presentation in his memoir of the civil war. For Messalla as historical source

for Tacitus, see Morgan, *69 AD: The Year of Four Emperors*, 282–83; Ash, *Tacitus: Histories, Book II*, 28–29.
20 Goldberg, 'Appreciating Aper'.
21 William A. Johnson, *Readers and Reading Culture in the High Roman Empire: A Study of Elite Communities* (Oxford: Oxford University Press, 2010), 65.
22 Christopher van den Berg, *The World of Tacitus'* Dialogus de Oratoribus: *Aesthetics and Empire in Ancient Rome* (Cambridge: Cambridge University Press, 2014), 131–35.
23 Aper in fact juxtaposes the solid pleasure of delivering a well-prepared speech with the keener delights of spontaneity. Aper himself, we are told at his introduction, conceals his erudition in order to appear more unrehearsed (*Dial.* 2), so he is playing up to that reputation here.
24 T. J. Luce, 'Reading and Response in the *Dialogus*', in *Tacitus and the Tacitean Tradition*, ed. A. J. Woodman and T. J. Luce (Princeton, NJ: Princeton University Press, 1993), 31.
25 van den Berg, *The World of Tacitus'* Dialogus de Oratoribus, 133–34, provides a perceptive analysis of the different routes to power in this chapter.
26 Luce, 'Reading and Response in the *Dialogus*', 36.
27 *Histories* 4.8, 4.43.2; *Annals* 16.28–29.
28 van den Berg, *The World of Tacitus'* Dialogus de Oratoribus, 151–52, argues, on different grounds, that Marcellus and Crispus fail to achieve the autonomy enjoyed by Aper and Maternus.
29 See *Ann.* 16.25–26 for Thrasea's deliberation on whether to attend his trial, with discussion of the possible emotive effects of his presence.
30 Woodman and Martin, *The Annals of Tacitus, Book 3*, 451–56, for various interpretations of this passage.
31 This was discussed in chapter three.
32 T. J. Luce, 'Tacitus on "History's Highest Function": *Praecipuum Munus Annalium* (*Ann.* 3.65)', *ANRW* II 33, no. 4 (1991): 2904–27.
33 Rusticus' praise of Thrasea as *sanctissimus* (Suet., *Dom.* 10.3) or *hieros* (Dio 67.13.2) leads to his condemnation under Domitian.
34 Jonas Grethlein, *Experience and Teleology in Ancient Historiography: Futures Past from Herodotus to Augustine* (Cambridge: Cambridge University Press, 2013), 1–23.
35 Grethlein, *Experience and Teleology in Ancient Historiography*, 168.
36 Talbert, *The Senate of Imperial Rome*, 202–7.
37 Pliny finds it difficult to ascribe wit to these proposals (Plin., *Ep.* 8.5.3): cf. Stewart Irvin Oost, 'The Career of M. Antonius Pallas', *American Journal of Philology* 79, no. 2 (1958): 130–32.

38 Compare Licinius Caecina's ill-advised attack on Eprius Marcellus, undertaken to make a name for himself at the start of his senatorial career (*Hist.* 2.53.1).
39 Some of Quintilian's comments on Afer, who was his teacher: Quint., *Inst.* 10.1.118, 12.11.3.
40 Chapter one.
41 Woodman and Martin, *The Annals of Tacitus, Book 3*, 461, on the word order, diction, and ironic Sallustian allusion.
42 Hammer, *The Iliad as Politics*, 172, quoted earlier.
43 Marcellus in his riposte to Helvidius reclaims the term *constantia* as a term to denote the philosophical, intransigent senators of the civil wars, Cato and Brutus (*Hist.* 4.8.3). For a discussion of these attempts to cast Thrasea and Helvidius as 'Stoic opposition', see chapter five.
44 Similarly, in the second senate meeting, Helvidius makes a new attempt against Marcellus by commencing his speech with praise of Cluvius Rufus.
45 Pigoń, 'Helvidius Priscus, Eprius Marcellus, and *Iudicium Senatus*', 236.
46 Woodman, *The Annals of Tacitus, Book 4*, 142–44, for the Sallustian parallels in this passage; 3–12 for the Sallustian structure of *Annals* 4 overall.

Chapter 5

1 Sailor, *Writing and Empire in Tacitus*, 106–10.
2 O'Gorman, 'Conspicuous Absence'.
3 R. M. Ogilvie and I. A. Richmond, *De Vita Agricolae* (Oxford: Clarendon Press, 1967), 315. Followed by A. R. Birley, *Tacitus: Agricola and Germany* (Oxford: Oxford World's Classics, 1999), 33; Haynes, 'Survival and Memory in the *Agricola*', 169. The phrase is rare, and mostly used in juristic contexts. Sailor, *Writing and Empire in Tacitus*, 107, renders it more closely to my interpretation; cf. Aul. Gell., *NA*. 7.5.9.
4 Stephen J. Harrison, 'From Man to Book: The Close of Tacitus' *Agricola*', in *Classical Constructions: Papers in Memory of Don Fowler, Classicist and Epicurean*, ed. Stephen J. Harrison, Peta G. Fowler, and Stephen J. Heyworth (Oxford: Oxford University Press, 2007), 315.
5 Woodman, *Agricola*, 67.
6 Woodman, *Agricola*, 110–12.
7 The two passages where repudiation of Thrasea *et al.* are adduced are, most explicitly, Tacitus' dismissal of those who actively seek a martyrdom which is no good to the state (*Agr.* 42.4) and, more implicitly, the anecdote about Agricola's early excessive love of philosophy (*Agr.* 4.3).

8 Cf. Andrew M. Riggsby, 'Self and Community in the Younger Pliny', *Arethusa* 31, no. 1 (1998): 76–81; Roy K. Gibson and Ruth Morello, *Reading the Letters of Pliny the Younger* (Cambridge: Cambridge University Press, 2012), 136–68.
9 Jacqueline Carlon, *Pliny's Women: Constructing Virtue and Creating Identity in the Roman World* (Cambridge: Cambridge University Press, 2010), 40–41.
10 Neil W. Bernstein, 'Each Man's Father Served as His Teacher: Constructing Relatedness in Pliny's Letters', *Classical Antiquity* 27, no. 2 (2008): 203–30.
11 See the introduction on the politics of happiness, understood as plenitude.
12 Bartsch, *Actors in the Audience*, 63–66. See also the introduction.
13 Thomas E. Strunk, 'Domitian's Lightning Bolts and Close Shaves in Pliny', *Classical Journal* 109, no. 1 (2013): 93–95.
14 Rhiannon Ash, 'Drip-Feed Invective: Pliny, Self-Fashioning, and the Regulus Letters', in *The Author's Voice in Classical and Late Antiquity*, ed. Anna Marmodoro and Jonathan Hill (Oxford: Oxford University Press, 2013), 214–21.
15 See, e.g., Quint., *Inst.* 1, *pr.* 15; *Ann.* 16.22.2 (hypocrisy); Quint., *Inst.* 12.3.12; *Hist.* 4.5.1 (laziness); Sen., *Ep.* 73.1; *Ann.* 15.57.3 (disruptiveness).
16 See chapter two.
17 Also a topic of Domitianic satire: Juvenal, *Sat.* 5.36–37; Martial, *Epig.* 1.8.
18 Christopher Whitton, '"Let Us Tread Our Path Together": Tacitus and the Younger Pliny', in *A Companion to Tacitus*, ed. Victoria Emma Pagán (Malden, MA: Wiley-Blackwell, 2012), 353. See also the sensible observations of Dészpa, 'The Flavians and the Senate', 167–68. Marcus Wilson, 'After the Silence: Tacitus, Suetonius, Juvenal', in *Flavian Rome: Culture, Image, Text*, ed. A. J. Boyle and William Dominik (Leiden: Brill, 2003), 538: 'If anyone can be said to have created the "Stoic opposition" it was surely Eprius Marcellus.'
19 See, for instance, on Rusticus in *Histories*, Kathryn Williams, 'Tacitus' Senatorial Embassies of 69 CE', in *A Companion to Tacitus*, ed. Victoria Emma Pagán (Malden, MA: Wiley-Blackwell, 2012), 224–28.
20 Thrasea's daughter Fannia may also be present.
21 The metaphor of thirst for *libertas* occurs only twice elsewhere: Cic., *Rep.* 1.66 (of the Roman people); Livy, *Epit.* 39.26.7 (of the Thessalians).
22 Sailor, *Writing and Empire in Tacitus*, 15–16.
23 Thrasea has already discussed with his wife the suitability of her following a parental *exemplum*; cf. Rebecca Langlands, *Exemplary Ethics in Ancient Rome* (Cambridge: Cambridge University Press, 2018), 118–19.
24 My discussion of exemplarity here draws on Matthew Roller, *Models from the Past in Roman Culture: A World of* Exempla (Cambridge: Cambridge

University Press, 2018), and Langlands, *Exemplary Ethics in Ancient Rome*.

25 A hostile tradition is represented by Dio 75.12.3. On creative imitation of *exempla*, see Langlands, *Exemplary Ethics in Ancient Rome*, 86–111 and *passim*.

26 Action which is *ambitiosus* is ostentatious because it explicitly directs itself to an onlooker for approval.

27 Woodman, *Agricola*, 303, and Strunk, *History after Liberty*, 14–18, resist the identification of *plerique* with Thrasea and Helvidius; Sailor, *Writing and Empire in Tacitus*, 16–17, sees it as a rejection of a category of activity, separate from Tacitus' praise for individuals.

28 Syme, *Tacitus*, 555–62, and Strunk, *History after Liberty*, 104–5, articulate the primacy of the political; Peter Brunt, 'Stoicism and the Principate', *Papers of the British School at Rome* 43 (1975): 7–35, and William Turpin, 'Tacitus, Stoic Exempla, and the *Praecipuum Munus Annalium*', *Classical Antiquity* 27 (2008): 359–404, represent philosophically-inflected interpretations. See also John L. Penwill, 'Expelling the Mind: Politics and Philosophy in Flavian Rome', in *Flavian Rome: Culture, Image, Text*, ed. A. J. Boyle and William Dominik (Leiden: Brill, 2003).

29 Even the suicide of his father-in-law, Caecina Paetus, is overlooked in Tacitus' cursory account of the conspiracy of Scribonianus against Claudius in 42 (*Ann.* 12.52.1–2).

30 Further discussion of this passage in the introduction.

31 Mayer, 'Oratory in Tacitus' *Annals*', 288, reminds us that Capito was not a member of senate in AD 58.

32 An overview of imperial limits on gladiatorial games is provided by Koestermann, *Cornelius Tacitus: Annalen, Band III*, 332.

33 A comparable example of a statement made outside of senate but likely intended to reach senatorial ears is Tiberius' (*Ann.* 3.65.3), discussed in chapter three; 'private' conversations among Thrasea's circle in Tacitus' narrative could be drawn from the biography of Rusticus (e.g. *Ann.* 16.25–26).

34 Keitel, '*Sententia* and Structure in Tacitus *Histories* 1.12–49', 226–27.

35 Strunk, *History after Liberty*, 106–7.

36 This passage is extensively discussed. See particularly Martin and Woodman, *Tacitus: Annals Book IV*, 169–71; Moles, 'Cry Freedom', 106–11; O'Gorman, *Irony and Misreading in the Annals of Tacitus*, 101–2.

37 Koestermann, *Cornelius Tacitus: Annalen, Band III*, 299, suggests that Tacitus delays mention of this detail until it becomes meaningful, as it does at *Ann.* 16.21.3.

38 Olivier Devillers, 'Les passages relatifs à Asinius Gallus dans les *Annales* de Tacite', *Revue des Études Latines* 87 (2009): 156, on the careful structuring of Gallus' appearances in *Annals*.
39 Bhatt, 'Useful Vices: Tacitus's Critique of Corruption', 325–29.
40 David Shotter, 'Tiberius and Asinius Gallus', *Historia* 20 (1971): 443–57, sees Gallus as primarily hostile to Tiberius (cf. Geraldine Herbert-Brown, 'C. Asinius Gallus, Ti: Claudius Nero, and a Posthumous Agrippa in Ephesus (*ILS* 8897)', *Syllecta Classica* 15 (2004): 131–51); A. B. Bosworth, 'Asinius Pollio and Augustus', *Historia* 21, no. 3 (1972): 441–73, maintains that historical accounts of Gallus are coloured by the rebellion of his son against Claudius. See also Devillers, 'Les passages relatifs à Asinius Gallus'.
41 Shotter, 'Tiberius and Asinius Gallus', 448.
42 See chapter three.
43 Hence Tacitus comments on the *ferocia* which he has inherited from his father (*Ann*. 1.12.4).
44 See Woodman, *The Annals of Tacitus, Books 5 and 6*, 185–88, for an insightful reading of the passage.
45 Dio 57.2.5, 58.3.1. On the association of *ferocia* and *libertas* or *parrhesia*, see H. W. Traub, 'Tacitus' Use of *Ferocia*', *Transactions of the American Philological Association* 84 (1953): 250–61; Vielberg, *Pflichten, Werte, Ideale*, 159–63.
46 Mayer, 'Oratory in Tacitus' *Annals*', 283.
47 Ginsburg, 'Speech and Allusion in Tacitus', 540.
48 Thomas E. Strunk, 'Saving the Life of a Foolish Poet: Tacitus on Marcus Lepidus, Thrasea Paetus, and Political Action under the Principate', *Syllecta Classica* 21 (2010): 137; cf. Strunk, *History after Liberty*, 112–13.
49 Cowan, 'Contesting Clementia', 94–96.
50 Talbert, *The Senate of Imperial Rome*, 440 and 511–12, implies that this pertains to all senatorial decrees. Tacitus' narrative suggests the moratorium is for decrees of capital punishment. Cowan, 'Contesting Clementia', 94–96, argues persuasively for the moratorium as formalizing the exercise of imperial *clementia*.
51 See Bauman, *Impietas in Principem*, 62–65, for the interpretation of this proposal.
52 Soranus and Thrasea are together identified as 'virtue itself' by Tacitus at *Ann*. 61.21.1; in *Hist*. 4.10 he refers to the 'sacred memory' of Soranus in the senate, a clear parallel to the 'venerable image' of Thrasea that arose in the senate's mind during the trial itself (see chapter four).
53 Heubner, *P. Cornelius Tacitus: Die Historien, Band IV*, 95.
54 His proposal to restore honours to Piso Caesar as well as to Galba is ignored, but is perhaps a suitable intervention from one junior senator on behalf of another young man.

55 See also the suggestion of R. H. Martin, 'The Speech of Curtius Montanus: Tacitus, *Histories* IV, 42', *Journal of Roman Studies* 57 (1967): 109–14, and Whitton, 'Let Us Tread Our Path Together', 361, that Montanus is configured as Pliny in his attack on Regulus.
56 See esp. Plin., *Ep*. 4.22.3–6.
57 Elizabeth Keitel, 'Speech and Narrative in *Histories* 4', in *Tacitus and the Tacitean Tradition*, ed. T. J. Luce and A. J. Woodman (Princeton, NJ: Princeton University Press, 1993), 45.
58 Note also Aper in *Dialogus*, who refers to Eprius' *eloquentia* running rings around Helvidius – possibly an allusion to their altercation or to their final confrontation in *Hist*. 4.43 (*Dial*. 5.7).
59 Against this, Curtius Montanus concludes his attack on Regulus by suggesting that the senate has acted too late: *optimus est post malum principem dies primus* (*Hist*. 4.42.6).
60 Stanley E. Hoffer, *The Anxieties of Pliny the Younger* (Atlanta, GA: Scholars Press, 1999), 87, suggests that Pliny could have been acting as an agent for others in bringing charges against Certus.
61 John Bodel, 'The Publication of Pliny's Letters', in *Pliny the Bookmaker*, ed. Ilaria Marchesi (Oxford: Oxford University Press, 2015), 74–83.
62 On the literary interactions between the two, see Ilaria Marchesi, *The Art of Pliny's Letters* (Cambridge: Cambridge University Press, 2008), 97–206; Whitton, 'Let Us Tread Our Path Together'.
63 Whitton, 'Let Us Tread Our Path Together', 355–62.
64 Whitton, 'Pliny, *Epistles* 8.14'; O'Gorman, 'Conspicuous Absence'.
65 Sir Ronald Syme, 'The Ummidii', *Historia* 17 (1968): 84–99.
66 On the significance of juxtaposed letters, see Gibson and Morello, *Reading the Letters of Pliny the Younger*, 12–52.

Conclusion

1 Moles, 'Cry Freedom'; O'Gorman, *Irony and Misreading in the Annals of Tacitus*, 100–102; Sailor, *Writing and Empire in Tacitus*, 250–313.
2 Alexandra Gajda, 'Tacitus and Political Thought in Early Modern Europe, c. 1530–c. 1640', in *The Cambridge Companion to Tacitus*, ed. A. J. Woodman (Cambridge: Cambridge University Press, 2009); Daniel J. Kapust, *Republicanism, Rhetoric, and Roman Political Thought* (Cambridge: Cambridge University Press, 2011).

3 Dean Hammer, *Roman Political Thought and the Modern Theoretical Imagination* (Norman, OK: University of Oklahoma Press, 2008); Dean Hammer, *Roman Political Thought, from Cicero to Augustine* (Cambridge: Cambridge University Press, 2014); and Connolly, *The Life of Roman Republicanism*.
4 See especially Jacob Soll, *Publishing the Prince: History, Reading, and the Birth of Political Criticism* (Ann Arbor, MI: University of Michigan Press, 2005).

Bibliography

Ahl, Frederic. 'The Art of Safe Criticism in Greece and Rome'. *American Journal of Philology* 105, no. 2 (1984): 174–208.

Alcorn, Marshall W. 'Self-Structure as a Rhetorical Device: Modern *Ethos* and the Divisiveness of the Self'. In *Ethos: New Essays in Rhetorical and Critical Theory*, edited by James S. Baumlin and Tita French Baumlin, 3–35. Dallas, TX: Southern Methodist University Press, 1994.

Aldrete, Gregory. *Gestures and Acclamations in Ancient Rome*. Baltimore, MD: Johns Hopkins University Press, 1999.

Alföldy, G. 'Augustus und die Inschriften: Tradition und Innovation'. *Gymnasium* 98 (1991): 289–324.

Alston, Richard. 'Foucault's Empire of the Free'. *Foucault Studies* 22 (2017): 94–112.

Ando, Clifford. *Imperial Ideology and Provincial Loyalty in the Roman Empire*. Berkeley, CA: University of California Press, 2000.

Ando, Clifford. *Roman Social Imaginaries: Language and Thought in Contexts of Empire*. Toronto: University of Toronto Press, 2015.

Ando, Clifford. 'Tacitus, *Annales* VI: Beginning and End'. *American Journal of Philology* 118, no. 2 (1997): 285–303.

Ash, Rhiannon. 'At the End of the Rainbow: Nero and Dido's Gold (Tacitus *Annals* 16.1–3)'. In *Fame and Infamy: Essays on Characterization in Greek and Roman Biography and Historiography*, edited by Rhiannon Ash, Judith Mossman, and Frances B. Titchener, 269–83. Oxford: Oxford University Press, 2015.

Ash, Rhiannon. 'Drip-Feed Invective: Pliny, Self-Fashioning, and the Regulus Letters'. In *The Author's Voice in Classical and Late Antiquity*, edited by Anna Marmodoro and Jonathan Hill, 207–32. Oxford: Oxford University Press, 2013.

Ash, Rhiannon. *Ordering Anarchy: Armies and Leaders in Tacitus' Histories*. London: Duckworth, 1999.

Ash, Rhiannon. *Tacitus: Histories, Book II*. Cambridge: Cambridge University Press, 2007.

Bablitz, Leanne. *Actors and Audience in the Roman Courtroom*. Abingdon and New York: Routledge, 2007.

Balbo, Andrea. *I frammenti degli oratori romani dell'età augustea e tiberiana. Parte seconda: Età tiberiana*, 2 vols. Alessandria: Edizioni dell'Orso, 2007.

Bartsch, Shadi. *Actors in the Audience: Theatricality and Doublespeak from Nero to Hadrian*. Cambridge, MA: Harvard University Press, 1994.

Batstone, William. 'The Drama of Rhetoric at Rome'. In *The Cambridge Companion to Ancient Rhetoric*, edited by Erik Gunderson, 212–27. Cambridge: Cambridge University Press, 2009.

Bauman, Richard A. *Impietas in Principem: A Study of Treason against the Roman Emperor with Special Reference to the First Century AD*. Munich: C. H. Beck, 1974.

Baumlin, James S., and Craig A. Meyer. 'Positioning Ethos in/for the Twenty-First Century: An Introduction to Histories of Ethos'. *Humanities* 7, no. 78 (2018). https://doi.org/10.3390/h7030078.

Bernstein, Neil W. 'Each Man's Father Served as His Teacher: Constructing Relatedness in Pliny's Letters'. *Classical Antiquity* 27, no. 2 (2008): 203–30.

Bernstein, Neil W. *Ethics, Identity, and Community in Later Roman Declamation*. Oxford: Oxford University Press, 2013.

Bhatt, Shreyaa. 'The Augustan Principate and the Emergence of Biopolitics: A Comparative Historical Perspective'. *Foucault Studies* 22 (2017): 72–93.

Bhatt, Shreyaa. 'Useful Vices: Tacitus's Critique of Corruption'. *Arethusa* 50, no. 3 (2017): 311–33.

Birley, A. R. *Tacitus: Agricola and Germany*. Oxford: Oxford World's Classics, 1999.

Bloomer, W. Martin. *The School of Rome: Latin Studies and the Origins of Liberal Education*. Berkeley, CA: University of California Press, 2011.

Bodel, John. 'The Publication of Pliny's Letters'. In *Pliny the Bookmaker*, edited by Ilaria Marchesi, 13–108. Oxford: Oxford University Press, 2015.

Bosworth, A. B. 'Asinius Pollio and Augustus'. *Historia* 21, no. 3 (1972): 441–73.

Brunt, Peter. 'Stoicism and the Principate'. *Papers of the British School at Rome* 43 (1975): 7–35.

Burgers, Peter. 'The Role and Function of Senatorial Debate: The Case of the Reign of Tiberius AD 14–37'. *Latomus* 58 (1999): 564–73.

Carlon, Jacqueline. *Pliny's Women: Constructing Virtue and Creating Identity in the Roman World*. Cambridge: Cambridge University Press, 2010.

Champlin, Edward. 'Seianus Augustus'. *Chiron* 42 (2012): 361–88.

Chilver, G. E. F., and G. B. Townend. *A Historical Commentary on Tacitus' Histories IV and V*. Oxford: Clarendon Press, 1985.

Coffee, Neil. *Gift and Gain: How Money Transformed Ancient Rome*. Oxford: Oxford University Press, 2017.

Connolly, Joy. 'Fear and Freedom: A New Interpretation of Pliny's Panegyricus'. In *Ordine e sovversione nel mondo greco e romano*, edited by Gianpaolo Urso, 247–66. Pisa: Edizioni ETS, 2008. http://www.fondazionecanussio.org/atti2008/15_connolly.pdf.

Connolly, Joy. *The Life of Roman Republicanism*. Princeton, NJ: Princeton University Press, 2015.

Connolly, Joy. 'The Politics of Rhetorical Education'. In *The Cambridge Companion to Ancient Rhetoric*, edited by Erik Gunderson, 126–41. Cambridge: Cambridge University Press, 2009.

Connolly, Joy. *The State of Speech: Rhetoric and Political Thought in Ancient Rome*. Princeton, NJ: Princeton University Press, 2007.

Consigny, Scott. 'Rhetoric and Its Situations'. *Philosophy & Rhetoric* 7, no. 3 (1974): 175–86.

Cooley, Alison E. 'Paratextual Perspectives upon the *SC de Pisone Patre*'. In *The Roman Paratext: Frame, Texts, Readers*, edited by Laura Jansen, 143–55. Cambridge: Cambridge University Press, 2014.

Corbeill, Anthony. 'Rhetorical Education and Social Reproduction in the Republic and Early Empire'. In *A Companion to Roman Rhetoric*, edited by William Dominik and Jon Hall, 69–82. Malden, MA: Wiley-Blackwell, 2007.

Cornwell, Hannah. *Pax and the Politics of Peace: Republic to Principate*. Oxford: Oxford University Press, 2017.

Cowan, Eleanor. 'Contesting Clementia: The Rhetoric of Severitas in Tiberian Rome before and after the Trial of Clutorius Priscus'. *Journal of Roman Studies* 106 (2016): 77–101.

Cowan, Eleanor. 'Tacitus, Tiberius, and Augustus'. *Classical Antiquity* 28, no. 2 (2009): 179–210.

Damon, Cynthia. *The Mask of the Parasite: A Pathology of Roman Patronage*. Ann Arbor, MI: University of Michigan Press, 1997.

Damon, Cynthia. *Tacitus: Annals*. London: Penguin Books, 2012.

Damon, Cynthia. *Tacitus: Histories, Book I*. Cambridge: Cambridge University Press, 2003.

Dészpa, Loránd. 'The Flavians and the Senate'. In *A Companion to the Flavian Age of Imperial Rome*, edited by Andrew Zissos, 166–85. Malden, MA: Wiley-Blackwell, 2016.

Devillers, Olivier. 'The Concentration of Power and Writing History: Forms of Historical Persuasion in the *Histories* (1.1–49)'. In *A Companion to Tacitus*, edited by Victoria Emma Pagán, 162–86. Malden, MA: Wiley-Blackwell, 2012.

Devillers, Olivier. 'Les passages relatifs à Asinius Gallus dans les *Annales* de Tacite'. *Revue des Études Latines* 87 (2009): 154–65.

Donaldson, Peter S. *Machiavelli and Mystery of State*. Cambridge: Cambridge University Press, 1988.

Dressler, Alex. 'Poetics of Conspiracy and Hermeneutics of Suspicion in Tacitus's *Dialogus de Oratoribus*'. *Classical Antiquity* 32, no. 1 (2013): 1–34.

Dunkle, J. Roger. 'The Rhetorical Tyrant in Roman Historiography: Sallust, Livy and Tacitus'. *Classical World* 65, no. 1 (1971): 12–20.

Elkins, Nathan T. *The Image of Political Power in the Reign of Nerva, AD 96–98.* Oxford: Oxford University Press, 2017.

Enos, Richard Leo, and Karen Rossi Schnakenberg. 'Cicero Latinizes Hellenic Ethos'. In *Ethos: New Essays in Rhetorical and Critical Theory*, edited by James S. Baumlin and Tita French Baumlin, 191–209. Dallas, TX: Southern Methodist University Press, 1994.

Flaig, Egon. 'A Coherent Model to Understand the Roman Principate: "Acceptance" instead of "Legitimacy" and the Problem of Usurpation'. In *Il princeps romano: Autocrate o magistrato? Fattori giuridici e fattori sociali del potere imperiale da Augusto a Commodo*, edited by Jean-Louis Ferrary and John Scheid, 81–100. Pavia: IUSS Press, 2015.

Flaig, Egon. *Den Kaiser herausfordern: Die Usurpation im Römischen Reich.* Frankfurt: Campus Verlag, 1992.

Flaig, Egon. 'How the Emperor Nero Lost Acceptance in Rome'. In *The Emperor and Rome: Space, Representation, and Ritual*, edited by Christian Ewald Bjorn and Carlos F. Noreña, 275–88. Cambridge: Cambridge University Press, 2011.

Foucault, Michel. *The Courage of the Truth (The Government of Self and Others II): Lectures at the Collège de France, 1983–1984*, edited by Frédéric Gros, translated by Graham Burchell. Basingstoke: Palgrave-Macmillan, 2011.

Foucault, Michel. *On the Government of the Living: Lectures at the Collège de France, 1979–1980*, edited by Michel Senellart, translated by Graham Burchell. Basingstoke: Palgrave-Macmillan, 2014.

Foucault, Michel. 'Truth and Power'. In *Power/Knowledge: Selected Interviews and Other Writings, 1972–1977*, edited by Colin Gordon, 109–33. Brighton: Harvester Press, 1980.

Freyburger, Gérard. 'La supplication d'action de grâces sous le Haut-Empire'. *ANRW* II 16, no. 2 (1978): 1418–39.

Gajda, Alexandra. 'Tacitus and Political Thought in Early Modern Europe, c. 1530–c. 1640'. In *The Cambridge Companion to Tacitus*, edited by A. J. Woodman, 253–68. Cambridge: Cambridge University Press, 2009.

Gallia, Andrew B. *Remembering the Roman Republic: Culture, Politics and History under the Principate.* Cambridge: Cambridge University Press, 2012.

Gibson, Roy K., and Ruth Morello. *Reading the Letters of Pliny the Younger.* Cambridge: Cambridge University Press, 2012.

Gildenhard, Ingo. *Creative Eloquence: The Construction of Reality in Cicero's Speeches.* Oxford: Oxford University Press, 2010.

Ginsburg, Judith. 'Speech and Allusion in Tacitus, *Annals* 3.49–51 and 14.48–49'. *American Journal of Philology* 107 (1986): 525–41.

Goldberg, Sander. 'Appreciating Aper: The Defence of Modernity in Tacitus' *Dialogus de Oratoribus*'. In *Oxford Readings in Tacitus*, edited by Rhiannon Ash, 155–79. Oxford: Oxford University Press, 2012 [1999].

González, Julián. 'Tacitus, Germanicus, Piso, and the Tabula Siarensis'. *American Journal of Philology* 120, no. 1 (1999): 123–42.

Gotoff, Harold. 'Cicero's Caesarian Orations'. In *Brill's Companion to Cicero: Oratory and Rhetoric*, edited by J. M. May, 219–71. Leiden: Brill, 2002.

Grethlein, Jonas. *Experience and Teleology in Ancient Historiography: Futures Past from Herodotus to Augustine*. Cambridge: Cambridge University Press, 2013.

Griffin, Miriam. 'Claudius in Tacitus'. *Classical Quarterly* 40, no. 2 (1980): 482–501.

Griffin, Miriam. *Seneca: A Philosopher in Politics*, Oxford: Clarendon Press, 1976.

Guérin, Charles. *La voix de la vérité: Témoin et témoignage dans les tribunaux romains du 1er siècle avant J.-C.* Paris: Les Belles Lettres, 2015.

Gunderson, Erik. *Declamation, Paternity, and Roman Identity: Authority and the Rhetorical Self*. Cambridge: Cambridge University Press, 2003.

Gunderson, Erik. *Staging Masculinity: The Rhetoric of Performance in the Roman World*. Ann Arbor, MI: University of Michigan Press, 2000.

Habinek, Thomas N. *The Politics of Latin Literature: Writing, Identity, and Empire in Ancient Rome*. Princeton, NJ: Princeton University Press, 1998.

Hammer, Dean. 'Foucault, Sovereignty, and Governmentality in the Roman Republic'. *Foucault Studies* 22 (2017): 49–71.

Hammer, Dean. *The* Iliad *as Politics: The Performance of Political Thought*. Norman, OK: University of Oklahoma Press, 2002.

Hammer, Dean. *Roman Political Thought and the Modern Theoretical Imagination*. Norman, OK: University of Oklahoma Press, 2008.

Hammer, Dean. *Roman Political Thought, from Cicero to Augustine*. Cambridge: Cambridge University Press, 2014.

Hardie, Philip. 'Crowds and Leaders in Imperial Historiography and in Epic'. In *Latin Historiography and Poetry in the Early Empire: Generic Interactions*, edited by John F. Miller and A. J. Woodman, 9–27. Leiden: Brill, 2010.

Harries, Jill. *Law and Crime in the Roman World*. Cambridge: Cambridge University Press, 2007.

Harrison, Stephen J. 'From Man to Book: The Close of Tacitus' *Agricola*'. In *Classical Constructions: Papers in Memory of Don Fowler, Classicist and Epicurean*, edited by Stephen J. Harrison, Peta G. Fowler, and Stephen J. Heyworth, 310–19. Oxford: Oxford University Press, 2007.

Hawhee, Debra. *Rhetoric in Tooth and Claw: Animals, Language, Sensation.* Chicago, IL: University of Chicago Press, 2016.

Haynes, Holly. *The History of Make-Believe: Tacitus on Imperial Rome.* Berkeley, CA: University of California Press, 2003.

Haynes, Holly. 'Survival and Memory in the *Agricola*'. *Arethusa* 39 (2006): 149–70.

Haynes, Holly. 'Tacitus' Dangerous Word'. *Classical Antiquity* 23, no. 1 (2004): 33–61.

Herbert-Brown, Geraldine. 'C. Asinius Gallus, Ti. Claudius Nero, and a Posthumous Agrippa in Ephesus (*ILS* 8897)'. *Syllecta Classica* 15 (2004): 131–51.

Herz, Peter. 'Emperors: Caring for the Empire and their Successors'. In *A Companion to Roman Religion*, edited by Jörg Rüpke, 304–16. Malden, MA: Wiley-Blackwell, 2007.

Heubner, Heinz. *P. Cornelius Tacitus: Annales.* Stuttgart: B. G. Teubner, 1983.

Heubner, Heinz. *P. Cornelius Tacitus: Dialogus de Oratoribus.* Stuttgart: B. G. Teubner, 1983.

Heubner, Heinz. *P. Cornelius Tacitus: Die Historien, Band I.* Heidelberg: Carl Winter Universitätsverlag, 1963.

Heubner, Heinz. *P. Cornelius Tacitus: Die Historien, Band II.* Heidelberg: Carl Winter Universitätsverlag, 1968.

Heubner, Heinz. *P. Cornelius Tacitus: Die Historien, Band IV.* Heidelberg: Carl Winter Universitätsverlag, 1976.

Heubner, Heinz. *P. Cornelius Tacitus: Historiarum Libri.* Stuttgart: B. G. Teubner, 1978.

Hoffer, Stanley E. *The Anxieties of Pliny the Younger.* Atlanta, GA: Scholars Press, 1999.

Hurlet, Frédéric. 'Les Sénateurs dans l'entourage d'Auguste et de Tibère: Un complément à plusieurs synthèses récentes sur la cour impériale'. *Revue de philologie* 74 (2000): 123–50.

Johnson, William A. *Readers and Reading Culture in the High Roman Empire: A Study of Elite Communities.* Oxford: Oxford University Press, 2010.

Jones, A. H. M. *The Criminal Courts of the Roman Republic and Principate.* Oxford: Basil Blackwell, 1972.

Kapust, Daniel J. *Flattery and the History of Political Thought: That Glib and Oily Art.* Cambridge: Cambridge University Press, 2018.

Kapust, Daniel J. *Republicanism, Rhetoric, and Roman Political Thought.* Cambridge: Cambridge University Press, 2011.

Keitel, Elizabeth. '"Is Dying so Very Terrible?": The Neronian *Annals*'. In *The Cambridge Companion to Tacitus*, edited by A. J. Woodman, 127–43. Cambridge: Cambridge University Press, 2009.

Keitel, Elizabeth. '*Sententia* and Structure in Tacitus *Histories* 1.12–49'. *Arethusa* 39 (2006): 219–44.

Keitel, Elizabeth. 'Speech and Narrative in *Histories* 4'. In *Tacitus and the Tacitean Tradition*, edited by T. J. Luce and A. J. Woodman, 39–58. Princeton, NJ: Princeton University Press, 1993.

Keitel, Elizabeth. 'The Structure and Function of Speeches in Tacitus *Histories* I–III'. *ANRW* II 33, no. 4 (1991): 2772–94.

Kemezis, Adam. *Greek Narratives of the Roman Empire under the Severans: Cassius Dio, Philostratus and Herodian*. Cambridge: Cambridge University Press, 2014.

Kemp, Jerome. 'Flattery and Frankness in Horace and Philodemus'. *Greece & Rome* 57 (2010): 65–76.

Koestermann, Erich. *Cornelius Tacitus: Annalen, Band III, Buch 11–13*. Heidelberg: Carl Winter Universitätsverlag, 1967.

Laird, Andrew. *Powers of Expression, Expressions of Power: Speech Presentation and Latin Literature*. Oxford: Oxford University Press, 1999.

Langlands, Rebecca. *Exemplary Ethics in Ancient Rome*. Cambridge: Cambridge University Press, 2018.

Latour, Bruno. *Reassembling the Social: An Introduction to Actor-Network-Theory*. Oxford: Oxford University Press, 2005.

Lausberg, Heinrich. *Handbook of Literary Rhetoric*. Translated by D. F. Orton and R. D. Anderson. Leiden: Brill, 1998.

Lavan, Myles. *Slaves to Rome: Paradigms of Empire in Roman Culture*. Cambridge: Cambridge University Press, 2013.

Lendon, J. E. *Empire of Honour: The Art of Government in the Roman World*. Oxford: Clarendon Press, 1997.

Levene, David S. 'God and Man in the Classical Latin Panegyric'. *Proceedings of the Cambridge Philological Society* 43, no. 1 (1997): 66–103.

Levene, David S. 'Tacitus' *Histories* and the Theory of Deliberative Oratory'. In *The Limits of Historiography: Genre and Narrative in Ancient Historical Texts*, edited by Christina Shuttleworth Kraus, 197–216. Leiden: Brill, 1999.

Levick, Barbara. 'Tacitus in the Twenty-First Century: The Struggle for Truth in *Annals* 1–6'. In *A Companion to Tacitus*, edited by Victoria Emma Pagán, 260–81. Malden, MA: Wiley-Blackwell, 2012.

Levick, Barbara. *Tiberius the Politician*. Rev. ed. London: Routledge, 1999.

Lobur, John. *Consensus, Concordia, and the Formation of Roman Imperial Ideology*. New York: Routledge, 2008.

Lorenzini, Daniele. 'Foucault, Regimes of Truth, and the Making of the Subject'. In *Foucault and the Making of Subjects*, edited by Laura Cremonesi, Orazio Irrera, Daniele Lorenzini, and Martina Tazzioli, 63–75. London: Rowman & Littlefield, 2016.

Luce, T. J. 'Reading and Response in the *Dialogus*'. In *Tacitus and the Tacitean Tradition*, edited by A. J. Woodman and T. J. Luce, 11–38. Princeton, NJ: Princeton University Press, 1993.

Luce, T. J. 'Tacitus on "History's Highest Function": *Praecipuum Munus Annalium* (*Ann.* 3.65)'. *ANRW* II 33, no. 4 (1991): 2904–27.

Luce, T. J. 'Tacitus' Conception of Historical Change: The Problem of Discovering the Historian's Opinions'. In *Oxford Readings in Tacitus*, edited by Rhiannon Ash, 339–56. Oxford: Oxford University Press, 2012 [1983].

Luke, Trevor S. 'From Crisis to Consensus: Salutary Ideology and the Murder of Agrippina'. *Illinois Classical Studies* 38 (2013): 207–28.

Luke, Trevor S. *Ushering in a New Republic: Theologies of Arrival at Rome in the First Century BCE*. Ann Arbor, MI: University of Michigan Press, 2014.

Malloch, S. J. V. *The Annals of Tacitus, Book 11*. Cambridge: Cambridge University Press, 2013.

Marchesi, Ilaria. *The Art of Pliny's Letters*. Cambridge: Cambridge University Press, 2009.

Martin, James. 'A Feeling for Democracy? Rhetoric, Power and the Emotions'. *Journal of Political Power* 6 (2013): 461–76.

Martin, James. *Politics and Rhetoric: A Critical Introduction*. London: Routledge, 2014.

Martin, R. H. 'The Speech of Curtius Montanus: Tacitus, *Histories* IV, 42'. *Journal of Roman Studies* 57 (1967): 109–14.

Martin, R. H., and A. J. Woodman. *Tacitus: Annals Book IV*. Cambridge: Cambridge University Press, 1989.

Master, Jonathan. *Provincial Soldiers and Imperial Instability in the Histories of Tacitus*. Ann Arbor, MI: University of Michigan Press, 2016.

Matthews, John. 'Tacitus, *Acta Senatus*, and the Inauguration of Tiberius'. In *Roman Perspectives: Studies in the Social, Political and Cultural History of the First to Fifth Centuries*. Swansea: Classical Press of Wales, 2008.

May, James M. *Trials of Character: The Eloquence of Ciceronian Ethos*. Chapel Hill, NC: University of North Carolina Press, 1988.

Mayer, Roland. 'Oratory in Tacitus' *Annals*'. In *Form and Function in Roman Oratory*, edited by D. H. Berry and Andrew Erskine, 281–93. Cambridge: Cambridge University Press, 2010.

Millar, Fergus. *The Emperor in the Roman World*. London: Duckworth, 1977.

Miller, Susan. *Trust in Texts: A Different History of Rhetoric*. Carbondale, IL: Southern Illinois University Press, 2008.

Milnor, Kristina. 'Augustus, History, and the Landscape of the Law'. *Arethusa* 40 (2007): 7–23.

Moles, John. 'Cry Freedom: Tacitus *Annals* 4.32–35'. *Histos* 2 (1998): 95–184.

Morello, Ruth. 'A Correspondence Course in Tyranny: The *Cruentae Litterae* of Tiberius'. *Arethusa* 39, no. 2 (2006): 331–54.

Morgan, Gwyn. *69 AD: The Year of Four Emperors*. Oxford: Oxford University Press, 2006.

Morstein-Marx, Robert. *Mass Oratory and Political Power in the Late Roman Republic*. Cambridge: Cambridge University Press, 2004.

Neocleous, Mark. *Imagining the State*. Maidenhead: Open University Press, 2003.

Noreña, Carlos F. *Imperial Ideals in the Roman West: Representation, Circulation, Power*. Cambridge: Cambridge University Press, 2011.

Noreña, Carlos F. 'Self-Fashioning in the *Panegyricus*'. In *Pliny's Praise: The Panegyricus in the Roman World*, edited by Paul Roche, 29–43. Cambridge: Cambridge University Press, 2011.

Oakley, Stephen. '*Res olim dissociabiles*: Emperors, Senators and Liberty'. In *The Cambridge Companion to Tacitus*, edited by A. J. Woodman, 184–94. Cambridge: Cambridge University Press, 2009.

Ogilvie, R. M., and I. A. Richmond. *De Vita Agricolae*. Oxford: Clarendon Press, 1967.

O'Gorman, Ellen. 'Conspicuous Absence: Tacitus' *Republic*'. In *Unspoken Rome: Absence in Latin Literature and Its Reception*, edited by Tom Geue and Elena Giusti. Cambridge: Cambridge University Press, forthcoming.

O'Gorman, Ellen. 'Intertextuality and Historiography'. In *The Cambridge Companion to the Roman Historians*, edited by Andrew Feldherr, 231–42. Cambridge: Cambridge University Press, 2009.

O'Gorman, Ellen. *Irony and Misreading in the Annals of Tacitus*. Cambridge: Cambridge University Press, 2000.

O'Gorman, Ellen. 'The Noise, and the *People*: Popular *Clamor* and Political Discourse in Roman Historiography'. In *Complex Inferiorities: The Poetics of the Weaker Voice in Latin Literature*, edited by Stephen Harrison and Sebastian Matzner, 128–48. Oxford: Oxford University Press, 2018.

Oost, Stewart Irvin. 'The Career of M. Antonius Pallas'. *American Journal of Philology* 79, no. 2 (1958): 113–39.

Pagán, Victoria Emma. *Tacitus*. London and New York: I.B. Tauris, 2017.

Pandey, Nandini B. *The Poetics of Power in Augustan Rome: Latin Poetic Responses to Early Imperial Iconography*. Cambridge: Cambridge University Press, 2018.

Peachin, Michael. 'Augustus' Emergent Judicial Powers, the "Crimen Maiestatis", and the Second Cyrene Edict'. In *Il princeps romano: Autocrate o magistrato? Fattori giuridici e fattori sociali del potere imperiale da Augusto a Commodo*, edited by Jean-Louis Ferrary and John Scheid, 497–553. Pavia: IUSS Press, 2015.

Peachin, Michael. 'Exemplary Government in the Early Roman Empire'. In *Crises and the Roman Empire*, edited by Olivier Hekster, Gerda de Kleijn, and Daniëlle Slootjes, 75–93. Leiden: Brill, 2007.

Pelling, Christopher. 'The Spur of Fame: Annals 4.37–8'. In *Ancient Historiography and Its Contexts: Studies in Honour of A. J. Woodman*, edited by Christina Shuttleworth Kraus, John Marincola, and Christopher Pelling, 364–84. Oxford: Oxford University Press, 2010.

Pelling, Christopher. 'Tacitus' Personal Voice'. In *The Cambridge Companion to Tacitus*, edited by A. J. Woodman, 147–67. Cambridge: Cambridge University Press, 2009.

Penwill, John L. 'Expelling the Mind: Politics and Philosophy in Flavian Rome'. In *Flavian Rome: Culture, Image, Text*, edited by A. J. Boyle and William Dominik, 345–68. Leiden: Brill, 2003.

Perry, Matthew. 'Quintus Haterius and the "Dutiful" Freedman'. *The Ancient History Bulletin* 25, no. 3–4 (2011): 133–48.

Pettinger, Andrew. *The Republic in Danger: Drusus Libo and the Succession of Tiberius*. Oxford: Oxford University Press, 2012.

Pigoń, Jakub. 'Helvidius Priscus, Eprius Marcellus, and *Iudicium Senatus*: Observations on Tacitus, Histories 4.7–8'. *Classical Quarterly* 42, no. 1 (1992): 235–46.

Plass, Paul. *Wit and the Writing of History: The Rhetoric of Historiography in Imperial Rome*. Madison, WI: University of Wisconsin Press, 1988.

Potter, David. 'Tacitus' Sources'. In *A Companion to Tacitus*, edited by Victoria Emma Pagán, 125–40. Malden, MA: Wiley-Blackwell, 2012.

Poulsen, Aske Damtoft. 'The Language of Freedom and Slavery in Tacitus' *Agricola*'. *Mnemosyne* 70, no. 5 (2017): 834–58.

Rees, Roger. 'Panegyric'. In *A Companion to Roman Rhetoric*, edited by William Dominik and Jon Hall, 136–48. Malden, MA: Wiley-Blackwell, 2007.

Rich, John. 'Consensus Rituals and the Origins of the Principate'. In *Il princeps romano: Autocrate o magistrato? Fattori giuridici e fattori sociali del potere imperiale da Augusto a Commodo*, edited by Jean-Louis Ferrary and John Scheid, 101–38. Pavia: IUSS Press, 2015.

Richardson, J. S. 'The Senate, the Courts, and the *SC de Cn. Pisone Patre*'. *Classical Quarterly* 47, no. 2 (1997): 510–18.

Riggsby, Andrew M. 'Self and Community in the Younger Pliny'. *Arethusa* 31, no. 1 (1998): 75–97.

Roche, Paul. 'Pliny's Thanksgiving: An Introduction to the *Panegyricus*'. In *Pliny's Praise: The* Panegyricus *in the Roman World*, edited by Paul Roche, 1–28. Cambridge: Cambridge University Press, 2011.

Rogers, R. S. 'The Tacitean Account of a Neronian Trial'. In *Studies Presented to Daniel Moore Robinson on His Seventieth Birthday*, edited by George E. Mylonas and Doris Raymond, 711–18. St. Louis, MO: Washington University Press, 1953.

Roller, Matthew. *Constructing Autocracy: Aristocrats and Emperors in Julio-Claudian Rome*. Princeton, NJ: Princeton University Press, 2001.

Roller, Matthew. 'The Difference an Emperor Makes: Notes on the Reception of the Republican Senate in the Imperial Age'. *Classical Receptions Journal* 7, no. 1 (2015): 11–30.

Roller, Matthew. *Models from the Past in Roman Culture: A World of Exempla*. Cambridge: Cambridge University Press, 2018.

Roller, Matthew. 'The Rise of the Centumviral Court in the Augustan Age'. In *The Alternative Augustan Age*, edited by Josiah Osgood, Kit Morrell, and Kathryn Welch, 266–81. Oxford: Oxford University Press, 2019.

Rowe, Greg. *Princes and Political Cultures: The New Tiberian Senatorial Decrees*. Ann Arbor, MI: University of Michigan Press, 2002.

Ruch, Michel. *M. T. Ciceronis Pro Marcello Oratio*. Paris: Presses Universitaires de France, 1965.

Russell, Amy. 'The Augustan Senate and the Reconfiguration of Time on the Fasti Capitolini'. In *Augustus and the Destruction of History: The Politics of the Past in Early Imperial Rome*, edited by Ingo Gildenhard, Ulrich Gotter, Wolfgang Havener, and Louise Hodgson, 157–86. London: Oxbow Books, 2019.

Russell, Amy. 'Inventing the Imperial Senate'. In *The Alternative Augustan Age*, edited by Josiah Osgood, Kit Morrell, and Kathryn Welch, 325–42. Oxford: Oxford University Press, 2019.

Rutledge, Steven. 'Delatores and the Tradition of Violence in Roman Oratory'. *American Journal of Philology* 120, no. 4 (1999): 555–73.

Rutledge, Steven. *Imperial Inquisitions: Prosecutors and Informants from Tiberius to Domitian*. London: Routledge, 2001.

Sailor, Dylan. *Writing and Empire in Tacitus*. Cambridge: Cambridge University Press, 2008.

Scott, James C. *Domination and the Arts of Resistance: Hidden Transcripts*. New Haven, CT: Yale University Press, 1990.

Shotter, David. 'Tiberius and Asinius Gallus'. *Historia* 20 (1971): 443–57.

Severy, Beth. 'Family and State in the Early Imperial Monarchy: The Senatus Consultum de Pisone Patre, Tabula Siarensis, and Tabula Hebana'. *Classical Philology* 95, no. 3 (2000): 318–37.

Sinclair, Patrick. *Tacitus the Sententious Historian: A Sociology of Rhetoric in Annales 1–6*. University Park, PA: Pennsylvania State University Press, 1995.

Soll, Jacob. *Publishing the Prince: History, Reading, and the Birth of Political Criticism*. Ann Arbor, MI: University of Michigan Press, 2005.

Soni, Vivasvan. 'A Classical Politics without Happiness? Hannah Arendt and the American Revolution'. *Cultural Critique* 74 (2010): 32–47.

Strunk, Thomas E. 'Collaborators amongst the Opposition? Deconstructing the Imperial *Cursus Honorum*'. *Arethusa* 48, no. 1 (2015): 47–58.

Strunk, Thomas E. 'Domitian's Lightning Bolts and Close Shaves in Pliny'. *Classical Journal* 109, no. 1 (2013): 88–113.

Strunk, Thomas E. *History after Liberty: Tacitus on Tyrants, Sycophants, and Republicans*. Ann Arbor, MI: University of Michigan Press, 2017.

Strunk, Thomas E. 'Saving the Life of a Foolish Poet: Tacitus on Marcus Lepidus, Thrasea Paetus, and Political Action under the Principate'. *Syllecta Classica* 21 (2010): 119–39.

Sumi, Geoffrey S. *Ceremony and Power: Performing Politics in Rome between Republic and Empire*. Ann Arbor, MI: University of Michigan Press, 2005.

Syme, Sir Ronald. 'Marcus Lepidus, *Capax Imperii*'. In *Ten Studies in Tacitus*, 1–10. Oxford: Clarendon Press, 1970.

Syme, Sir Ronald. *Tacitus*. 2 vols. Oxford: Clarendon Press, 1958.

Syme, Sir Ronald. 'The Ummidii'. *Historia* 17 (1968): 72–105.

Talbert, Richard J. A. *The Senate of Imperial Rome*. Princeton, NJ: Princeton University Press, 1984.

Tedeschi, Antonella. *Lezione di buon governo per un dittatore. Cicerone*, Pro Marcello: *Saggio di commento*. Bari: Edipuglia, 2005.

Tempest, Kathryn. 'An Ethos of Sincerity: Echoes of *de Re Publica* in Cicero's *Pro Marcello*'. *Greece & Rome* 60, no. 2 (2013): 262–80.

Townend, Gavin. 'The Consuls of AD 69–70'. *American Journal of Philology* 83, no. 2 (1962): 113–29.

Traub, H. W. 'Tacitus' Use of *Ferocia*'. *Transactions of the American Philological Association* 84 (1953): 250–61.

Tsouna, Voula. *The Ethics of Philodemus*. Oxford: Oxford University Press, 2007.

Turpin, William. 'Tacitus, Stoic Exempla, and the *Praecipuum Munus Annalium*'. *Classical Antiquity* 27 (2008): 359–404.

van den Berg, Christopher. 'Deliberative Oratory in the *Annals* and the *Dialogus*'. In *A Companion to Tacitus*, edited by Victoria Emma Pagán, 189–211. Malden, MA: Wiley-Blackwell, 2012.

van den Berg, Christopher. *The World of Tacitus' Dialogus de Oratoribus: Aesthetics and Empire in Ancient Rome*. Cambridge: Cambridge University Press, 2014.

van der Blom, Henriette. *Oratory and Political Career in the Late Roman Republic*. Cambridge: Cambridge University Press, 2016.

Vielberg, Meinolf. *Pflichten, Werte, Ideale: Eine Untersuchung zu den Wertvorstellungen des Tacitus*. Stuttgart: Franz Steiner Verlag, 1987.

Walker, B. *The Annals of Tacitus*. Rev. ed. Manchester: Manchester University Press, 1960.

Wallace-Hadrill, Andrew. 'Civilis Princeps: Between Citizen and King'. *Journal of Roman Studies* 72 (1982): 32–48.

Wallace-Hadrill, Andrew. 'Roman Arches and Greek Honours: The Language of Power at Rome'. *Proceedings of the Cambridge Philological Society* 36 (1990): 143–81.
Wallace-Hadrill, Andrew. *Rome's Cultural Revolution*. Cambridge: Cambridge University Press, 2008.
Weinstock, Stefan. *Divus Julius*. Oxford: Clarendon Press, 1971.
Wellesley, Kenneth. *Cornelius Tacitus: The Histories, Book III*. Sydney: Sydney University Press, 1972.
Whitton, C. L. 'Pliny, *Epistles* 8.14: Senate, Slavery and the *Agricola*'. *Journal of Roman Studies* 100 (2010): 118–39.
Whitton, Christopher. *The Arts of Imitation in Latin Prose: Pliny's* Epistles/Quintilian *in Brief*. Cambridge: Cambridge University Press, 2019.
Whitton, Christopher. '"Let Us Tread Our Path Together": Tacitus and the Younger Pliny'. In *A Companion to Tacitus*, edited by Victoria Emma Pagán, 345–68. Malden, MA: Wiley-Blackwell, 2012.
Williams, Kathryn. 'Tacitus' Senatorial Embassies of 69 CE'. In *A Companion to Tacitus*, edited by Victoria Emma Pagán, 212–36. Malden, MA: Wiley-Blackwell, 2012.
Wilson, Marcus. 'After the Silence: Tacitus, Suetonius, Juvenal'. In *Flavian Rome: Culture, Image, Text*, edited by A. J. Boyle and William Dominik, 523–42. Leiden: Brill, 2003.
Winterbottom, Michael. 'Quintilian and the *Vir Bonus*'. *Journal of Roman Studies* 54 (1964): 90–97.
Wisse, Jakob. *Ethos and Pathos: From Aristotle to Cicero*. Amsterdam: Adolf M. Hakkert, 1989.
Woodman, A. J. *Agricola*, with C. S. Kraus. Cambridge: Cambridge University Press, 2014.
Woodman, A. J. *The Annals of Tacitus, Book 4*. Cambridge: Cambridge University Press, 2018.
Woodman, A. J. *The Annals of Tacitus, Books 5 and 6*. Cambridge: Cambridge University Press, 2017.
Woodman, A. J. *Tacitus Reviewed*. Oxford: Oxford University Press, 1998.
Woodman, A. J. *Tacitus: The Annals*. Indianapolis, IN: Hackett, 2004.
Woodman, A. J., and R. H. Martin. *The Annals of Tacitus, Book 3*. Cambridge: Cambridge University Press, 1996.
Yavetz, Zvi. *Plebs and Princeps*. Oxford: Oxford University Press, 1969.

Index

Spelling and inversion of Roman names follow the forms given in the text. Page references for notes are in the format 183 n.2.

accountability 63, 94–5. *See also* responsibility
accusation. *See delatio*
action 27–8
    and *delatio* 57–9, 70–2, 73–5, 96
    and ethos 127–8, 130–1
    generation of 49
    obstruction of 39–40
    political 2, 18, 24, 130–1, 140–1
    representation of 116, 157, 160, 162, 163
    ritualized 18
adulatio (flattery) 20, 25–6, 31–51, 123–4, 183 n.2
    and agency 34–7
    contagious 40–1
    countering of 82–92
    damage caused by 32–3, 37–8, 43–4, 81
    delatio, compared with 53
    ethics of 34–43
    failures of 45–6
    and friendship 36–7
    and *honor* 21, 47–51
    rhetorical art of 43–7
    and truth 38–41
    and unequal power 32–3
Afer, Domitius 128–9
agency
    and *adulatio* 34–7
    and *delatio* 26
    distributed 57–66, 94–5
    divided between speakers 36–7, 40
    and *felicitas* 13, 14–15
    of imperial subjects 7, 33
    limited by tyranny 34–5
    loss of 15
    and *mores* 141
    of rulers 64–5
    senatorial 5–6, 13–14, 15, 33, 63–4, 113
agonistic discourse 26, 33, 81–2, 92, 97, 99.
    See also delatio
Agricola 14, 190 n.7
    and counter-speech 95–6
    and *delatio* 61
    and ethos 111
    and *mores* 139, 140–2, 147, 156
alacritas (joy/eagerness) 89
alienation, political 16
ambiguity 4, 11, 12–13, 61–2, 97–8
animals/animality 35, 38, 176 n.11
Annals 2, 9, 123–4, 170 n.15
    and *adulatio* 20, 31–2, 35–6, 83–7
    and counter-speech 83–7, 93, 94, 96–9, 102–5
    and *delatio* 59–63, 64–71, 73–8
    and ethos 121–3, 128–9, 134, 135
    and *honor* 20, 47, 49–50
    and *mores* 144, 146–7, 148–56
Antistius Sosianus 101, 102
Aper, Marcus 76, 116–21, 189 n.23, 194 n.58
argument 43–4, 63–4, 81, 95, 131–2, 154–6.
    See also eloquentia
arrogance 90
Asiaticus, Valerius 68–9, 182 n.31
attentiveness 150–1
audiences 110, 111–12, 126–7
    emotional response of 111, 122–3
    empathy of 120–1
    pleasure of 115, 132
    reception of speakers 127
    responsiveness to 114–15
    See also readers/reading
Augustus (emperor) 50, 70, 89, 179 n.51
    and Asinius Gallus 151–2
    and *delatio* 73–4

and Marcus Lepidus 134
authority
    of emperors 48
    loss of 129
    of the senate 48, 49
    of speaker 22–3
autocracy 4–5, 34–5, 37–8, 64

Bartsch, Shadi 11
Bauman, Richard A. 67
Berg, Christopher van den 117
Bernstein, Neil 143
brutality (*saevitia*) 94–5, 154

Caecina, C. Silius 100
Caesar, Augustus. *See* Augustus
Caesar, Julius 53–6
Capito, Ateius 129
Capito, Cossutianus 64–5, 70–1, 77–8, 144–5
Catus, Firmius 60–1
Celer, Publius 157–8
Celsus, Marius 43
censorship 76–7
ceremonies of thanksgiving 48, 49–50
Certus, Publicius 160–2
character. *See* ethos
characterization 116, 126–7, 128
Cicero, Marcus Tullius 35, 122, 170 n.14
    De Inventione 113–14
    De Officiis 57–8
    De Oratore 114
    Pro Marcello 53–6
citizenship 58–9, 101–2
civilis princeps (citizenlike ruler) 89–90, 92–4
Claudius (emperor) 9, 93
    and *adulatio* 31, 44
    and *delatio* 68–9, 76, 93, 94
clementia (clemency) 104, 105, 154, 187 n.52, 193 n.50
Clutorius Priscus 100–3, 153
collaboration 86–7, 153, 157–8, 184 n.11
community
    judgement, formation of 86–7, 134, 153
    and *mores* 141–3
    political 111–12, 140–8, 157–8
compliance (*obsequium*) 89–90
complicity 38, 61–3, 152

and *delatio* 68–9, 76–7
Connolly, Joy 55
consensus 134–7
consensus rituals 19, 48
consistency (*constantia*) 132, 145, 147, 159, 163, 190 n.47
conspiracy 8, 67, 68–9, 74
constantia (consistency) 132, 145, 147, 159, 163, 190 n.47
consuls/consulate 14, 22, 58, 128
    and *adulatio* 31–3, 43
    and counter-speech 87–90
    and *mores* 151, 161–2
conversation, private 67, 86–7
co-production 32–3, 68–9, 76–7
counter-speech 26–7, 81–106, 131–2
    against *adulatio* 82–92
    against *delatio* 92–106
Cowan, Eleanor 154
Crispinus, Caepio 62, 63
Crispus, Vibius 119–20
critical archive
    of *ethos* (character) 123–37
    historiography as 24–5, 27, 125

death 147
    execution 49–50, 67, 101, 103, 187 n.46
    suicide 9, 64, 93, 146
debate, political 131–2, 148–58, 160–1, 179 n.51
    individual contribution to 20–1
    and *mores* 148–56
declamation 16, 86–7
decorum 47–8, 50, 91
deficiency (*elleipsis*) 47
dehumanization 35, 38
delatio (predatory accusation) 26–7, 53–79
    accountability for 63, 94–5
    adulatio, compared with 53
    and citizenship 58–9
    countering of 92–106
    criticism of 58, 75, 76–7
    damage caused by 81–2
    defence of *delatores* 112–16
    and distributed agency 57–66
    judgement 99–105
    justifications for 77–9

and *maiestas* 66–73
  monetary reward for 58, 76–8, 96–7, 98–9, 101
  origins of 53–7
  process of 57–9, 99–105
  punishment 99–100, 101–2, 104–5
  ruler-*delator* symbiosis 68–9, 76–7
  speech of 73–9
depersonalization 60–1, 62, 98–9
deprecatio 113–14
Dészpa, Loránd 53
Dialogus de Oratoribus 16, 194 n.58
  and *adulatio* 36
  and *delatio* 76, 77
  and ethos 116–21
dignity
  of rulers 84–6
  of senators 152–3
Dio Chrysostom 38
discordia 159
discourse
  agonistic 26, 33, 81–2, 92, 97, 99 (*See also delatio*)
  construction of rulers in 105
  construction through 105, 113–14
  private 67, 86–7
  public 86–7
  truth, production of 5–7, 13
  See also speech
discrepancy 61–2
dishonour 32
disinterestedness. *See* objectivity
distributed agency 57–66, 94–5
divinity, of rulers 54, 56, 83–4
Dolabella, Cornelius 46, 84–5, 178 n.38
Domitian (emperor) 37–8, 61, 65, 112, 160, 164
Drusus, Nero Claudius (Drusus Julius Caesar) 45, 84
duty, dereliction of 71–2

eagerness (*alacritas*) 89
elleipsis (deficiency) 47
eloquentia (eloquence) 46, 69–70, 117, 165, 194 n.58
  and *ethos* 118–20
  and values 109–10
emotion
  alacritas (joy) 89

  of audience response 111, 122–3
  and ethos 110–11, 121–3
  fear 32, 37–8, 122–3
  felicitas (happiness) 13–15
  in oratory 120–1
empathy 111, 120–1
emperors
  authority of 48
  bodyguard, senators as 55, 56
  delatio trials, blamed for 59, 94–5
  and *honor* 47–50
  senators, relationships with 36–7
  senators as danger to 75–6
  sententiae of 84–5
  See also Augustus; Claudius; Domitian; Gaius; Galba; Nero; Nerva; Otho; Tiberius; Trajan; Vespasian; Vitellius
empty speech 33–4, 41, 84–5
enthusiasm 42, 89
entrapment 66–7
epigrams 28, 46, 168
ethos 27, 109–37
  and action 127–8, 130–1
  contingency of 110
  critical archive of 123–37
  critique of 128–30
  debate of 130–4
  and *eloquentia* 118–20
  and emotion 110–11, 121–3
  and historiography 126–37
  judgement of 123–7, 130
  and narrative 127–8
  and oratory 116–21
  performance of 112–16, 165
  and rhetoric 113–15
evaluation. *See* judgement
exaggeration 20, 42, 54–5
excess 46–7
execution 49–50, 67, 101, 103, 155
exemplarity 146–8, 163–4, 191 n.24

Faianius 61, 62
falsehood 42
fear 32, 37–8, 122–3
felicitas (happiness) 13–15
Flaig, Egon 19
flattery (*adulatio*) 20, 25–6, 31–51, 123–4, 183 n.2

214 *Index*

and agency 34–7
contagious 40–1
countering of 82–92
damage caused by 32–3, 37–8, 43–4, 81
delatio, compared with 53
ethics of 34–43
failures of 45–6
and friendship 36–7
and *honor* 21, 47–51
rhetorical art of 43–7
and truth 38–41
and unequal power 32–3
Fonteius, Agrippa 60–1
Foucault, Michel 3–4, 11–12
friendship 32, 36–7, 67–8. *See also* social networks

Gaius (emperor) 31, 32, 34–5, 69–70
Galba (emperor) 38–9, 41, 63, 76
Galla, Sosia 1, 2, 100
Gallio, Iunius 85–6
Gallus, Annius 43
Gallus, Asinius 151–3, 193 n.40
Gallus, Togonius 129
genealogies of practice 148–56
generalization 31–2, 84, 149
Germanicus (Germanicus Julius Caesar) 20, 40, 174 n.68
Ginsburg, Judith 153–4
Grethlein, Jonas 125

Hammer, Dean 110, 131
happiness (*felicitas*) 13–15
Haterius, Quintus 45–6, 129, 178 n.36
Helvidius Priscus (father) 20, 26, 27, 190 n.47, 190 n.48
and *adulatio* 77, 88–91
and ethos 130–4
as example 163–4
and *mores* 145–6, 157–8
as philosopher 146–7
Helvidius Priscus (son) 95–6, 160–2
hierarchy 22, 69, 74, 128–9, 160–1
Hispo, Romanius 62
Histories 4–9, 12–13, 14, 20, 184 n.10
and *adulatio* 35, 38–9, 41–3, 88–91
and counter-speech 88–91, 93–5
and *delatio* 76, 77

and ethos 110, 112–13, 126–7, 131–4
and *mores* 145, 157–60
historiography
as critical archive 24–5, 27, 125
and ethos 126–37
experiential 125–6
and judgement 110, 124–5
and political speech 7–8
teleological 125–6
and triviality 150–1
and truth 5–6, 11, 12
history 11–12, 24–5, 111
honor (honours) 17–20
and *adulatio* 21, 47–51, 90–1
improperly applied 49–50
and truth 90–1
hubris 90
humanity
dehumanization 35, 38
of rulers 37, 83–4
humility 34–5
hyperbole 46–7

imitation 144, 147, 153, 154
indecorum 50
independence
historiographical 5–6
lack of 25–6, 33, 35, 159
and *mores* 145–6
senatorial 35, 148–9, 152
indictment 57, 59, 67–8, 96, 160–1
inequality, of power 18–19, 32–3
infamy 129, 130
inheritance 2, 100–2, 105
insults 75, 102
interdependence
ruler-*delator* 68–9, 76–7
ruler-populace 54–5
of subjectivity 141
interiority 140–1
interpretation 10–11, 12–13
invective 75, 102
irony 4, 8–9, 159, 170 n.15
isolation 37–8, 121

joy (*alacritas*) 89
judgement 21, 22
collective 86–7, 134, 153
in *delatio* 99–105

of ethos 123–7, 130
historical 110, 124–5, 129–31
and selfhood 104
senatorial 103–5, 157
Julius Caesar 53–6

Kapust, Daniel 32
Keitel, Elizabeth 157–8
knowledge 3–4, 5–6

Latiaris, Latinius 66–8
law and legal systems 1–2, 9, 179 n.51, 184 n.17, 185 n.32
  lex Cincia 77, 96–7
  lex maiestatis 61, 104–5
  violence of 49–50, 67, 75, 101, 103, 155
  See also *delatio*; indictment; praetors/praetorship; punishment; trials
Lentulus, Cn. (Gnaeus Cornelius Lentulus) 99–100, 101, 102
Lepidus, Marcus 1, 2, 27, 28
  and counter-speech 99–105
  and ethos 130–1, 134–7
  Thrasea, compared to 153–6
Levene, David 54–5
Libo, Scribonius 59–61
lies 42
Luce, T. J. 118

magic 74
maiestas (treason) 1, 2, 53, 61, 92–3
  and *delatio* 66–73
  trials 59–65, 70–3, 75–6, 95–6, 99–105
  verbal 73–9
Mamercus Scaurus 130
Marcellus, Eprius 26, 190 n.47, 190 n.48, 194 n.58
  and counter-speech 94–5, 99
  and *delatio* 63–5, 72–3, 77
  and ethos 118–23, 124–5, 133
  and *mores* 157–8, 164
Marcellus, Granius 61, 62, 63
Maternus, Curiatius 36, 76, 77, 120–1
Mauricus, Iunius 142–3, 158
Mayer, Roland 153
meaning
  lack of 33–4, 35, 41, 84–5
  suspended 9–11
memory 111

Messalina, Valeria 9, 94–5
Messalinus, Catullus 65
Messalla, Vipstanus 110, 112–16, 164, 188 n.19
metaphor 65, 72–3, 78
Metellus (Quintus Caecilius Metellus Numidicus) 136
Montanus, Curtius 77, 122, 157–8, 186 n.35, 194 n.59
monuments 48–9, 184 n.11
mores 27–8
  and community 141–3
  cultivation of 142–3
  and political debate 148–56
  and social networks 140–8
  transmission of 145–8, 151, 156–65
Mucianus, Gaius Licinius 90

narrative 27–8, 111–12
  and depersonalization 60–1, 62
  discrepancy in 61–2
  and ethos 127–8
  experiential effect of 125–6
  and *mores* 142
  political sense of 126
  repetition in 35, 153–6
  See also style
Nero (emperor) 49, 78, 160
  and *delatio* 63–5, 69, 70–3, 76
Nerva (emperor) 14–15, 159–60
networks, social 140–8, 157–8. See also friendship
Noreña, Carlos 13

Oakley, Stephen 15
oaths 71, 76–7, 93–4, 158, 162
obedience (*obsequium*) 89–90
objectivity 4, 6, 60–2, 64, 96–9, 127–9
obsequium (compliance/obedience) 89–90
Octavia (Claudia Octavia) 49–50
Octavius. See Augustus
oppositional speech. See counter-speech
oratory 25, 76–7, 116–21, 130–1, 143–4, 168. See also style
Otho (emperor) 41, 43–4

Paetus, Thrasea. See Thrasea Paetus
panegyric 7–8, 17–18, 21–2, 91, 135–7. See also *adulatio*; honor

paradox 68, 74–5
paranoia 54–5, 85–6
passive voice 60, 62, 98–9
Paterculus, Velleius 70, 134–5
Paulinus, Suetonius. *See* Suetonius
    Paulinus
performance
    emotive 121–3
    of ethos 165
    politics as 48–9
    and reception 127
    of selfhood 109–10, 115–16, 129
    See also oratory; rhetoric
persona. See ethos
persuasion 116
Philodemus of Gadara 35, 36, 37, 83
philosophy 144–6, 190 n.7
Pigoń, Jakub 133
pleasure
    of audiences 115, 132
    of oratory 116–18, 189 n.23
Pliny the Younger 14–15, 17, 18, 28, 63
    de Helvidi ultione 161–4
    Epistulae 65, 142–3, 160–5, 189 n.37
    Panegyricus 21–2, 38, 41, 173 n.72,
        180 n.6
    and Tacitus, Publius Cornelius 162–3
Plutarch 35, 36, 37, 38, 176 n.11
political action 2, 18, 24, 130–1, 140–1
political community 111–12, 140–8
political debate 131–2, 148–58, 160–1,
    179 n.51
    individual contribution to 20–1
    and *mores* 148–56
    as performance 48–9
Poppaea Sabina 9
populace 7, 33, 41–3, 47, 50, 54–5
posterity 139, 141–2, 156–65, 168
postulatio (request for trial) 59, 60, 64, 70
power
    inequality of 18–19, 32–3
    and knowledge 5–6
    of senate 22–3, 48, 49, 167–8
    and truth 2–3
practice, genealogies of 148–56
praetors/praetorship 56, 87, 101–2, 160–1
praise 7–8, 17–18, 21–2, 91, 135–7. *See also*
    adulatio; *honor*
predatory accusation (*delatio*) 26–7, 53–79

accountability for 63, 94–5
adulatio, compared with 53
and *civilitas* 58–9
countering of 92–106
criticism of 58, 75, 76–7
damage caused by 81–2
defence of *delatores* 112–16
and distributed agency 57–66
judgement 99–105
justifications for 77–9
and *maiestas* 66–73
monetary reward for 58, 76–8, 96–7,
    98–9, 101
origins of 53–7
process of 57–9, 99–105
punishment 99–100, 101–2, 104–5
ruler-*delator* symbiosis 68–9, 76–7
speech of 73–9
princeps 3, 6, 24–5, 53
    safety of 58, 68
    and senate 105
    status of 69–70
    See also adulatio; *honor*
Principate
    autocratic rule of 4–5
    status of 84–5
    truth regime of 4–6
    use of history in 24–5
Priscus, Clutorius. *See* Clutorius Priscus
Priscus, Helvidius. *See* Helvidius Priscus
    (father); Helvidius Priscus (son)
private conversation 67, 86–7
private space 67–8
Proculus, Licinius 43
property 155
    inheritance 2, 100–2, 105
    state as 5–6
prosecution 57–8. *See also* indictment;
    predatory accusation; trials
punishment 99–100, 101–2, 104–5, 155

Quadratus, Ummidius 164–5
quaestors 145, 146, 147
Quintilian, Marcus Fabius 47

rank 22, 69, 74, 128–9, 160–1
readers/reading 9, 12–13, 127–8, 156–7
reception 110, 111, 127
redemption 160–2, 163

Index

Regulus, Aquilius 77, 112–16, 143–4, 164, 186 n.35, 194 n.59
relatedness 142–3
remembrance
   historical 111
   monuments 48–9, 184 n.11
repetition 35, 153–6
representation
   of action 116, 157, 160, 162, 163
   layers of 110, 115–16
   of transmission 153–6
Republic/Republicanism 16, 23–4, 48, 147–8, 167
reputation 115–16, 127, 129, 134
resistant speech 36–7
responsibility 33–6, 94, 95
   for *delatio* 62–3
   judicial 153
   of senators 96, 103
   See also accountability
res publica 6, 92–3, 102
   safety of 53–6, 68–9, 71
rhetoric 25
   and *adulatio* 43–7
   declamation 16, 86–7
   deprecatio 113–14
   and ethos 113–15
   passive voice 60, 62, 98–9
   and values 109–10
   violent 72–3, 97–8
rituals, consensus 19, 48
Roller, Matthew 17, 23
Rome 6, 92–3
   autocracy 4–5, 34–5, 37–8, 64
   co-production of regime 32–3
   Republic/Republicanism 16, 23–4, 48, 147–8, 167
   safety of 53–6, 68–9, 70–1
   subjects 7, 33, 41–3, 47, 50, 54–5
   See also Principate; *res publica*; rulers; senate/senators
Rubrius 61, 62
Rufus, Suillius. *See* Suillius Rufus
rulers
   agency of 64–5
   construction of 105
   dignity of 84–6
   humanity of 37, 83–4
   influence on 22–3
   interdependence with populace 54–5
   modes of address 82–3, 88–9
   quasi-divine 54, 56, 83–4
   safety of 26, 53–8, 68, 180 n.6
   self-presentation of 89, 90
   senate, relationship with 105
   supremacy of 69–70, 74
   tyranny 4–5, 34–5, 37–8, 64
   See also emperors; princeps
rumour 38–9
Russell, Amy 19
Rusticus, Arulenus 142–3, 144
Rutledge, Steven 60

Sabinus, Titus 66–8
Sacrovir, Julius 47
saevitia (brutality) 94–5, 154
safety
   of rulers 26, 53–7, 68–9, 180 n.6
   of state 53–6, 68–9, 70–1
Sallust 136
Saturninus, Aponius 39–40
Scaurus, Mamercus. *See* Mamercus Scaurus
Scipio, Cornelius 9
Scott, James 36
secessio (secession) 71–2
Sejanus, Lucius Aelius 37, 40, 56, 70, 85–6, 182 n.37
selfhood
   and judgement 104
   and oratory 116–18
   performance of 27, 109–10, 115–16, 129
   rhetorical construction of 113–14
   See also ethos; subjectivity
self-sufficiency 117, 120, 121
senate/senators 1–2, 15–17, 179 n.51
   agency of 5–6, 13–14, 15, 33, 63–4, 113
   attentiveness 150–1
   authority of 48, 49
   censorship of 76–7
   as collective 143–4, 157–8, 184 n.11
   criticism of 42–3
   dignity of 152–3
   duties of 55
   emperors, danger to 75–6
   emperors, relationships with 36–7, 105

as emperors' bodyguard 55, 56
failures of 159, 160
genealogies of practice 148–56
independence of 35, 148–9, 152
judgement of 103–5, 157
mores, transmission of 156–65
oaths 71, 76–7, 93–4, 158, 162
power of 22–3, 48, 49, 167–8
quaestors 145, 146, 147
responsibility of 96, 103
selection of 133–4
social networks 143–4, 157–8
status of 33–4
See also consuls/consulate
Seneca the Elder (Lucius Annaeus) 46
sententiae 28, 31–2, 167–8
in counter-speech 89–91, 99–101, 104–5
of emperors 84–5
in historiography 49–50, 123–4
judicial 154–8, 161
servility 31, 32, 35–6
severitas 154
Silanus, C. 99–100, 130
Silius, C. 96–8, 186 n.40
Sinclair, Patrick 31–2
slavery 33, 35–6, 42
social networks 140–8, 157–8. *See also* friendship
Soni, Vivasvan 13–14
Soranus, Barea 128, 157–8, 193 n.52
Sosianus, Antistius
space, private 67–8
speech
abusive 67
agonistic 26, 33, 81–2, 92, 97, 99
authority of 22–3
damaging modes of 25–6
empty 33–4, 41, 84–5
figured 8–9, 171 n.28
improper 73–9
militaristic 70
as performance 27
private conversation 67, 86–7
reported 186 n.34
resistant 36–7
rights to 152
senatorial 7–8, 9–11, 16–17
and subjectivity 11–12

See also adulatio; counter-speech; *delatio*; oratory; rhetoric
Spurinna, Vestricius 143–4
state, Roman 6, 92–3
autocracy 4–5, 34–5, 37–8, 64
co-production of regime 32–3
Republic/Republicanism 16, 23–4, 48, 147–8, 167
safety of 53–6, 68–9, 70–1
subjects 7, 33, 41–3, 47, 50, 54–5
See also Principate; *res publica*; rulers; senate/senators
status 22, 69, 74, 128–9, 160–1
Stoicism 144–5
Strunk, Thomas 24, 154, 171 n.33
studia 132, 134
style 28, 44–7, 72, 85, 89, 135–7
subjectivity
interdependent 141
of speaker 11–12, 127–9
subjects 7, 33, 41–3, 47, 50, 54–5
Suetonius (Gaius Suetonius Tranquillus) 69, 74, 85
Suetonius Paulinus 43–4, 126–8
suicide 9, 64, 93, 146
Suillius Rufus 76–9, 93–7, 185 n.32
supremacy, of rulers 69–70, 74
symbiosis, ruler-*delator* 68–9, 76–7

Tacitus, Publius Cornelius
and *maiestas* trials 95–6
and Pliny the Younger 162–3
See also Agricola; *Annals*; *Dialogus de Oratoribus*; *Histories*
tastelessness 45
temporalities, interaction of 156–65
Terence 35
thanksgiving ceremonies 48, 49–50
Theophrastus, *Characters* 36
Thrasea Paetus 23, 27–8, 193 n.52
and counter-speech 99, 101–3, 105
and *delatio* 63–5, 70–3
and ethos 121–3, 124–5
as *exemplum* 146–8
Lepidus, compared with 153–6
and *mores* 144–8
Tiberius (emperor) 1, 20–1, 47–8, 55–6, 184 n.10

Index

and *adulatio* 31, 35–6, 37, 40, 44–5, 82–7
and *delatio* 56–7, 60–2, 66–8, 70, 76
and *maiestas* 74–5
Principate, status of 84–5
time periods, interaction of 156–65
Titianus, L. Salvius Otho 43
Trajan (emperor) 41, 171 n.33
transmission
   to the future 139, 141–2, 156–65
   of *mores* 145–8, 151, 156–65
   representation of 153–6
   See also audiences; readers/reading; reception
treason (*maiestas*) 1, 2, 53, 61, 92–3
   and *delatio* 66–73
   trials 59–65, 70–3, 75–6, 95–6, 99–105
   verbal 73–9
trials 16, 158–62
   maiestas 7, 59–65, 70–3, 75–6, 95–6, 99–105
   postulatio (request for trial) 59, 60, 64, 70
   show 94–5
   See also *delatio*; judgement
Trio, Fulcinius 60–1
triviality 150–1
truth
   and *adulatio* 38–41
   assertion of 11–12, 13
   and historiography 5–6, 12
   and *honor* 90–1
   lack of 42
   and power 2–3
   produced in discourse 4–7, 13
   truth regimes 3–6, 15, 81
tyranny 4–5, 34–5, 37–8, 64

ultio (vengeance) 93

Valerius Asiaticus 68–9, 182 n.31
values 109–10
   decorum 47–8, 50, 91
   and *eloquentia* (eloquence) 109–10
   See also ethos
vengeance (*ultio*) 93
Vescularius, Flaccus 60–1
Vespasian (emperor) 74, 131
   and *adulatio* 45
   and counter-speech 88–91, 93–4
   and *delatio* 76–7
victims 74–5, 93
violence
   of *delatio* 57, 58–9, 65, 68, 77
   of judicial system 49–50, 67, 75, 101, 103, 155
   rhetorical 72–3, 97–8
visualization 122–3
Vitellius (emperor) 38–40, 44
Vitellius, Lucius 10, 31–3, 34–5
voice 95
voice, passive 60, 62, 98–9
Votienus 75

Wallace-Hadrill, Andrew 3–4, 19, 49
Whitton, Christopher 163

youth 112–13

CPSIA information can be obtained
at www.ICGtesting.com
Printed in the USA
LVHW081138160422
716296LV00039B/1178

9 781350 195011